THE
BLOOMBERG
WAY

Bloomberg Press imprint (non-Financial Series)
Since 1996, Bloomberg Press has published books for financial professionals, as well as books of general interest in investing, economics, current affairs, and policy affecting investors and business people. Titles are written by well-known practitioners, BLOOMBERG NEWS® reporters and columnists, and other leading authorities and journalists. Bloomberg Press books have been translated into more than 20 languages.

For a list of available titles, please visit our Web site at www.wiley.com/ go/bloombergpress.

THE
BLOOMBERG
WAY

A Guide for
Reporters and Editors

Matthew Winkler

BLOOMBERG PRESS
An Imprint of
 WILEY

Published by John Wiley & Sons, Inc., Hoboken, New Jersey.
Published simultaneously in Canada.

The Bloomberg Way was previously published in eleven editions by Bloomberg for its employees.

For general information on our other products and services or for technical support, please contact our Customer Care Department within the United States at (800) 762-2974, outside the United States at (317) 572-3993 or fax (317) 572-4002.

Wiley also publishes its books in a variety of electronic formats. Some content that appears in print may not be available in electronic books. For more information about Wiley products, visit our web site at www.wiley.com.

Library of Congress Cataloging-in-Publication Data:

Winkler, Matthew.
   The Bloomberg way : a guide for reporters and editors / Matthew Winkler. — 12
      p.   cm. — (Bloomberg ; 149)
   ISBN 978-1-118-03017-2 (hardback); ISBN 978-1-118-14988-1 (ebk);
   ISBN 978-1-118-14989-8 (ebk); ISBN 978-1-118-14990-4 (ebk)
      1. Journalism, Commercial—Style manuals.   2. Bloomberg News (Firm)   I. Title.
   PN4784.C7W56   2011
   070.4'4965—dc23   2011022707

Printed in the United States of America

10 9 8 7 6 5 4 3 2 1

Contents

Introduction

ON THE SECOND Wednesday in November 1989, I got a phone call that would mark the birth of an implausible news organization led by an unlikely publisher: "Hi, it's Bloomberg. I need some advice. What would it take to get into the news business?" Michael Rubens Bloomberg, former partner of Salomon Brothers and now president and founder of Bloomberg Financial Markets, was asking me, at the time probably the happiest reporter at the *Wall Street Journal*.

The question was intriguing. Bloomberg had no experience in journalism. His almost two decades of selling securities would prove to be an advantage. The computer terminal he created in 1982 with his name on it already used an array of historical and current data to show investors and traders how to buy the cheapest securities and to sell the most expensive ones—a service unmatched by any news company and as valuable as any Pulitzer Prize–winning story, or so I thought.

Mike Bloomberg also had plenty of opinions. Here's one: "If reporters are any good, what do we need editors for?" I happened to be the first journalist who considered him qualified as a newsman, even if I disagreed with him about editors.

And he surprised me when I parried his initial query about what it would take to get into the news business with another question bereft of dollar signs: "All right," I said. "You have just published a story that says the chairman—and I mean chair*man*—of your biggest customer has taken $5 million from the corporate till. He is with his secretary at a Rio de Janeiro resort, and the secretary's spurned boyfriend calls to tip you off. You get an independent verification that the story is true. Then the phone rings. The customer's public-relations person says, 'Kill the story or we will return all the terminals we currently rent from you.' "

"What would you do?" I asked.

"Go with the story," Mike said. "Our lawyers will love the fees you generate."

That was the deciding moment. I could then say, "You and the few hundred people working at Bloomberg know more about money, markets and balance sheets than any collection of journalists. You show this knowledge daily on your electronic screens. If you can somehow marry this knowledge to prose and attach comprehensive data to each published story, you will have something that doesn't exist anywhere."

Bloomberg intuitively knew as much. Here was an opportunity to make the world of money more transparent—non-stop, throughout the day, throughout the year—as only people who had the experience of buying and selling money could. The journalists who would join Bloomberg would be the translators and narrators. If we could make Bloomberg's printed and spoken word lucid enough, even to Aunt Agatha, Bloomberg would become a journalistic benchmark for instant perspective on money. And money increasingly was becoming the mother of all stories. For those who recall Watergate, the best advice any two reporters received in the 20th century was: "Follow the money!"

The first Bloomberg byline appeared June 14, 1990, on 9,500 leased computer terminals delivering real-time data and news to people with the most at stake. That byline came at the end of four paragraphs exemplifying the essence of the Bloomberg Way—a new model for the news business at the end of a century celebrated for the journalism that brought down governments, created celebrities and encouraged everyone to be masters of money. None of the dozen Bloomberg reporters and editors in New York and London in their initial summer would have dared to predict that they would become a hundred times more numerous in scores of bureaus or that their global regimen would serve hundreds of thousands of customers wired to Bloombergs in so many countries that no one can identify all of them two decades later.

The Bloomberg Way, a guide to reporting and editing the story of money in all its forms, initially was a 30-page manifesto for writing about currencies, bonds, stocks, commodities and the economy. It aspired to create the sensibility for an electronic newspaper, and it was inspired by an exquisite little book, *The Elements of Style*, by William Strunk Jr. and E. B. White. This expanded *Bloomberg Way* remains true to its origins.

The electronic newspaper began when Mike Bloomberg created the first computerized system that provided the relative value of bonds. For someone who had traded only equity securities, this was especially noteworthy and it would prove unique in 1982, when Merrill Lynch became the first customer of the so-called Market Master from the startup Innovative Market Systems. Less than eight years later, he decided his now-eponymous company couldn't prosper without news.

The Bloomberg by then was ubiquitous among Merrill's customers and competitors. It leveled the playing field between buyers and sellers in a keystroke during the 1980s, just as the bond market was telling every other market what to do. Mike Bloomberg's Wall Street world consisted of buying money for a living, selling money for a living, trading money for a living, investing money for a living and analyzing money for a living. Now he was providing information about money for a living. He wasn't a newsman. Yet he became the only publisher who seized the opportunity to computerize current and historical data with unlimited what-if scenarios attached to every event worthy of an extraordinary anecdote in a reporter's notebook. When he asked me to join him, Bloomberg News was born.

That was four years before Netscape introduced the Internet to the world, marking the beginning of the end of newspapers as the essential medium with a captive embrace of advertisers. We didn't know that when Bloomberg Business News, as it was then called, published its first story. What we did know when we started a news service is that people in the bond, stock, currency, commodities, energy and derivatives markets needed to know everything worth knowing on a real-time basis.

Until that point, such reporting was dominated by a handful of traditional news wires whose pedigrees began around the time of Abraham Lincoln and who ruled the real-time journalistic landscape as quasi-monopolies. They left narrative reporting, so vital to understanding the meaning of events, to newspapers and magazines. The people who needed real-time news received little more than staccato headlines, and this was long before there was Twitter. For context and perspective, these traders, investors and fiduciaries still had to wait for their favorite newspaper the next day.

About the same time that newspapers found themselves literally enslaved by the printing press with the legacy costs of mass circulation and daily distribution of harvested forests, Bloomberg News conceived itself as an electronic newspaper dedicated to providing everything a newspaper does well with none of the drawbacks of once-a-day delivery. The need for a second-by-second valuation of companies, governments and individuals made the electronic newspaper compelling. When the instantaneous importance of the credit market converged with readers' need for something far more substantial than your father's news service, Bloomberg News became a necessity for several hundred thousand readers concentrated in half a dozen of the biggest money centers.

That's why Bloomberg News was substantially staffed by journalists who migrated from the once-a-day, once-a-week, once-a-month and on-the-hour platforms in journalism—otherwise known as newspapers, magazines, radio and television—to the real-time platform that begged for the best practices of the profession. To succeed, we needed a Bloomberg Way because there was no curriculum in journalism schools or manual that provided a step-by-step guide for the growing, and increasingly rigorous, demands of real-time producers of multimedia news. The Bloomberg Way obligates reporters to be the agent of their readers and never the agent of their sources. Bloomberg users are the most educated and affluent community of men and women from anywhere. They are internationally minded because their interests—cultural, political and financial—are global. They go wherever they choose, whenever they decide and for anything they want. Bloomberg users awake knowing that whatever they don't know might ruin them.

Providing news for Bloomberg users is a serious undertaking that requires news judgment, or the obligation to provide exactly what they need precisely at the moment when their need is greatest. In the Bloomberg Way, five words that begin with F govern news judgment: Being the First word, because news is a surprise. Being the most Factual word, as something isn't news unless it's true. Being the Fastest word, as every event is shaped by subsequent action. Being the Final word, as every story should be complete. Being the Future word, because the meaning of today's event is enhanced by its relevance tomorrow.

In order to fulfill the Five Fs, each Bloomberg News story must include Five Easy Pieces, because every event is shaped by forces derived from markets, the economy, government, politics and companies. No story is complete without these five elements. Similarly, every subject needs to be defined by its scope and size. Every story must provide the Bloomberg user with enough relevant functionality based on specific data so there is no doubt about the factual basis for what is reported and how each report can be replicated with a panoply of data by a keystroke or two. To be most influential, every story must be exceptional and definitive.

Fulfilling the Five Fs with Five Easy Pieces requires relentless preparation. In an age when information vies with misinformation, the truth is obscured. Bloomberg News resists the temptation to embrace spontaneous expression and mistake it for considered thinking and accurate reporting. The Bloomberg Way insists that reporters show, not tell, and not rely on modifiers, because adjectives and adverbs are imprecise. At a point when technology can deliver so many words instantly, editing still matters. The Bloomberg Way has little patience for throat-clearing *indeeds* and *howevers* and other extraneous words. Instead of saying, "You disappoint me, but I'll always love you," the Bloomberg Way says: "You disappoint me, and I'll always love you." The difference in meaning is profound. Reporting should never be restrained by unnecessary qualification and qualification should never be ambiguous.

The Bloomberg Way insists that every assertion should be substantiated by a fact, example or anecdote and that names make news. Our handiwork is demonstrated in stories slugged Chart of the Day and Real M&A, which fuse the Bloomberg's archival data, analytical prowess and news into a unique perspective. The Bloomberg Way demands that news be a basis for action. The Bloomberg Way asks its reporters and editors to aspire to produce literature in a hurry while delivering the first draft of history. As moral force makes journalism a calling for those who embrace it, the Bloomberg Way necessitates a respect for life, peace and harmony, education, family stability, social responsibility, transparency, free trade and free markets.

So much of the reporting that proves exceptional begins with headlines such as these:

Never Have So Many Short Sellers Made So Much Money With Stocks
Libor Signals Credit Seizing Up as Banks Balk at Money Lending
Obama Is First Black, Last Black President: David M. Kennedy
Evil Wall Street Exports Boomed With 'Fools' Born to Buy Debt
Wall Street Lawyers Asking Barclays, Can You Spare $250,000?
Ten Days Changed Wall Street as Bernanke Saw Massive Failures
Mizuho $7 Billion Loss Turned on Toxic Aardvark Made in America

As we chronicled the worst financial shakeout of our lifetime, caused mostly by the abuse and misuse of credit, it is revealing to know how we came to publish the most-read story on the Bloomberg in 2008 and how we applied elements of the Bloomberg Way to make it so.

On Sunday, Sept. 21, 2008, many millions of Americans watched the Green Bay Packers fritter away several opportunities and lose to the Dallas Cowboys, 27–16, before a hometown crowd at Lambeau Field. That afternoon, Bloomberg News reported that the Federal Reserve was about to allow Morgan Stanley and Goldman Sachs to become deposit-taking institutions. At a news meeting that evening, editors were considering another story about Morgan Stanley and Goldman Sachs for the next morning. The headline and first sentence of the story matter-of-factly reported that the Fed was about to let Goldman Sachs and Morgan Stanley become more regulated commercial banks, ending 75 years of history. During the discussion of the headline and lead, editors decided that this approach insufficiently captured the significance of that Sunday afternoon in September. So we started over with a new headline:

Goldman, Morgan Stanley Bring Down Curtain on Wall Street Era

. . . and rewrote the first four paragraphs of the story:

Sept. 22 (Bloomberg) -- The Wall Street that shaped the financial world for two decades ended last night, when Goldman Sachs Group Inc.

and Morgan Stanley concluded there is no future in remaining investment
banks now that investors have determined the model is broken.

The Federal Reserve's approval of their bid to become banks ends the
ascendancy of the securities firms, 75 years after Congress separated them
from deposit-taking lenders, and caps weeks of chaos that sent Lehman
Brothers Holdings Inc. into bankruptcy and led to the rushed sale of
Merrill Lynch & Co. to Bank of America Corp.

"The decision marks the end of Wall Street as we have known it,"
said William Isaac, a former chairman of the Federal Deposit Insurance
Corp. "It's too bad."

Goldman, whose alumni include Henry Paulson, the Treasury sec-
retary presiding over a $700 billion bank bailout, and Morgan Stanley,
a product of the 1933 Glass-Steagall Act that cleaved investment and
commercial banks, insisted they didn't need to change course, even as their
shares plunged and their borrowing costs soared last week.

This proved to be the most-read story on the Bloomberg that year because
the event had far more significance than two iconic securities firms winning
approval to take deposits. While every other news organization on Monday,
Sept. 22, reported that Goldman Sachs and Morgan Stanley were becoming
banks, Bloomberg News seized the day to report the end of an era on Wall
Street. By Tuesday, Sept. 23, that theme finally was reported by the news
organizations that still buy their ink by the barrel.

The Bloomberg Way is a distillation of weekly notes distributed to the
2,735 reporters, editors, anchors, producers and engineers of Bloomberg
News since 1991, when the first edition was published. For the first time, we
share the twelfth edition with the public through John Wiley & Sons. *The
Bloomberg Way* is our guide to learning. May the learning never end, because
the best is yet to come.

—Matthew Winkler
August 2011

Acknowledgments

Three words characterize the people who follow the Bloomberg Way: *integrity, commitment* and *gratitude.*

Without integrity, there is no value in anything we do. Without commitment, there is no assurance of our integrity. As every endeavor is derived from the assistance of those who come before us and those among us, our sense of integrity and commitment is inspired by our gratitude to them. Collaboration is the essence of the Bloomberg Way and therefore depends on integrity, commitment and gratitude.

Mike Bloomberg understood as much when he insisted not long after he started the company that we could dispense with titles on our business cards as only our names mattered. While we may be forgiven for being inept, there is no reason why we should expect to be forgiven for a lack of integrity. If we don't acknowledge our gratitude for the generosity of those who forgive our carelessness, we can't expect customers to remain loyal to us.

Integrity, commitment and *gratitude*—no other words matter as much as we go forth unafraid.

The Bloomberg Way has its origin in thousands of discussions about what's news and how to write the news. As the flaws of this guide are entirely mine, no one has suffered more slings and arrows of Winkler misfortune than Galen Meyer, who (forgive the modifiers) was tireless, patient and always pleasantly persistent helping me prepare the Weekly Notes that inform *The Bloomberg Way* for eight years. Brenda Batten has never flagged in her commitment to precision in language as a matter of Bloomberg News style. The Bloomberg Way was first applied by David Wilson, who proved during our initial learning programs in 1991 that young men and women with no training as journalists or knowledge of economics and markets can become proficient reporters and editors. Some of the graduates from the Wilson classroom are themselves managing and teaching the next generation of Bloomberg journalists today. Wilson's work continues so ably with Paul Addison, Leah Harrison Singer, Marybeth Sandell, Chris Thompson, Vyola Willson, Bob Brennan and Shin Pei. Charles Glasser, who is the model of probity as our newsroom counselor, remains indispensable as the legal authority in *The Bloomberg Way*. Tom Goldstein has no peer as the arbiter of best practices in journalism. If he didn't exist for Bloomberg News, we would have had to invent him. Similarly, Brendan Moynihan brings the rare sensibility derived from doing everything our customers have done as the master of the Bloomberg News Brain Trust. As hiring is perhaps the most important thing we do, no one has done as much to bring the best and brightest under the auspices of the Bloomberg Way as Tom Contiliano, whose knowledge of accounting figures prominently throughout this book.

Whatever benefits may come from the many hours I applied to making this guide, they must be attributed to mentors now, then and long ago. There is Mike Bloomberg, of course, and the sponsors I can only consider divine intervention: Peter Grauer, Dan Doctoroff, Norman Pearlstine, Reto Gregori, Marty Schenker, Tammi Snyder, Jerry Bell, Lex Fenwick, Beth Mazzeo, Tom Secunda, Patti Roskill, Martin Geller, Arthur Levitt, Dick DeScherer and Tom Golden. The success of the Bloomberg Way is entirely dependent on the leadership of executive editors Amanda Bennett, Chris Collins, Susan Goldberg, Laurie Hays, Ronald Henkoff, Daniel Hertzberg, Manuela Hoelterhoff, Albert Hunt, Kenneth Kohn, John McCorry, Daniel Moss, Tim Quinson, James Rubin, Marty Schenker, David Shipley and Josh Tyrangiel.

—MW

1

The Bloomberg Way

THE MANDATE OF Bloomberg News is to provide definitive coverage of economies, markets, companies and industries worldwide. This is the greatest opportunity in journalism today. We are dedicated to providing this news 24 hours a day, 365 days a year, with the depth and sensibility of a well-written newspaper or magazine.

Economies, markets, companies and industries are little understood, much less appreciated. The public—our readers, viewers and listeners—suffers the consequence of journalism's traditional ignorance of these subjects and the arrogance of reporters and editors reveling in their ignorance.

Once all of us understand this challenge, we will be on the road to a prosperous destiny, because it is the road least traveled by our peers and the most direct way to news that most people can use.

Following that road requires precision in language, scrupulous attention to detail, an insatiable hunger for knowledge, persistence in getting any task accomplished no matter how daunting, the humility to recognize that none of us is infallible and the decency to address anyone and everyone with concern and kindness.

And, because education is what remains after all that we've learned has been forgotten, as Albert Einstein said, we are dedicated to continuous education.

Our mission at Bloomberg News requires us to be:

First with the news of money, markets, companies, commodities, economies, government, culture, science and man-made and natural disasters.

As comprehensive as any publication on these subjects.

Written so that a layman can understand and a professional can appreciate.

Accurate and convincing in our presentation.

Skilled enough to be meticulous with details, because they give a story its authority.

Persistent in our pursuit of information as it relates to shareholders, bondholders and folks who have deposits at banks.

Honest enough to admit our mistakes as soon as we discover them.

Diligent enough to correct our mistakes as soon as we discover them.

Thoughtful enough to understand that the sum of us is greater than our parts.

Humble enough to know we can always do better.

These 10 principles bridge the gulf between those who say "Just get the news out" and those who insist on getting it right the first time. We can and should do both. The more knowledgeable and skilled we are, the easier the task becomes.

2

Principles

BLOOMBERG NEWS IS shaped by these principles. Reporters and editors who put them into practice stand to reap the rewards that go with success.

It isn't news if it isn't true. Accuracy is the most important principle in journalism. There is no such thing as being first with news if we're wrong.

News is not a commodity. The critical thinking we apply to reporting, writing and editing can make every story unique.

We are defined by our words. Writing to the highest standard is in the best interests of the reporter, the editor, Bloomberg News and our customers.

Show, don't tell. Back up statements and assertions with facts, figures and anecdotes. Write with nouns and verbs; shun adjectives and modifiers.

News is a surprise. What do we know today that we didn't know yesterday? That question will offer guidance when deciding which facts to highlight first.

Names make news. People want to read and hear about people—the actors and the victims. The bigger the name, the bigger the audience.

Not invented here. We immediately report news from other organizations and then seek to advance the story. We don't accept the frequent lapse in journalism that if we didn't break the news, it didn't happen, and we should never fail to acknowledge who did.

Follow the money. Explaining the role of money in all its forms—from capital flows to executive compensation to the cost of an acquisition to election spending—reveals the true meaning of the news.

One story for all. Think globally, not locally. Write with a style and simplicity that anyone, anywhere can understand.

The more we prepare, the luckier we will be. We report, write and edit stories in advance so we're prepared to deliver our best news judgment, which is what readers, listeners and viewers want and need most at the moment their interest is greatest.

3

The Five Fs

Bloomberg News is defined by these words:

Factual word. Be the most factual. Rely on nouns and verbs, because they are more precise than adjectives and adverbs. Strive for 100 percent accuracy. Use the Bloomberg terminal to obtain facts and context, and use our reporting to develop anecdotes. We want to impress with the quality of our information, not the intricacy of our prose.

First word. Be the first to report the news. This is essential to satisfy our audience, whose livelihoods depend on the timeliness of information. It's easiest to be first if we develop the necessary sources and knowledge in advance of the news. We also have to provide the fastest delivery of key information from news sources that are readily accessible to our rivals, such as economic reports and corporate releases.

Fastest word. Be the fastest to report the details. By being prepared, we can beat others every time with the latest facts, anecdotes and examples. Through the last update of a story, make every effort to provide the supporting information before anyone else.

Final word. Be the definitive source. At the end of a day, a Bloomberg News story ought to have as much context and perspective as any account published by major newspapers, if not more. It should be worthy of publication in any of the hundreds of publications worldwide that receive our stories.

Future word. Explain today's news in the context of tomorrow's. What does an event indicate? The answer is often vital to people deciding whether to buy, sell or hold stocks, bonds, currencies or commodities, because future events will determine whether their decisions are right or wrong. They need to know what they can expect, and they will have an appetite for our stories if we tell them.

Our existential angst with each story is how we get the first and fastest words to be the final and future words. That's why our achievement is greatest when we deliver stories that can be considered complete in the first published version. Readers shouldn't have to settle for only one of the Five Fs.

TOP <Go>, the front page of Bloomberg News on the Bloomberg terminal, is at its best when the factual, first, fastest, final and future words are embodied in each story and these stories are indistinguishable in their presentation.

At our best, we have proven that the Five Fs are compatible. We can break news and follow events with stories that are as insightful as anything in tomorrow's newspapers.

4

The Four-Paragraph Lead

BLOOMBERG NEWS STORIES have a structure as immutable as the rules that
govern sonnets and symphonies. The structure begins with the lead. We have
identified the ideal lead as having four paragraphs.

Here's a guide to what belongs there. Learn how to apply this to stories—
all stories—and you will know how to succeed.

Theme. This consists of two elements: the *what* and *why*, or sometimes
the *what* and *so what*.

What: The key piece(s) of information that the story will provide. Stories
about economic indicators, corporate earnings and markets must convey a
sense of direction: rose, fell or little changed. Include a comparison with historical performance or expectations to help show the surprise. Stories about
companies and people often begin with their names and provide a size-and-
scope reference that tells something about the subject to show why it matters
or how the news is relevant.

Why: Explains the key piece(s) of information. The explanation establishes
the narrative that the details and quote can support. Which components of
an economic indicator, segments of a company's business or securities in a

market were most responsible for the performance? Why is a company or person doing something?

So what: Explains why the news matters. Sometimes an event's significance is more newsworthy than explaining why it happened. Whenever that is true, the lead ought to mention what is at stake, either in place of the *why* element or in addition to it.

Details. Provide the other pieces of information that back up the theme or provide essential facts, such as statistics from an economic report or company financial statement, the location of the subject or the performance of a benchmark security or index.

Quotation. A statement in plain English from an authority who provides support for the theme. It gives the reader more confidence about the story's credibility. In some cases, we want an independent voice, preferably someone with a financial interest, such as a stock owner or bondholder.

Nut paragraph. What's at stake? This paragraph, sometimes called the cosmic paragraph, explains why people ought to care about a story even if they don't have a direct relationship to its subject. The nut paragraph provides context and perspective that make the story easy to understand and interesting to a wider range of customers. How does today's news relate to the past and future? What could happen as a result?

Aside from the *what* element of the theme, the order of the elements in the four-paragraph lead is flexible. The first paragraph can explain why, mention what's at stake or provide both. The quote can go in the second paragraph if it supports the lead or in the fourth paragraph if it needs a nut paragraph to set up the topic. The details can go in any paragraph where they best support the theme.

Stories that have only these four paragraphs can put events in perspective. A fifth paragraph may be included when needed to supply more breaking news or add more context.

Apply this formula to every story and readers won't miss much.

Here are some of the tasks that reporters and editors must perform in order to conform to the four-paragraph lead format:

Determine the key piece(s) of information. Failing to include the most important facts, or including too many facts, makes it difficult to attract and to hold the audience's attention.

Select an appropriate size and scope. What defines the subject? While most will cite a company's size in its industry, another reference often can do a better job. What makes the subject unique? What makes it unique to this story?

Include the *why* or the *so what* along with the *what*. Unless the explanation is part of the theme, the story won't have a well-established narrative that the quotation and details can support.

Add details that relate directly to the theme. Good writing involves deciding not only whether information belongs in a story, but also where it belongs. Details put in the wrong place can sidetrack the narrative. Too many details lumped together can stop a reader.

Have a quotation that backs up the theme. Sometimes quotes refer to details that aren't central to the story or undermine the theme rather than support it. When that happens, the reader can get confused and the writing loses credibility.

Tune your ear to key quotes. Good first quotes vividly summarize the story's theme, back up the writer's authoritative voice, deliver a promised punch line and set up the story to come.

Explain the news sufficiently before providing context. To understand why a story matters, people must first have an idea of what the story is. Otherwise, the context and perspective become meaningless.

It is important to appreciate why we are obsessed with leads, details, quotes and nut paragraphs. There is nothing like great writing. It does so many things for people. It keeps the morale high, because it's one thing we can take pride in every day. It has a way of sustaining people year in and year out, inspiring them. Competitors who look at something done elsewhere that is more precise and graceful are humbled by that comparison.

That proverb "On the day of victory, nobody is tired" is what we're after. Here's an example from 2010:

Druckenmiller Calls It Quits After 30 Years as Job Gets Tougher
(Names, surprise and tension attract readers.)

Aug. 19 (Bloomberg) -- Hedge-fund icon Stanley Druckenmiller is quitting the business after three decades, telling investors he'd been worn down by the stress of trying to maintain one of the best trading records in the industry while managing an "enormous amount of capital."
(Includes the *what, why* and *so what.*)

"For 30 years I've been responsible for managing client money and it's been a joy, but at some point I need to move on," Druckenmiller, who made $1 billion for George Soros by forcing a devaluation of the British pound in 1992, said in a two-hour interview in his New York City office on Aug. 17. "Thirty years is enough."
(The voice is that of the protagonist. In other cases, it may be appropriate to quote a fund manager or someone with something at stake.)

Druckenmiller, 57, said he's frustrated by his failure in the past three years to match returns that had averaged 30 percent annually since 1986. His Duquesne Capital Management LLC, which oversees $12 billion and has never had a losing year, is down 5 percent in 2010.
(Includes the supporting details, more of the *why*, and the background that any reader needs to know before going further.)

Druckenmiller built his reputation making large bets on macroeconomic themes that he spotted before others, a skill he shares with legendary traders Bruce Kovner, Michael Steinhardt and Soros, the Hungarian-born billionaire. The decision to shut Duquesne suggests that in an era in which the biggest *hedge funds oversee $30 billion and are adding more assets, they may no longer be able to routinely outperform conventional funds by wide margins.* (The context fits today's news with the bigger picture.)

Headlines

Write a dynamic headline and the story has the best chance of becoming influential.

Headlines matter because they are the first words our customers see, whether they are for a story that was written in five minutes after a news release or a 2,000-word profile that took six months to report, write and edit.

We don't have a monopoly on headlines. Ours compete against at least half a million other headlines a day on statements, analysts' reports and stories from other news organizations that scroll across the Bloomberg terminal screen.

Before reporters write a word of narrative—even the lead—they should write the headline. Nothing focuses a story better than the discipline of first having to report its contents in 63 characters. Asking, "What's the headline?" helps to focus leads, which often are too long or have too many thoughts. "What's the headline?" will help identify which facts and figures should be provided in the first four paragraphs. "What's the headline?" will help determine a nut paragraph that explains what's at stake.

These are the elements that make the best headlines:

Names. The names that make news should come first in a headline, because the reader sees them first. The bigger the name, the greater the chance the story will be read. The exception is when the subject is the surprise.

Before:
Obama Names Goolsbee to Lead White House Economic Advisers Panel
After:
Goolsbee to Direct Obama's Economic Panel Advising on Job Growth

Surprise. If news is defined as a surprise, then the headline should be surprising or present enough of a conflict to provoke curiosity about its outcome.

Before:

Payrolls in U.S. Increase 290,000 in April; Unemployment at 9.9%

After:

U.S. Payrolls Rise Most in Four Years as Private Jobs Exceed Forecasts

Before:

New York City Region Purchasers February Index Reaches 69.8

After:

New York City Businesses Expand at Fastest Pace in Decade

What's at stake? The headline should explain why the news matters, even to readers who might not otherwise have an interest in the topic.

Before:

Three-Month Dollar Libor Rises to a Seven-Year High

After:

Libor Rises to a Seven-Year High on Subprime Concern

Before:

New U.S. Lawmakers Tap Corporate Pipeline to Amass Funds

After:

U.S. Lawmakers Raise Campaign Funds to Intimidate Foes

Conflict and conflict resolution. Framing headlines around the action and consequences will set up the drama and tension.

Before:

House and Senate Face Tough Negotiations Over Tax Measure

After:

Congress Risks $30 Billion Budget Shortfall With Tax Cuts

Before:

Hedge-Fund Managers' Taxes Might Be a Medicare Shot in the Arm

After:

Hedge-Fund Billionaires Eyed by Congress for More Medicare Tax

A headline that has two, three or more of these elements will probably entice customers to read the story.

Leads

A lead has to be compelling enough to make people want to know more. Capturing the theme—what the news is and why it is important—is usually the best way to accomplish this. Most leads start with the story's most important name—a company, an organization, a person—because names make news. Put Bill Gates at the beginning, and the story will get the attention of Microsoft Corp.'s managers, employees, customers, suppliers, competitors and investors, as well as people who want to know what one of the world's richest men is doing.

Leads about an industry or market, especially the stock market, benefit from naming companies. Industries consist of companies, as do stock markets. The more companies we cite, the more newsworthy our story becomes. Each company has holders of its shares and bonds who will read any story that mentions their investments. The details confer credibility and authority.

U.S. stocks rose the most in six months amid signs that fourth-quarter earnings will exceed analysts' estimates. Boeing Co., General Motors Corp. and Caterpillar Inc. led the advance.

By mentioning the three companies in the lead, the story begins its seduction of the reader. It isn't just that some numerical measures known as indexes rose. Specific stocks advanced, and for each there is a story.

Leads need to be clear and straightforward, demonstrating an obvious cause and effect. This lead doesn't meet any of these standards . . .

U.S. bonds rose as traders awaited reports this week that may provide more evidence on whether the economy is growing fast enough to cause inflation to accelerate.

. . . because it wades through several thoughts without a pause. Worse, it doesn't explain why bond prices rose. Our job is to find at least one plausible reason, and preferably several, for any price change. If people in the market say they are looking forward to economic reports, we must explain what they expect the reports to show. To write that traders are waiting for inflation reports is like saying they are waiting for the sun to rise.

Be sure the reason is specific. *Company A is acquiring Company B for $2 billion to expand its business* is obvious. Of course the company is expanding. That's the result of most acquisitions. Why this acquisition at this time? *Company A is acquiring Company B, its biggest competitor, to double its share of the market for widgets* says something that isn't so obvious.

Add context and perspective to explain why the news is significant.

Before:

President Barack Obama said his plan to refashion supervision of the U.S. financial system is needed to fix lapses in oversight and excessive risk taking that helped push the economy into a prolonged recession.

After:

President Barack Obama proposed the most sweeping overhaul of the U.S. financial regulatory system in 75 years, seeking to correct a "cascade of mistakes" that toppled Merrill Lynch & Co. and Lehman Brothers Holdings Inc., sparked the worst economic crisis since the Great Depression, froze credit markets and destroyed $26.4 trillion in stock market value.

Only the most newsworthy numbers belong in a lead. Numbers distract the eye. Cite a percentage change or a size and scope for the figure when possible, rather than the actual numbers. Actual figures are meaningful only if readers, viewers and listeners know everything there is to know about the subject—and if that is the case, they probably know what happened to the numbers.

Compare the first lead after this economic figure was released . . .

Japan's economy expanded at an annualized 0.4 percent pace in the three months ended June 30, the Cabinet Office said today in Tokyo. The median estimate of 19 economists surveyed by Bloomberg News was for 2.3 percent.

. . . with this update that puts the percentage change into perspective . . .

Japan's economy expanded at the slowest pace in three quarters, missing the estimates of all economists surveyed as global demand cooled and the government's stimulus wore off.

. . . and with this lead that puts Japan's economy into a global context . . .

China surpassed Japan as the world's second-largest economy last quarter, capping the nation's three-decade rise from Communist isolation to emerging superpower.

Leads should be actionable and definitive. The original lead advertised what we didn't know.

Before:

The death of Massachusetts Senator Edward M. Kennedy is likely to set off an intense battle for a seat that has been held for almost 55 of the past 57 years by a member of his famous family.

After:

Massachusetts Governor Deval Patrick could temporarily replace the late U.S. Senator Edward Kennedy as early as the fourth week in September under a timetable being considered by Democratic members of the Legislature.

Leads that contain multiple clauses can be difficult to understand.

Before:

U.S. bonds surged, gaining for a seventh day in eight, as evidence of slower wage growth boosted expectations that the Federal Reserve won't raise interest rates for a third time this year on Nov. 16.

After:

U.S. bonds extended their rally as slower wage growth suggested that the Federal Reserve has fewer reasons to raise interest rates.

Breaking leads into two sentences can make them more compelling.

Before:

European stocks gained, with banks such as Spain's Banco Bilbao Vizcaya SA and Italy's Banca di Roma SpA leading benchmark indexes higher, amid optimism interest rates won't rise.

After:

European stocks gained on speculation that interest rates won't rise soon. Spain's Banco Bilbao Vizcaya SA and Italy's Banca di Roma SpA were among the biggest winners.

Be flexible and creative. Some of the best leads take fewer than 20 words. Strive for brevity and simplicity while attempting to surprise.

China's economy finally achieved its Great Leap Forward—overnight.

Ben Bernanke, Ivy League economist and monetary theorist, meet Ben Bernanke, White House economic adviser. You might have some difficulty recognizing one another.

The U.S. government agency that promotes corporate transparency has some secrets. Lots of them.

Ahmed Hanafi was born in a Cairo cemetery in 1975. He still lives there.

While the rewrite of the next lead doesn't follow the typical format, it provides the theme well enough to make the reader want to know more. It captures the tension and the conflict.

Before:

U.S. retailers' earnings will rise in the fiscal third quarter, led by demand for brand-name goods at discount retailers such as Wal-Mart Stores Inc. and fashions at specialty shops including Gap Inc.

After:

U.S. consumers want their goods creative—and cheap.

Leads that begin with anecdotes work best when they are short and the story's theme develops immediately.

John Reed said he was scrubbing his new Beneteau Ombrine motorboat last Friday afternoon in a village on Ile de Re, off the southwest coast of France, when an old friend called.

It was Henry Paulson, chairman and chief executive officer of Goldman Sachs Group Inc., phoning to ask him to come back to the U.S. and save the world's biggest stock exchange.

"John, we have a little problem," said Paulson, who sits on the New York Stock Exchange board. The exchange, in turmoil and leaderless after the forced departure of Chairman Richard Grasso, needed a replacement seen as neutral and free of any conflict of interest.

"I knew that Grasso had been sacked but that didn't matter much to me. I read it in the newspapers," Reed said in an interview yesterday at Les Colonnes, his favorite cafe, more than three years and thousands of miles from his own departure in April 2000 as chairman of Citigroup Inc. following a power struggle with its current chairman, Sanford Weill.

Size and Scope

Whenever people are introduced, it is necessary to explain what these people do: "I'd like you to meet Fred, who was a reporter for 10 years at the *Daily Planet* in New York before he became editor of the *International Review.*"

That description is the size and scope. We insist on size and scope for the subjects in our stories because they explain something significant or exceptional about the person, company or event that we're introducing to the reader. Names are more newsworthy when we remind readers why newsmakers are important.

The size-and-scope element is the defining characteristic of the subject, helping put it into perspective.

The sooner the size-and-scope element appears, the faster the tale unfolds. The size-and-scope clause often includes a superlative, such as a subject's ranking or importance:

> *Coca-Cola, the world's most valuable brand,*
> *Credit Suisse Group, the first major European bank to market*
> *mutual funds developed and managed by competitors,*
> *Wal-Mart Stores Inc., the largest private employer in the U.S.,*
> *Wal-Mart Stores Inc., the biggest importer of goods into the U.S.,*
> *The U.S. Northeast, which burns 75 percent of the nation's heating fuel,*
> *Lehman Brothers Holdings Inc., which filed the world's largest*
> *bankruptcy case,*
> *Barack Obama, the first black U.S. president,*
> *Franklin Resources Inc., the biggest publicly traded U.S.*
> *mutual-fund company,*
> *China, which accounted for one 10th of the world's economic growth*
> *last year,*

We normally define size by sales. If we're defining by any other measure—assets, market value, number of subscribers, etc.—show the measure in the story.

Look beyond size or ranking. Scope can provide immediate context, help explain why the story is important, or capture the irony.

Italian Prime Minister Silvio Berlusconi, who controls the country's biggest private broadcaster, says television coverage of him is unfair.

Veritas Software Corp., whose name is Latin for "truth," said Kenneth Lonchar resigned as chief financial officer after admitting he lied about having a master's degree in business administration from Stanford University. The company's shares fell 19 percent.

The articles *a* and *an* are often ineffective in defining the subject. Referring to a company as *a maker* of something means it's one of many. *The* is definitive when followed by labeling or action that is unique.

Before:

Monsanto Inc., a maker of agricultural products,

After:

Monsanto Inc., the maker of top-selling herbicide Roundup,

Avoid saying two things in the same size-and-scope clause or packing in too many thoughts.

Before:

Waterford Wedgwood Plc, the Irish maker of luxury crystal that said in October it may bid for Royal Doulton Plc, will go ahead with an offer that values the British producer of porcelain figurines at 39.9 million pounds ($77 million).

After:

Waterford Wedgwood Plc, the Irish maker of crystal and china whose roots date back to the 18th century, plans to bid 39.9 million pounds ($77 million) for Royal Doulton Plc, the 190-year-old British producer of porcelain figurines.

Separating the size-and-scope element from what it is modifying may confuse the reader. The size-and-scope clause should be a direct reference, not an indirect one that forces the reader to connect the dots or assumes knowledge on the reader's part. In this example, will most readers know that Japan is the second-largest economy in the world?

Before:

> *Japanese household spending fell in September as stagnant wages prevented consumers from making purchases, sapping growth in the world's second-largest economy.*

After:

> *Household spending in Japan, the world's second-largest economy, fell in September as stagnant wages sapped growth by preventing consumers from making purchases.*

Reinforcing the Lead

Every successful story supports the lead's theme with authoritative details, quotes or anecdotes. Second paragraphs are convenient for this purpose. They should amplify, not say the same thing.

> *Lehman Brothers Holdings Inc., the fourth-largest U.S. investment bank, succumbed to the subprime mortgage crisis it helped create in the biggest bankruptcy filing in history.*
> *The 158-year-old firm, which survived railroad bankruptcies of the 1800s, the Great Depression in the 1930s and the collapse of Long-Term Capital Management a decade ago, filed a Chapter 11 petition with U.S. Bankruptcy Court in Manhattan today. The collapse of Lehman, which listed more than $613 billion of debt, dwarfs WorldCom Inc.'s insolvency in 2002 and Drexel Burnham Lambert's failure in 1990.*

When we head in one direction in the lead and go in another with the second paragraph, we're confusing readers. The elements shouldn't clash.

Before:

Crude oil fell the most in almost two months in New York on concern the U.S. economy will slow and reduce demand at a time of rising supplies.

Oil prices climbed to a record this year partly because U.S. and Chinese economic growth spurred energy consumption.

After:

Crude oil fell the most in almost two months in New York on concern the U.S. economy will slow and reduce demand at a time of rising supplies.

Oil prices have fallen 7.1 percent from the record $78.77 a barrel on Aug. 1 amid signs that losses in the mortgage market may reduce growth in the U.S., the world's biggest energy consumer.

Quotations

Stories that provide opinions uttered by newsmakers who have the most at stake—chief executives, chief financial officers, shareholders, bondholders, prime ministers and presidents—inspire more confidence. Quoting those whose voices matter is a sure way to persuade people to rely on Bloomberg News.

People interested in the stock market will never tire of a market report that has Warren Buffett saying something in the second paragraph. Anyone interested in computers will never tire of a story that has Bill Gates opining in the second paragraph. Who is the Buffett or Gates in your industry, market, economy, country or area of coverage? Get to know them and get their comments into stories.

The bigger the name, the tougher the access. That's what makes getting such opinions appealing.

Easy-to-reach sources are a great temptation because they are helpful, are quick to pick up the phone and give vivid comments. They are also dangerous because all they ever give is the sound bite—and they probably will give the same sound bite to the many other journalists who call. Better to get an opinion from someone with something at stake in the news.

It is essential for reporters to learn how to listen for quotes, how to get people to utter them, how to use them to inspire writing, and how to structure articles around them. You may have to needle and wheedle your subjects. Joke with them. Rephrase the question. Return to the point again and again. Never feel guilty about pushing for an articulate point of view. No one wants to sound stupid.

Quotes must provide some form of human content—opinion, analysis or interpretation—rather than information that a computer or news release could spit out. Choose remarks that contain a special energy and clarity.

"It's the most revolutionary thing to happen since the Industrial Revolution—there's no question."
(Jack Welch, former chairman of General Electric Co., speaking about the Internet.)

"I've had all the fun I can stand in investment banking."
(Bank of America Chief Executive Officer Kenneth Lewis, announcing plans to cut 3,000 jobs at the bank's corporate and investment banking unit.)

"I'm not boasting, but I think I'm the greatest lawyer in the world."
(Willie Gary, a Florida lawyer, after he won a $500 million verdict in a lawsuit against a funeral-home company.)

Not all quotes are this dazzling. While no one would save the following quote for posterity, it tells how a stakeholder views the company. In that sense, the quote is human:

"I'm absolutely giddy," said Jane Snorek, who helps manage $40 billion at US Bancorp. "Business is so strong that this is definitely not seasonality."
(Snorek spoke after Intel Corp. said sales would increase as much as 22 percent.)

Quotation marks promise flesh-and-blood and character. To deliver only numerical data is false advertising.

"Something like 60 percent of the card charges are actually cash advances," said Sam Chin, a banking analyst at ABN Amro Securities Ltd.

Pointing out the actions and performance of people who provide analysis and make predictions helps establish their credibility and authority.

"This company can go a long way for a long, long time," said Hugh Evans, an analyst at T. Rowe Price Associates Inc. The Baltimore-based mutual-fund company owns more than 1.5 million shares of Cabot, or a 6.5 percent stake, Evans said. Since September, T. Rowe Price has almost quadrupled its holdings.

Put comments into context to help explain why the person's opinion matters.

Before:
"They have pushed the DNA of the Gucci brand very fast and very aggressively," said Concetta Lanciaux, an industry consultant.
After:
"They have pushed the DNA of the Gucci brand very fast and very aggressively," said Concetta Lanciaux, an industry consultant and former aide to the chairman of competitor LVMH.

Analysts typically encourage a firm's customers to buy, sell and trade securities and help investment bankers arrange security sales. When we cite an analyst, explain why the person's opinion matters, such as whether he or she ranks at the top of the lists of influential analysts or whether past recommendations have moved the stock. Also note whether the analyst owns any of the shares.

"It is all about the economy at this point in attempting to value bank stocks," said Paul Miller, who ranked first among more than 3,000 stock-picking analysts worldwide in 2008, according to data compiled by Bloomberg. Miller, an analyst for FBR Capital Markets in Arlington, Virginia, cut his estimate for Bank of America's annual earnings by 40 percent to 45 cents a share.

Details

Details that support the theme are essential to any story. Our readers are pressed for time. Asking a reader to press the page-forward button is like asking a newspaper reader to go from the front page to an inside page to finish an article. Many won't.

If a lead says *XYZ Corp.'s earnings rose 20 percent in the third quarter*, the numbers used to calculate the change often should be in the first four paragraphs. Stories about mergers and acquisitions typically provide an offer's terms. In market reports, include at least one quotation for stock indexes, bonds, currencies or commodity futures that shows whether prices rose or fell. Economic stories need to provide key statistics.

Be sparing. A wall of facts and figures will discourage readers.

News judgment means deciding where information belongs, not just what should be included. Give enough details to back up the theme and add the rest later.

What is left out can be as important as what is included. The following lead purposely omitted the numbers:

China's economic expansion slowed for the first time in a year as Premier Wen Jiabao curbed investment to keep the world's fastest-growing major economy from overheating.
Gross domestic product in the third quarter rose 10.4 percent from a year earlier after gaining 11.3 percent in the prior three months, the statistics bureau said in Beijing today. Second-quarter growth was the fastest in more than a decade.

Providing details can be a matter of fairness. It would be unfair to report that a bank president was arrested on charges of embezzlement without mentioning that the district attorney had failed to secure any convictions after six similar and transparently political arrests.

These details should be on the first screen of any story:

Location. Specify where a company is based, where a government official spoke, where trading occurred, where an investor is based, where a battle happened, where a conference took place. This is important because we don't include locations in datelines.

If an article about a Paris-based company's earnings includes a comment from a shareholder in New York, make the locations clear. If the chief executive of a Seattle-based retailer was interviewed while attending a conference in Tokyo, report where the executive spoke.

When the location isn't familiar, help pinpoint it for our worldwide audience. Motorola Inc. is based in Schaumburg, Illinois. Mentioning that Schaumburg is a suburb of Chicago makes it easier for people to recognize.

Time element. Most stories should include what day the news happened, which is almost always today. The day should appear on the first screen and often will fit well in the second paragraph. The day doesn't belong in the lead unless it is germane to the news. Market stories are an exception. We don't need to specify today because readers know that reports about trading are that day's news.

Attribution. Always tell the reader how we know what we know. Attribution should be precise, ubiquitous and transparent. Was it from an interview? A news release? A press conference? An e-mail? A memo? A note to clients? How was it distributed?

We give credit where credit is due. When another organization breaks a story, we cite it in our stories. As the day goes on and the news grows stale, that credit can move lower. Once the news is announced, we no longer need to note who scored the scoop.

People. Names make news. Highlight stakeholders in the news. The success of a chief executive officer's strategy can be measured by the performance of earnings, sales, market share, stocks and bonds. The same is true for heads of state, central bankers and others who run organizations.

Nut Paragraphs

Readers need a sense of what's at stake to know why they ought to care about an event, and the nut paragraph provides it, especially when there is a superlative such as most, worst, biggest, smallest and so on.

It isn't sufficient for a story to rewrite the news release that says XYZ Co. will introduce a product line next month. We need to report the estimated revenue, the reasons for marketing the product, the effect on the company's outlook, changes in employment, the company's track record with new products, the reaction of shareholders and analysts and so on. It shouldn't just be background or history pulled from the Bloomberg's archives.

A nut paragraph should put the breaking news into perspective and explain why it's significant. What does the news mean, show, suggest, reflect or illustrate? The nut paragraph should convey ideas, not just facts. It should conjure images, not just numbers. It should look forward, not just backward, and use the history as a secondary theme.

Writing a nut paragraph is a challenge under deadline. The more we emphasize context in each story, the easier it will be to meet the challenge.

Start by asking these questions:

What's at stake? The nut paragraph should explain why the news in the lead is important.

What was the biggest event in the life of this company, institution or person in the past 12 months?

Who will be hurt? Who will benefit? Identify the winners and losers.

Where do we go from here? Better or worse? If so, how so? What's the outlook?

The nut paragraph may spring from the answers to one or more of those questions. The answers may be anecdotes: *The company lost more money in the past 12 months than at any time in its history. It fired 25 percent of its workers, closed half of its offices and may seek bankruptcy.*

Context comes from persistently explaining why something is so and why it matters. It comes from knowing the story of the beat.

> *Boeing Co., General Electric Co. and other companies share interests with China on issues such as lower tariffs and a stable currency. Their willingness to go to bat for the country illustrates China's growing importance to U.S. companies, which imported $70 billion of Chinese goods and components last year, more than half of the nation's exports to the U.S.*

5

Five Easy Pieces

For people with the most at stake, no story is complete without some reporting of the relationship between markets, economy, government, politics and companies. These five pieces provide the context and perspective necessary to comprehend the meaning of events.

The latest economic figures become more understandable when our reporting includes examples about the relevant markets, companies and government initiatives. Reporting about companies is more meaningful when the narrative consists of anecdotes about the economy, markets and politics and policy. Markets are best understood when the perspective is informed by examples about companies, economies, politics and policy.

Including these pieces in every story, with varying degrees of emphasis, is essential to providing the most influential news. The following example of a daily economic report includes each of the five pieces, showing how they converge with the First word, Factual word, Fastest word, Final word and Future word.

Employers Cut Most Jobs in Five Years as Crisis Hits Main Street

(The economic piece:)
Oct. 3 (Bloomberg) -- U.S. payrolls plunged in September, signaling that the economy may be heading for its worst recession in at least a quarter-century as the 13-month-long credit crisis on Wall Street finally hits home on Main Street.

Employers cut the most jobs in five years in September as cash-squeezed companies pulled back to bolster pinched profits. In its last employment report before Americans choose their next president, the Labor Department said the unemployment rate was 6.1 percent, a climb of 1.4 percentage points from a year before.

"If credit markets remain dysfunctional, the current recession could turn out to be as severe as any in the postwar period," said Lyle Gramley, a former Federal Reserve governor, in a telephone interview from Washington.

(The political piece:)
Polls show that voters increasingly see Democrat Barack Obama as the candidate best able to steer the U.S. through economic travails. The unemployment rate has risen only twice in the year leading up to elections since World War II, and in each case the incumbent party lost.

"This country can't afford Senator McCain's plan to give America four more years of the same policies that have devastated our middle class and our economy for the last eight," Obama, 47, said in a statement.

McCain's Reaction

Arizona Senator John McCain, a 72-year-old Republican, called his opponent a tax-and-spend liberal whose prescriptions would exacerbate the crisis.

"Unlike Senator Obama, I do not believe we will create one single American job by increasing taxes, going on a massive spending binge, and closing off markets," McCain said in a statement. "Our nation cannot afford Senator Obama's higher taxes."

Americans will go to the polls on Nov. 4.

(The government piece:)
*The credit crisis deepened last month, forcing the failure or
government takeovers of Lehman Brothers Holdings Inc., Fannie Mae,
Freddie Mac and American International Group Inc.*

*The jobs figures came hours before the House of Representatives
passed a $700 billion rescue plan for the financial industry pushed by
Treasury Secretary Henry Paulson. The Senate approved the legislation two
days ago after the House rejected an initial version on Sept. 29.*

Market Reaction

(The market piece:)
*Stocks rose and Treasury securities fell. The Standard & Poor's
500 index climbed 1.8 percent to 1,134.6 at 1:39 p.m. in New York.
The yield on the benchmark 10-year note rose to 3.71 percent from 3.63
percent late yesterday.*

*Today's report showed that hours worked—a proxy for the state of
the economy—matched the lowest level since records began in 1964. That
indicates the recession may be at least as severe as the 1981–82 slump,
when the gross domestic product shrank 2.7 percent.*

*Edelmira Clark, a 53-year-old hotel housekeeper, said her hours have
been cut to two days a week and she is afraid she may lose her job.*

*"I'm trying to find a part-time job in the morning to balance, because I
can't do only two days of work," said Clark, who immigrated to Chicago from
Belize in 1997. "A lot of people, my friends, have lost their jobs for good."*

Payrolls Shrink

*Payrolls fell by 159,000 in September, the Labor Department said
in Washington. All major categories showed declines except government,
education and health care.*

*Health-care employment rose by 17,000, about half the average
monthly gain for the prior 12 months. Walgreen Co., the largest drugstore*

chain, reported Sept. 29 that its profit rose less than analysts estimated after the smallest sales increase in a decade. Factory payrolls fell by 51,000 after decreasing by 56,000 in August. Economists had forecast a drop of 57,000.

(The company piece:)
In the past month, Hewlett-Packard Co., the world's largest personal-computer maker, said it would cut 24,600 jobs, and auto-parts maker Federal-Mogul Corp. said it would eliminate 4,000. Without action from Congress, "the resulting credit squeeze could threaten businesses," said Arne Sorenson, chief financial officer for Marriott International Inc., the biggest U.S. hotel chain. There are "tens of thousands of jobs at stake in our company alone, and we are typical."

While reporting these five pieces is difficult for any individual under the most rigorous deadline, they become easier to deliver when there is communication, cooperation and collaboration. The editors in charge of markets, upon learning that a story about the economy is pending, should already be thinking about sharing the appropriate market piece that helps explain the impact. Through mutual assistance, we create a virtuous circle of excellence from Five Easy Pieces.

6

Show, Don't Tell

Show, don't tell is a simple rule for writing well. Rely on facts, anecdotes and examples, rather than characterizations and modifiers, to convince readers and listeners that we were there or know what we write is true.

Let the facts provide the *proof.* Including the evidence makes our stories instantly credible. A story is incomplete and untrustworthy when it includes unsupported assertions. Avoid adverbs that are loaded with assertions: *lavishly compensated, hugely successful, flatly denied, greatly underestimated.* The best reporters assemble the details, anecdotes and comments and then let the readers decide who's right, wrong, guilty or innocent. They don't rely on phrases such as *raises questions* or *raises eyebrows.*

The same goes for adjectives that are equally imprecise: *strong sales, robust economy, major rally, weak demand* and *steady rates.* What does strong mean? Is it a 20 percent sales increase? 50 percent? 75 percent? Is the economy robust when gross domestic product is growing at a 2 percent rate? 4 percent? 6 percent?

These leads show, rather than tell, because they rely on anecdotes and examples:

U.S. Treasuries rose on speculation that declines in stock prices may prompt the Federal Reserve to cut interest rates by half a percentage point as early as next week.

Spain's economy grew in the third quarter almost twice as much as the average of the nations sharing the euro, as rising employment and record low interest rates spurred consumer spending and construction.

Let nouns, verbs, facts, figures and anecdotes do the work. E.B. White once said an adjective hasn't been born that could pull a noun out of a tight spot. Mark Twain told a young correspondent, "When you can catch an adjective, kill it."

Before:

John Kerry is a decorated Vietnam War veteran.

After:

John Kerry was awarded a Silver Star, a Bronze Star and three Purple Hearts in the Vietnam War. He received the Silver Star for turning his boat back under fire in the Mekong Delta to rescue a soldier knocked overboard.

Before:

The vote was along party lines.

After:

The vote was 51–48 against the treaty, with all but four Republicans opposed.

Before:

The U.S. Federal Reserve cited sluggish business investment as a drag on economic growth.

After:

The U.S. Federal Reserve cited business investment, which has declined in nine of the past 11 quarters, as a drag on economic growth.

When referring to criticism, identify those making the assertion or explain instead of using the label.

Before:

Critics say the law would deny employees a secret ballot election and make them vulnerable to union scare tactics.

After:

Wal-Mart Stores Inc., the nation's largest retailer, and Republican lawmakers said last year that the law would deny employees a secret ballot election and make them vulnerable to union scare tactics.

Before:

The company, which has been criticized for assigning top grades to mortgage debt that proved worthless, said realized losses will probably be less than $1 billion.

After:

The company, criticized last year by Congress and the Securities and Exchange Commission for assigning top grades to mortgages that proved worthless, said realized losses will probably be less than $1 billion.

Characterizations

Characterizations are subjective judgments we shouldn't make. Our job is to report what people say or do.

Before:

InBev tried to calm fears of big cutbacks at Anheuser-Busch.

After:

InBev's chief executive officer, Carlos Brito, pledged in a letter to his counterpart at Anheuser-Busch that he wouldn't close any breweries for half a century.

Before:

Iran played down the significance of trade incentives offered by the European Union and the U.S., saying they won't deprive the country of its "right" to build up nuclear power.

After:

Iran said it won't give up its "legitimate right" to develop a nuclear power program, a day after the U.S. offered trade incentives to the Islamic republic as part of a policy to discourage the development of weapons of mass destruction.

Steer clear of words that suggest a subjective judgment by the reader, such as *seem* or *just.*

Before:

Blankfein never seemed to see a need to change the business model that helped Goldman Sachs set industry records for earnings and pay in 2006 and 2007.

After:

Blankfein has shown no inclination to change the business model that helped Goldman Sachs set industry records for earnings and pay in 2006 and 2007.

Before:

Tracy is just the second manager to win the award after being hired during the season, following Jack McKeon of the Marlins in 2003.

After:

Tracy is the second manager in the award's 26-year history to win after being hired during the season, following Jack McKeon of the Marlins in 2003.

Labels mean different things to different people. In politics, who decides whether someone is moderate, conservative, liberal, left wing, right wing? How can a reader in Singapore know the difference between a San Francisco liberal and a San Antonio liberal? Define people or organizations by specific events. Let characterizations come from the people or groups we profile, admirers and detractors, and their positions.

Before:

The center-right Berlusconi government said in May that it won't boost tax rates to reduce the 78 billion-euro ($98 billion) budget deficit for 2010.

After:

The Berlusconi government, which supports cutting the budget deficit, said in May that it wouldn't increase tax rates to reduce the 78 billion-euro ($98 billion) shortfall for 2010.

Before:

Obama generally has picked moderate "easily confirmable" nominees, said Nan Aron, president of the liberal advocacy group Alliance for Justice in Washington.

After:

Obama has picked "easily confirmable" nominees, said Nan Aron, president of Alliance for Justice, an association of 100 environmental, consumer and women's rights groups that helped thwart the nominations of judges nominated by President George W. Bush and supported Sonia Sotomayor as the first Hispanic woman justice on the U.S. Supreme Court.

Assertions

Assertions require examples, anecdotes, attribution or quotations that support the statement. Readers, listeners and viewers won't trust what we say without the proof.

Before:

Potential buyers are waiting for falling prices to hit bottom, causing the inventory of unsold properties to swell. People who are ready to buy face difficulty obtaining financing as lenders have tightened lending standards and cut back on the number of mortgages they are writing.

After:

Potential buyers are waiting for prices to hit bottom, causing the inventory of unsold properties to swell, said Paul Kasriel, the chief economist at Northern Trust Corp. and author of "Seven Indicators That Move Markets." People who are ready to buy face difficulty obtaining financing as lenders tighten standards and reduce the number of new mortgages, he said.

If we can't provide examples, the assertion should be discarded before publication.

Anecdotes

Anecdotes are the substance of depth reporting and unique storytelling. Anecdotes support whatever assertions are made. Anecdotes provide context. A story without anecdotes is a story at risk of becoming a commodity.

An anecdote conveys an event in the life of whatever or whomever we are writing about. It is an example of something that happened to a person or something he did that illustrates character or thinking.

The more specific the anecdote, the better. Saying someone is struggling is vague. Show it: *She fired 25 percent of the company's employees and canceled the free lunches.*

The anecdote should show the reader that you were there, or at least that your sources have been there.

When at a scene, write what you see: the titles of the books on the shelves (*Good to Great*), the paintings on the walls (René Magritte), the state of the person's desk (bare except for an 8-by-10 black-and-white photograph of her two daughters), the way she interacts with colleagues ("Nice to see you showed up, so we won't go broke today!").

If you interview by telephone, ask the person to describe the scene in as much detail as possible. How many people were at the meeting? Who was there? What was the size of the room? What floor? The shape of the table? Were people eating, smoking, drinking, laughing, all speaking at once, sitting in silence, secretly checking their e-mail?

For every assertion that the company is *customer-focused* and that the deal is *a win-win situation*, ask: Can you give me an example? Keep asking: How so?

How do you know that? What do you mean by that? Can you explain? Keep asking, even if you get a great quote. You may need to ask the same question, or some variation, two, three or more times. Sometimes, you'll have to circle back after the person has changed the subject. Often, you'll need to call back—maybe several times—for more details. Be relentless.

This excerpt from a profile of Richard Fuld, the former chief executive officer of Lehman Brothers Holdings Inc., shows the revelatory value of anecdotes:

> *While Fuld and his fellow traders were dismayed at the sale, Glucksman urged them not to disband and give up their franchise. One evening shortly after the Lehman board vote, Glucksman gathered his top traders—including Fuld, Pettit and Gregory, all of whom he had hired—in a conference room at the firm's headquarters at 55 Water Street.*
>
> *Glucksman had a fistful of pencils. He handed a single pencil to each man and instructed his perplexed deputies to snap them in half. Glucksman then handed a bunch of pencils to Fuld and directed him to try to break them all at once. He couldn't do it.*
>
> *"By staying together, you have done great things," Glucksman said. "Stay together and you will continue to do great things."*

The anecdote will stick with readers long after they have forgotten everything else in the story.

7

Writing Well Matters

In the 1930s, the *Wall Street Journal* and the *Journal of Commerce* had about the same circulation: 35,000. The *Wall Street Journal* grew to 2 million by 1982, dwarfing the influence and circulation of its competitor.

The reason: writing to the widest audience.

The Bloomberg News audience includes customers of the Bloomberg terminal, subscribers to *Bloomberg Markets* and *Bloomberg Businessweek* magazines, visitors to the Bloomberg.com and BloombergBusinessweek .com websites, subscribers to Bloomberg Government and Bloomberg Law, readers of newspapers that publish our stories, viewers of our television networks and those who listen to our radio station and affiliates. Many have an understanding of business and finance. Others have knowledge that is more general.

Write with the idea that you are telling a tale to your spouse, siblings, parents or friends.

George Orwell, in his 1946 essay *Politics and the English Language*, offered the following rules for writing well:

Never use a metaphor, simile or other figure of speech that you are used to seeing in print.

Never use a long word where a short one will do.

If it is possible to cut a word out, always cut it out.

Never use the passive where you can use the active.

Never use a foreign phrase, scientific word or jargon word if you can think of an everyday English equivalent.

Break any of these rules sooner than say anything outright barbarous.

Precision and Brevity

Prefer the short word to the long.

Prefer the familiar word to the fancy.

Prefer the specific word to the abstract.

Instead of *commence*, say *begin*; instead of *deactivate*, say *close* or *shut*; instead of *endeavor*, say *try*; instead of *finalize*, say *end* or *complete*; instead of *announced*, say *said*. And so on.

Words are special. They define us. Treat words with reverence and your writing will ring true.

Sentences deserve the same treatment. A sentence is too long if you have to pause for breath while reading it aloud. The remedy is simple: Break the sentence into shorter ones.

Clauses that start with *although, but, despite* or *however* often confuse more than they clarify, because the words connect dissimilar ideas in a single sentence.

Before:

Although the economy is in a nosedive, Obuchi said there would be a turnaround in the second quarter.

After:

The slumping economy will rebound in the second quarter, Obuchi said.

Before:

Despite assertions by leaders of Wall Street banks that the credit crunch is mostly over, the pain at places like Pee Wee's, in Brentwood, California,

50 miles east of San Francisco, is still ricocheting through the economy.
What began with the repackaging of subprime loans into AAA-rated
securities is unraveling on Main Street, wreaking havoc with businesses and
lives far from New York, as house prices continue to fall and foreclosures rise.
That, in turn, means more bad news for banks.

After:

The pain at places like Pee Wee's, in Brentwood, California, 50 miles
east of San Francisco, is still ricocheting through the economy. What
began with the repackaging of subprime loans into AAA-rated securities is
unraveling on Main Street, wreaking havoc with businesses and lives far
from New York, as house prices continue to fall and foreclosures rise. That
means more bad news for banks.

Before:

Donohue says he hears such complaints from local affiliates, but only
very rarely.

After:

Donohue says he rarely hears such complaints from local affiliates.

Before:

Some enmity remains, however, and Armstrong has been whistled at by
a few spectators.

After:

Some enmity remains. Armstrong has been whistled at by a few spectators.

Avoid pointless prepositional phrases by writing in parallel.

Before:

Ford said it was cutting production in Europe by 5,000 cars, with an
additional 4,000 cars cut by Ford factories in Asia.

After:
Ford said it is cutting production by 5,000 cars in Europe and 4,000 in Asia.

Guard against long subordinate clauses.

Before:
Norwegian Petroleum Directorate chief Bente Nyland said the recent lack of significant discoveries, which contributed to the agency today cutting the country's estimated undiscovered reserves by 21 percent to 2.6 billion cubic meters in oil equivalent, may impact Norwegian gas exports starting after 2015.

After:
Norwegian natural gas exports may fall after 2015 because the Scandinavian country hasn't made any recent significant discoveries, the head of the country's petroleum agency said.

Avoid long independent clauses linked by conjunctions such as *and* or *as.* Two sentences may work better.

Before:
Federal Reserve Chairman Alan Greenspan said the economy has probably passed the danger point for a recession, and he anticipated that it would grow for the rest of this year.

After:
Federal Reserve Chairman Alan Greenspan said the economy has probably passed the danger point for a recession. He forecast growth for the rest of this year.

Throat-clearing transitions such as *indeed, still, of course* and *meanwhile* delay the action, rarely improve the tale and often sound pompous. The first word in every paragraph is prime real estate.

Before:

Indeed, Sotomayor received nine Republican votes and Alito got four Democratic votes, and so far no Republican has announced support for Kagan.

After:

Sotomayor received nine Republican votes and Alito got four Democratic votes. No Republican has announced support for Kagan.

Before:

Still, the number of Americans filing claims for unemployment benefits unexpectedly rose last week, a reminder that companies will keep cutting staff even as the economy stabilizes.

After:

The unexpected increase in the number of Americans filing claims for unemployment benefits last week is a reminder that companies will keep cutting staff even as the economy stabilizes.

Watch for sentences that contain separate ideas bearing no logical relationship to each other.

Before:

Disney bought the studio for $32 million and said it may sell $300 million of debt by December.

After:

Disney bought the studio for $32 million. Separately, the company said it may sell $300 million of debt by December.

Understatement and specificity have a way of conferring greater authority than hype. There is a tendency to bombard the reader with verbs that are cousins of *rise, fall, advance, decline, gain* or *lose.* These include: *dived, surged, tumbled, plunged, plummeted* and *rocketed.* Say *declined 20 percent* or *fell the most in 10 years* instead of *plunged*. Once-meaningful words become trite from constant usage.

Jargon

The temptation to use the jargon of the industries and markets we cover is great. Resist it. Simple words are best because jargon leads to fuzzy thinking. Stories about the Federal Reserve should say the U.S. central bank *is prepared to raise interest rates*, not *tighten credit* or *tighten interest rates*. Stories about the stock market should say money managers are *increasing their holdings of entertainment companies*, not *overweight* in them. Instead of tobacco shares were *weighed down* by the threat of lawsuits and government restrictions against advertising, say the *Standard & Poor's tobacco index has declined this year*. People trust the news organization most that demystifies what the high and mighty do and say.

Before:

> *The stock was the fourth-biggest percentage decliner among the 1,677 comprising the MSCI World Index.*

After:

> *The stock had the fourth-biggest percentage decline among the 1,677 companies in the MSCI World Index.*

Paraphrase rather than use quotes containing jargon.

Before:

> *"They want to really focus on the over 90 percent of their business which is pharma," said Jeffrey Malcom, who manages about 500,000 Pfizer shares at Horan Capital Management in Towson, Maryland.*

After:

> *Pfizer wants to focus on pharmaceuticals, which account for more than 90 percent of its business, said Jeffrey Malcom, who manages about 500,000 Pfizer shares at Horan Capital Management in Towson, Maryland.*

Cliches

Cliches diminish our voice and message. Trite phrases show the writer is willing to settle for the first words that come to mind rather than what is fresh.

Before:

> *A weary Swiss couple trudged into the deserted lobby of the 12:01 East Backpackers hostel in Perth after a grueling eight-hour drive in Western Australia. Manager Winnie Kuwaja, sitting in a nearby office stuffed with tourism brochures, said they were a sight for sore eyes.*

After:

> *A Swiss couple trudged into the deserted lobby of the 12:01 East Backpackers hostel in Perth after an eight-hour drive in Western Australia. Manager Winnie Kuwaja, sitting in an office stuffed with tourism brochures, said he was pleased to see them.*

Before:

> *France Telecom shares have more than doubled since Breton took the helm in October.*

After:

> *France Telecom shares have more than doubled since Breton became chief executive officer in October.*

Before:

> *Obama may have fanned the town's hopes for relief by making it the poster child for his economic-stimulus bill.*

After:

> *Obama may have fanned the town's hopes for relief by scheduling his first primetime news conference the same day he traveled there, highlighting the trip in his opening remarks and mentioning it at least six times.*

Word Echoes

If the same word appears more than once in a paragraph, or even on a page, it's easy to notice. These word echoes are an invitation for the customer to seek out the competition. A lead that uses the same word repeatedly diminishes that word's value.

Before:

> Motorola Inc., the world's second-largest maker of mobile phones, said IT will cut 1,000 jobs as IT prepares to spin off ITS computer-chip business.

After:

> Motorola Inc., the world's second-largest maker of mobile phones, will cut 1,000 jobs in preparation for spinning off its computer-chip business.

Before:

> Bonds ROSE after Bank of Canada Governor David Dodge said the Canadian dollar's RISE to a 12-year high may curb economic growth, signaling that the central bank may not RAISE interest rates next month.

After:

> Canadian bonds rose after Bank of Canada Governor David Dodge said the currency's surge to a 12-year high may curb economic growth, signaling that the central bank may not increase interest rates next month.

Some words tend to echo throughout stories, including *it, its, it's, to, boost, cut, new, expect, bid, also, rise, gain, fall, expand.*

Words can echo when one paragraph after another starts the same way. Currency-market stories that start out with *The dollar, The U.S. currency, The decline* and *The economy* in the first four paragraphs may prove tiresome.

Tense and Voice

Rely on past tense and active voice: *he said, she said, he did, she did.* Writing that departs from this formula is often imprecise and misleading.

Consider this sentence, which uses present-perfect tense: *Winkler has said Bloomberg News wouldn't have more than 200 reporters and editors.* While Winkler might have said this in 1993, he didn't say it this year. We do readers a favor by using past tense instead: *Winkler said in 1993 that Bloomberg News wouldn't have more than 200 reporters and editors.*

Present tense creates room for error. A sentence such as *Wilson is bullish on the U.S. stock market* assumes that his view didn't change between the time our reporter spoke with Wilson and the time readers found out what he said. That may not be true. Writing that *Wilson said he was bullish on the stock market* avoids the possible inaccuracy.

The active voice (*fell 10 percent to 4.52, rose to a record, declined, advanced, gained*) is stronger than the passive voice (*losses were offset by, gains were moderated by, selling pressure was relieved by*). It doesn't rely on a modifier to convey the action. The verb does the work.

Passive voice is acceptable only to put the actor or victim first. *Argentina's Debt Rating Lowered to Caa3 by Moody's* is a better headline than *Moody's Lowers Rating on Argentina's Debt to Caa3.* The news is that Argentina became less creditworthy, not that Moody's Investors Service Inc. changed its rating. Mixing the past and present tenses in the same sentence is awkward and can be confusing.

Before:

> *Cerberus Capital Management LP and Carlyle Group sold (past tense) two investments valued at a combined $6.6 billion today, as private-equity firms find (present tense) overseas buyers because of a scarcity of financing for leveraged buyouts.*

After:

> *Cerberus Capital Management LP and Carlyle Group sold (past tense) two investments valued at a combined $6.6 billion today, finding overseas buyers as private-equity firms balked (past tense) because of a scarcity of financing for leveraged buyouts.*

Story Length

Stories may exceed 850 words when there's a consensus that depth reporting is required to provide the essential anecdotes, context and perspective.

Long stories consume more time than our busy readers can afford. We shouldn't ask them to give us that time unless the length is justified by exhaustive reporting that surprises, explains a complicated situation or tells a compelling tale of human interest.

Our newspaper clients don't have room for many 850-word stories. They're more likely to use 250 words, which means the four-paragraph lead will make a complete story.

8

Headlines

SUCCESSFUL HEADLINES get inside the heads of readers, betray their sensibilities and have one or more of these five elements:

Surprise

What's at Stake

Names That Make News

Conflict

Conflict Resolution

Every well-reported story has these elements, so it makes sense that a successful headline delivers the essence of the surprise. The more surprising the combination of words, especially the first four, the easier it is for readers to recognize news. When readers see a combination of words they can't remember seeing before, they're more willing to be enticed. A headline with none of these elements risks having the fewest readers.

The first four words are the most critical because they are what the eye sees first as it moves from left to right. Capturing the surprise at the start of the headline will help readers distinguish the reporting among thousands of alternative sources for news and information. Headlines do most of the heavy lifting to ensure readership. Each word must pull its weight because the average headline contains about nine words. Punctuation marks and conjunctions are disruptive and should be avoided to achieve the most aesthetic result.

Consider these examples:

Before:
U.S. Exported Financial Technology, Toxic Debt, Spread Havoc

After:
Evil Wall Street Exports Boomed With 'Fools' Born to Buy Debt

While the original headline is accurate, it's not compelling. Thousands of headlines a year begin with *U.S.* or *Export.* The first four words should surprise.

Short words pack a punch. Consider *evil.* In 1983, President Ronald Reagan described the Soviet Union as the *evil empire.* Nineteen years later, President George W. Bush called Iran, Iraq and North Korea the *axis of evil.* As the world plunged into the worst recession since the Great Depression partly because of American-made subprime mortgages and derivatives, people outside the U.S. began using that word to describe Wall Street. *Evil Wall Street xxx* was the first headline so worded at Bloomberg News.

The storytelling gets more compelling. The article included a Nobel Prize winner, Joseph Stiglitz, and his description of Wall Street's global search for "fools" willing to buy toxic securities. A story with several anecdotes provides many possibilities for the headline writer.

When comparing the first version to the published headline, it becomes clear that every comma, colon, semicolon, dash and quotation mark acts as a speed bump to greater appreciation.

Before:
Mizuho Wall Street Coup Became Japanese Subprime Nightmare

After:
Mizuho $7 Billion Loss Turned on Toxic Aardvark Made in America

The surprise should be clear at the beginning of the headline. *Mizuho Wall Street Coup* suggests that this is about a successful venture. As the story is about failure, the first four words are problematic. When was the last time that Mizuho, whose roots reach back to 1864 and name means "golden ears of rice" in Japanese, lost $7 billion so suddenly? That's the surprise.

In this story, Made in the U.S.A. is toxic. Mizuho is made in Japan and its difficulties are made in America.

Another possibility for the headline is the name of one of the toxic deals, called Aardvark after the squat animal with a pig-like snout that feeds on ants and termites. After making the story fit to print, the editor's job is to figure out how to make it most-read.

Before:
Buffett, Fed Scrutiny of Goldman Sachs Means Less Risk Taking, Pay
After:
Goldman Sachs Paydays Suffer on Lost Leverage With Fed Scrutiny

While the original headline includes a noun, a predicate and three attention-grabbing names, it doesn't describe the surprise and risks losing readers. The big idea isn't about Warren Buffett, the Federal Reserve, Goldman Sachs or risk-taking. It's about pay, a topic of great concern to most readers. Moving *Paydays* to the front of the headline sounds the alarm.

Before:
Shocked by UBS Losses, Swiss Pin Hopes on Singapore, Restructuring
After:
Zurichers Insist UBS 'Won't Go Bankrupt' Like Swissair Collapse

Shock is so often used that its impact is diminished, especially for UBS, which had reported losses for more than a year. The focus of the story is Zurich, and *Zurichers Insist* proved a unique combination of words.

That UBS, whose history dates back to 1862, could go bankrupt would have been unthinkable a year earlier. For Switzerland, the bank's failure would be another national trauma akin to the collapse of Swissair in 2001.

Singapore and *Restructuring* are a mouthful and a digression.

Before:

Fed Board Approves Goldman, Morgan Stanley Bid to Become Banks

After:

Goldman, Morgan Stanley Bring Down Curtain on Wall Street Era

Readers crave context and perspective, starting with the headline. The news broke on a Sunday night. The headline for the next day's story helped explain how the world changed overnight, 75 years after Congress separated securities firms from deposit-taking lenders—resulting in the year's most-read article.

Before:

Manas Hooks 10 Deals at Foros as Recruiting Poses Challenge in First Year

After:

Former Deutsche Bank M&A Chief Discovers Deals Easier to Land Than Bankers

Use words and names that attract attention. Neither Manas nor Foros is a global name. The rewritten headline attracted more than 1,100 readers to the story within a few minutes.

Before:

Robin Hood Counting on Wall Street's Goldman-Led Bonuses for 'Great Need'

After:
Robin Hood Says 'Hell Yeah' to Wall Street Recovery Led by Goldman Bonuses

The "Hell Yeah" quote surprises because the perception is that bonuses are bad.

Before:
Credit Swaps Traders Buy Distressed Debt Seeking Default Payoff
After:
Darth Wall Street Destroying Debtors With Credit-Default Swaps

Darth Wall Street Destroying proves to be a unique combination of words.

Paradox and conflict make these headlines work:

Fallen Soldiers' Families Denied Cash Payout as Insurers Profit
This Hedge Fund Manager Tries to Short Himself: Michael Lewis
Homeless Dropouts From High School Lured by For-Profit Colleges
Out of Lehman's Ashes Wall Street Gets Most of What It Wants

9

Preparation

Want a scoop? Prepare. Nothing makes people luckier than preparation. The people who win the race train the hardest. They are relentless. Winners are meticulous about preparing. They are obsessed with preparing. That is what builds confidence.

The more preparation that goes into what we report and write—before we have to report it, before we have to write it—the more confident we will be as reporters and writers. The more prepared we are, the better we will be able to deliver our best news judgment.

There is a reason why we say *smarter* means more, better, faster. If we are smarter, we can deliver more, better, faster. That's why there is no excuse for being unprepared.

Collecting String

The constant collecting of string—details about people, companies, markets and industries—is essential. The best reporters make every effort to obtain all sorts of facts. Details gathered on a rainy day, when there is little interest in a subject, will loom large when the subject is all-important.

The best reporters rely on details to write their stories. Best-selling books such as *Den of Thieves* and *When Genius Failed* are nothing if not collections of detail. These books are credible because their authors assembled an array of specific information.

All of us, no matter how difficult we find writing seamless prose, can be great reporters if we discipline ourselves to collect details, background and examples. Doing so will enable us to use them on the days when readers' appetites are greatest.

As the news developed, the writer of this story began collecting string on New York Stock Exchange Chairman Richard Grasso. That allowed for this instant perspective when the news broke:

NYSE's Grasso Kept $140 Million and 'Lost What Was Important'

Sept. 18 (Bloomberg) -- The New York Stock Exchange was everything to Richard Grasso.

It was his life for 36 of his 57 years. It's where he met his wife, the mother of his four children, and played court jester from the exchange's balcony to traders below at the 9:30 a.m. ringing of the bell that opened each day's session.

It's where he managed to get trading up and running six days after the Sept. 11 attacks that felled the Twin Towers of the World Trade Center, just blocks from the exchange floor. The city's mayor called the achievement "heroic."

His life at the exchange ended yesterday.

Grasso was ousted as chairman and chief executive officer of the world's largest equities market, the only place the college dropout from the New York City borough of Queens had worked during his adult life. Grasso was forced out by the furor over $140 million in deferred compensation, disclosed in late August, that had grown for years, hidden on the exchange's books.

Top 10s

Knowledge is power. Reporters should know the most important people and institutions on their beats and collect files and lists on each of them.

Industry reporters should draw up lists of the 10 most important companies, executives, investors and experts, and figure out what makes them influential. Visit and talk to them regularly. Find the top 10 companies in total revenue and sales growth, and the reasons why. The 10 most profitable. The 10 with the most debt and the least debt. The biggest winners and losers in stock price. Work up any number of lists and descriptions in advance that explain why this company matters. This is useful because it will remind us what's going on at the company and may provide relevant and timely size and scope.

For economic coverage, develop a list of the 10 most influential people and what makes them important, and keep track of their actions, strategies and recommendations. Who are the 10 most important inflation experts, Wall Street economists, scholars, former central bankers? Identify the 10 most-followed indicators and why they're important.

Political reporters should identify the 10 most important people in government, in Parliament, in the Senate. Who are the top 10 trade officials? Lobbyists?

Write all this down so it's there when the news breaks.

Curtain-Raisers

Much of what Bloomberg writes is based on scheduled events. Companies release their earnings reports every quarter or half year. Government departments schedule economic releases well in advance. Press conferences are announced hours or days before they happen. Elections and economic summits are scheduled long ahead of time.

Reporters have an easier time delivering the fastest and final words on these events when they have prepared perspective-laden copy. This often entails writing curtain-raisers that preview the event and the issues and handicap the potential outcome.

Write a curtain-raiser a couple of days in advance of the event. Ask people what they expect to happen. If those directly involved won't comment, focus on people with an interest, especially investors. Too often, curtain-raisers read like a calendar item . . .

Greenspan Faces Lawmakers' Questions on Rates, Housing, Jobs
July 20 (Bloomberg) -- Federal Reserve Chairman Alan
Greenspan, delivering what might be his last semiannual report to
Congress starting today, will face lawmakers' questions on housing prices,

jobs and whether the central bank is close to ending its drive to push interest rates higher.

. . . when they can be turned into something more newsworthy:

Greenspan's Outlook Seen Encouraging as Fed Raises Rates
July 20 (Bloomberg) -- Federal Reserve Chairman Alan Greenspan, delivering what might be his last semiannual report to Congress starting today, will probably say the U.S. economy is growing and needs gradual interest-rate increases to fight inflation.

Once the curtain-raiser is published, revise it for use as a template or background. Never cut and paste entire paragraphs, sentences or phrases into the new story. Every story ought to read as if it were freshly written.

When the outcome differs from the curtain-raiser, reconcile the stories so our coverage is credible and complete.

The curtain-raiser:

The Bank of England will end a five-month program of bond purchases as Europe's second-largest economy shows signs of emerging from a recession, said a majority of the firms that bid at government debt auctions.

The surprise:

The Bank of England expanded its bond purchase program beyond the original limit to spur lending and fight a recession that's deeper than previously anticipated.

How we explained the difference:

The Bank of England said that Britain's recession has been deeper than officials anticipated. Deputy Governor Charles Bean warned in July that the bank risks stoking inflation if it waits too long before withdrawing stimulus and Governor Mervyn King has said that the timing of an exit strategy will still be a "tricky judgment."

Eight of 12 primary dealers that bid at government debt auctions had predicted the central bank would end the program after announcing a pause yesterday.

Templates

Bloomberg News delivers stories loaded with anecdotes, examples and comments within seconds of the release of U.S. government reports on closely watched economic indicators. This also happens as a matter of course in other countries and with other events, such as the release of corporate earnings.

Reporters and editors could never do this if they waited until after an event to prepare stories. Instead, they put together several templates in advance that reflect their judgment of what a report may show and how it may compare with expectations. They decide which template fits the facts and assemble the final story when the news becomes available.

Templates consist of separate leads and follow-up paragraphs, including a comment from an authority, for each possible scenario. Prepare several paragraphs of details and background, often based on curtain-raisers, that will work with any of the leads.

Each template usually includes a comment about the scenario it describes, so it's essential to contact people and review the possibilities. Reporters may need to go through each scenario and ask what it would indicate about the state of the economy, the company and so on.

This template was prepared for use if the economic indicator fell, as economists had forecast:

Nov. 3 (Bloomberg) -- Orders placed with U.S. factories fell X.X percent in September, as bookings for aircraft, XXX and XXXX dropped, a government report showed.

The decline to $XXX.X billion followed a revised X.X percent // increase// in August, the Commerce Department said today in Washington. Excluding transportation equipment, orders rose/fell XX percent after rising/falling X.X percent.

Auto sales cooled as two hurricanes drove up energy costs, shut businesses and displaced thousands of people on the U.S. Gulf Coast. Boeing Co., the No. 2 maker of commercial aircraft, said its orders fell in September. A report this week showed that manufacturing expanded in October, and rebuilding on the Gulf Coast may buoy factory demand for equipment and materials in coming months.

"The dip in orders during September looks like it was temporary," Stuart Hoffman, chief economist at PNC Financial Services Group in Pittsburgh, said before the report. *"Outside of autos, manufacturing should show some decent growth over the next few quarters."*

For the same event, the team prepared this template for a surprise increase:

Nov. 3 (Bloomberg) -- Orders placed with U.S. factories unexpectedly rose X.X percent in September, as higher energy prices boosted the value of petroleum-based products such as chemicals, a government report showed.

The increase to $XXX.X billion followed a revised X.X percent // increase// in August, the Commerce Department said today in Washington. Excluding transportation equipment, orders rose/fell X.X percent after rising/falling X.X percent. Two hurricanes along the U.S. Gulf Coast drove up the costs of oil, natural gas and petrochemicals in September. A report this week showed that manufacturing expanded in October, and rebuilding on the Gulf Coast may buoy factory demand for equipment and materials in coming months.

"The need to rebuild inventories will lift production, employment and incomes this quarter, keeping the economy afloat while the consumer catches his breath," Joseph LaVorgna, chief U.S. fixed-income economist at Deutsche Bank Securities in New York, said in a note to investors before the report.

The indicator dropped as forecast, resulting in this story:

Nov. 3 (Bloomberg) -- Orders placed with U.S. factories fell 1.7 percent in September, as bookings for aircraft, computers and household appliances dropped, a government report showed.

The decline to $390 billion followed a revised 2.9 percent increase in August, the Commerce Department said today in Washington. Excluding transportation equipment, orders fell 1 percent after rising 3.2 percent.

Boeing Co., the No. 2 maker of commercial aircraft, said its orders fell in September. A report this week showed that manufacturing expanded in October. Order backlogs at record levels, and rebuilding after the Gulf Coast hurricanes, may buoy factory demand for equipment and materials in coming months.

"The need to rebuild inventories will lift production, employment and incomes this quarter, keeping the economy afloat while the consumer catches his breath," Joseph LaVorgna, chief U.S. fixed-income economist at Deutsche Bank Securities in New York, said in a note to investors before the report.

Templates need to specify when a person made the comments to make it clear that he didn't have a copy of the report. Starting with the first update, replace with a comment from someone contacted after the report, preferably from a different person.

Be ready to publish the template as soon as the news breaks. If the news is a surprise or the prepared story requires more than a few minutes of tinkering, abandon the template. Write a one- or two-sentence story and update immediately with relevant information from the template. The editing of a template shouldn't take precedence over a customer's need to know now.

10

Covering News

THINK OF Bloomberg News as an electronic newspaper, rather than a wire service in the traditional sense, because it provides the most complete perspective on events in a compelling, easy-to-understand style.

To do this, we update stories constantly. This may mean inserting comments from people who weren't available earlier in the day. It can mean providing the latest information about security, currency and commodity prices, or adding pertinent details about past moves or including details after examining documents.

Reporters need to send each update as soon as they have enough additional information to tell a more complete story. The first update ought to be completed within 15 minutes of the initial story. Begin immediately improving the reporting with more compelling quotes, anecdotes, details and more graceful word choices.

When inserting new paragraphs, discard or condense old ones. This means choosing one quotation as definitive and eliminating duplicates, or using three anecdotes rather than eight, which would dilute the value of the best three.

This process enables us to start with a one-paragraph item at 10 a.m. and turn it into a 750-word story by 4 p.m. In its final form, the piece doesn't have any holes, answers the most obvious questions and convinces the customer that we told all there is to tell.

No story can be abandoned after a flawed delivery with the excuse, "Well, the editor said we had to get it out fast." Editors are right to insist on speedy delivery. We would be out of business if they didn't. Editors want a complete story that adds perspective, provides details and explains why the event is important in the first place.

Editors ought to bend over backward to help the reporter deliver the context. This often requires a discussion when a paragraph doesn't fit. It may mean moving a truncated version of a story immediately and then, after consulting with the reporter, providing a more polished update.

Revise and rewrite. The first draft rarely is perfect. Abraham Lincoln scribbled many revisions of his 272-word Gettysburg Address, the greatest piece of writing in American literature. Read what you wrote aloud. Get a second opinion. Would your sibling understand it? Would she treasure it?

We strive for quality as well as speed. This is our competitive advantage, and we must make the most of it.

Breaking News

The skill and intelligence we bring to coverage of an unfolding event determine how competitive we are as a news organization. A combination of headlines and text is essential to providing the first and fastest words.

Publishing several headlines is the next best thing to an accompanying story because the reader can see the blocks of a story before they are assembled. Headlines can deliver whole chunks of a story much faster than 50-word bulletins.

When you become aware of possible market-moving information, the first thought must be: Have we told customers about this? If not, dictate at least one headline to an editor immediately. Deliver as many headlines as needed to make the important information available.

Make headlines specific. The more detail we provide on the traditional five Ws and H—who, what, when, where, why and how—the easier it will be to deliver the story. We flashed these headlines from an interview with former U.S. Treasury Secretary John Snow:

*SNOW SAYS U.S. ECONOMY GROWTH RATE IS 'TOO ANEMIC'
*SNOW SAYS GROWTH WILL EXCEED 3% IN 3RD, 4TH QUARTERS

*SNOW SAYS U.S. 'POISED FOR NICE PICKUP IN ECONOMIC ACTIVITY'
*SNOW SAYS THERE'S NO CHANGE IN STRONG U.S. DOLLAR POLICY
*SNOW SAYS FREDDIE MAC, FANNIE MAE NEED 'GOOD DISCLOSURE'
*SNOW SAYS U.S. ECONOMY 'IS STILL THE PLACE TO INVEST'
*SNOW SAYS CHINA CONSIDERING WIDENING YUAN TRADING BAND

Once the headlines are sent, explain the news in a seamless narrative. If the event is among the day's most important stories, make the first version no more than two sentences and send it within three minutes of the first headline so that Top menus can give the news the prominence it deserves. Then update within 15 minutes. Other first takes, of no more than four paragraphs, should be published within 15 minutes of the first headline—and the sooner the better.

These leads developed from those Snow headlines:

The U.S. economy is poised to gain strength in the second half as lower taxes and interest rates take effect, Treasury Secretary John Snow said.

The disclosure of accounting misstatements at Freddie Mac, the second-largest source of mortgage financing in the U.S., hasn't damaged U.S. markets, Treasury Secretary John Snow said.

U.S. Treasury Secretary John Snow said China should be encouraged to widen the trading band for its currency, a move that might help narrow the U.S. trade deficit by making exports cheaper and Chinese imports more expensive.

Many people won't trust headlines until they read a story that backs them up. They may question headlines about a central bank governor's views on interest rates until a story explains the context of the statement, shows where and to whom it was made, and provides enough detail to support the news judgment behind the headline.

News Releases

News releases are essential to news organizations. Many come from services such as PR Newswire, Business Wire and the Regulatory News Service. To deliver the fastest word, we track down and publish electronic versions of releases received via e-mail and facsimile or found on company and government websites.

The most newsworthy releases are used as the basis for a short story, edited and transmitted as quickly as possible. Then we strive to add value through background, context, perspective and voices.

In our hands, a company statement about a new product becomes a story that does many things. It explains how the shares have performed, how much sales and earnings have risen or fallen, how the company compares with competitors, how many and which analysts recommend the company or don't, who the biggest shareholders are—any number of details that, taken together, will provide more meaning.

Reporters and editors have to focus on the essentials of these releases. They have to provide sufficient perspective to allow anyone reading about the topic for the first time to understand the latest news.

Start by verifying the release to make sure it's authentic. As part of a news feed there is less risk. Look at the release for any information worthy of headlines. Check the release to determine whether any details needed for the story aren't provided. If so, call immediately to obtain them. If no one is available, say you will call back shortly. Use the Bloomberg to find background, context and perspective.

Write a brief story based on the release to incorporate the details gleaned thus far. If you still can't find anyone to answer questions, note in the story that officials declined to comment or couldn't be reached.

Make sure that Bloomberg's customers have access to the original release. Often this will mean transmitting the release to colleagues for scanning and publication, either in text form or as an electronic attachment. Then expand the search for information. Contact investors, analysts, traders, competitors, suppliers, customers and anyone else affected by the event. Incorporate their reactions.

Rumor and Speculation

The job of a Bloomberg journalist is to report and publish facts. We don't publish headlines, leads or other parts of stories based solely on rumors. We do report on speculation, which is when traders or investors buy or sell.

Speculation is different from rumor. We know for a fact that a price went up or down. The reason for the price fluctuation—the traders' motivation—may or may not be true. Their resulting action of buying or selling is factual. Before publishing any story, we must try to determine whether the information is accurate and give the individuals or organizations named a chance to respond.

When the speculation behind an action has been proven false, note that prominently in the story. We should also say that a report can't be confirmed if a market is still moving in reaction to unsubstantiated reporting such as a possible earthquake, bomb threat or capture of a terrorist.

Any story needs to provide evidence of the speculation in the first four paragraphs. Any story that mentions the speculation—including the movers and market columns—must include the comment/no comment/declined to comment from the people or organizations.

Carrefour SA, the world's second-largest retailer, rose the most in five months in Paris trading on speculation that larger competitor Wal-Mart Stores Inc. may offer to buy the French company.

"There is a rumor of a bid from Wal-Mart," Frederic Sauvegrain, managing director of European equities at Dexia Securities, said today. "This isn't completely unlikely."

Christian D'Oleon, a Carrefour spokesman, and Ray Bracy, vice president of international corporate affairs for Wal-Mart, declined to comment.

Carrefour rose 4.3 percent to 42.90 euros, the biggest one-day gain since the Paris-based retailer raised its sales forecast on Aug. 28.

Always check with the subject of the speculation. When shares in Bank Holding & Co. tumble 12 percent and traders say it's because Bank Holding can't pay its debts, we have to ask Bank Holding why the shares are falling and whether it has missed, or will miss, debt payments. If Bank Holding says "no comment," we are in a much better position with our customers, especially the company's shareholders. In many countries, Bank Holding would have a legal obligation to explain or disclose any causes for a decline in its shares. Responding to queries from us fulfills some of that obligation.

When attempting to confirm hearsay, make sure our questions distinguish Bloomberg News from the rumormongers. Indiscriminately aimed messages to a group of people aren't a responsible way to gather information because we have no intention of spreading the rumors. Conversations are best and reduce errors. If an e-mail is the only option, keep the questions specific.

When the company provides no reason and neither confirms nor denies our understanding of the cause of the share decline, we have enough information to provide an initial report in our story and headlines. Any company that doesn't say for the record that its finances are sound when it's buffeted by speculation to the contrary isn't serving the interests of its shareholders.

When competitors break news, we must make our audience instantly aware even when we can't verify the accuracy. The key is to identify their sources of information in our stories and headlines.

The purpose is to avoid giving credibility to a perception that may be inaccurate. Although prices may jump or plunge on a rumor, that doesn't make the rumor a worthy cousin of the truth. On slow days in the 1980s, bored commodity traders used to whisper that President Ronald Reagan had been shot, sending prices into convulsions.

Media Summaries

When Bloomberg News summarizes every newsworthy story from every newspaper and broadcast station, customers consider us a fast and complete news provider that needs no supplements. Every reporter and editor should be prepared to headline and summarize what news we don't have.

This process reminds us that there is always something we don't know— that our work is never done, our coverage is never complete and our news judgment will only get better when continuously and rigorously challenged.

If the story being summarized is about the economy, markets, money, companies or industries, or about policy that will affect any of these areas, we must rush to confirm it, advance the story and publish our own version.

If the *Local Gazette* says Company A will buy Company B, the first thing we do is summarize the report. Then we should call the companies and solicit their comments. Even if they can't be reached after our repeated attempts, we can publish our own story saying something beyond the summary, such as including reaction and comments. Readers depend on us to verify or dispute the contents of the *Local Gazette.*

Complete Coverage

As journalists providing the first draft of history, we have an obligation to deliver as much detail as we can about what was said and done. We should deliver related stories that run during the day and overnight to flesh out our reporting and highlight developments that might otherwise get overlooked in the main story.

Complete coverage goes beyond publishing a single story about an event. As much as they appreciate our stories, customers also want to read, see and hear news in its unadulterated and unfiltered form.

Original documents. Make copies of primary documents—press releases, regulatory filings, court papers, statements and texts of speeches—available on the system. Bloomberg News has no space limitations, so reporters and editors should make an effort to put every document on the Bloomberg.

Links. There is no better way for Bloomberg users to appreciate the scope of the system than through the clickable links to functions, source documents and news stories that we include throughout each article and in the so-called tour on how to find news and information at the end. Headlines linked to stories published by other organizations on the terminal or Internet give customers the first word with our news sensibility.

Voices. These brief articles capture important quotes that weren't used in stories. They are intended as quick fills of reaction and comment and aren't a substitute for a story.

Raw data. Our customers crave information, and raw data is often news they can use. Provide this in forms such as rankings, charts, at-a-glance boxes, bullet-point lists and timelines.

Multimedia. Speeches, press conferences and conference calls are broadcast in real time on the Bloomberg via LIVE <Go>. Broadcast, telephone or recorded interviews should be packaged as multimedia for AV <Go> so they can be viewed when it's convenient. Important interviews should be transcribed. Reporters should use video cameras found in bureaus worldwide to record interviews and events that complement stories.

Photographs. The Bloomberg is a visual medium. We have photo editors around the world who can assign photographers to shoot pictures that can be attached to stories and sent to our newspaper customers.

Graphics. Some information is best explained visually. Our graphics desk can break down complex issues or processes into charts and interactive graphics to be attached to stories for terminal readers and made available to newspaper clients.

Special reports. When a big story breaks, package the reports and multimedia in Top pages such as EXTRA <Go> or ELECT <Go>.

11

Ethics

Our name is Bloomberg. It is a good name and must never be tarnished by anything that we say or do.

The appearance of impropriety can be as damaging to a reputation as doing something improper. Because we hold others accountable for disclosure, we expect the same of ourselves. While disclosing errors of judgment may be embarrassing, the sooner the lapses are reported, the sooner there is nothing more to say.

A *conflict of interest* is an economic, personal or political relationship that may compromise a journalist's impartiality. Always discuss and try to resolve a conflict of interest before it becomes an issue. When it cannot be resolved, err on the side of disclosure.

We are in the often-difficult position of reporting on our customers. Altering a story because it embarrasses a company or individual would create the perception that we shade our news judgment under pressure, and that would cost us our integrity.

When exposing the wrongdoing of others, we should be above reproach. The greater the story's impact, the greater our obligation to withstand the most exacting scrutiny.

Bloomberg journalists don't break the law to gather news and, no matter what the law permits, aren't deceptive, duplicitous or dishonest. Although it isn't illegal to pay sources, Bloomberg never pays for information other than data or original reporting that is protected by copyright. We don't use another person or group to violate laws on our behalf.

Strive to achieve *balance* and *fairness* in all reporting and news decisions. Reporters and editors must set aside any *personal biases* and must never deceive or mislead. Make every effort to obtain a prompt and complete rebuttal to any accusation.

Sometimes the right thing to do is difficult to determine. Consult with a supervisor or our newsroom lawyer before acting.

Fairness

Readers, listeners and viewers will never put their faith in a news organization that isn't perceived as fair. Our policy is to give people, companies and organizations every chance to respond to allegations of wrongdoing, incompetence or unethical behavior before the story is published. The more serious the allegation of wrongdoing, the greater our effort should be to collect a response from the subjects or proxies such as their lawyers or spokesmen.

If the subjects of a story are surprised by what we publish, we have failed at making a good-faith effort. While a correction may satisfy the legal requirements, it won't restore the subject's reputation or Bloomberg's credibility. As Jim Lehrer, who anchored the Public Broadcast System's *NewsHour* program from 1975–2011, says: If we remember to imagine every story is about us as we report on others, we have a greater chance of achieving fairness.

When an analyst or investor pans a stock or bond, we should ask company officers whether they consider the assessment valid. When writing about legal charges, include any that have been defeated or withdrawn so that we report the whole story. When a politician accuses another of incompetence, pursue a response from the accused. If the allegations are included in a press release, complaint or other document, include a link in the story so that the reader can see the full comment in its original context.

Our efforts to contact the subjects must be transparent and verifiable: *Two messages left after hours at the chief executive officer's office and home weren't returned* or *Company spokeswoman Jane Smith couldn't be reached at her office or home.*

If we get a response or "no comment" after the story has been published, update the story as soon as possible. A delay might provoke suspicion that we aren't interested in telling the whole story.

When preparing to publish allegations from other news organizations that may stain a reputation or character, we must give the subjects a chance to deny or comment. Don't rely on any responses in the original story.

Legal-team editors must review all stories that contain allegations made in civil or criminal court proceedings or filings. They are trained to recognize our requirements, wade through legalisms and advise on how to get a response.

Any questions about our fairness should be discussed with a team leader. If issues of ethics or defamation are involved, raise them with a managing editor, executive editor or our newsroom's lawyer.

Public Responsibilities

Journalists are the face of Bloomberg LP and the public equates their behavior with the company.

Bloomberg respects the right of its editorial staff to vote, express their views in an appropriate manner and support parties or candidates. Bloomberg also acknowledges that individuals may belong to, or be involved in, *public-interest organizations.*

Journalists may not run for public office or serve on any quasi-governmental body that could affect any contract, bond issue or hiring decisions. Service with parent-teacher associations or similar groups focused on an individual school is acceptable.

News staff must not be involved in *political campaigns* or *contribute funds* to candidates, parties or political-action committees if that creates a possible conflict of interest with our reporting.

Journalists shouldn't participate in any political endeavor that compromises the integrity of our professional assignments. This could include any politically provocative action, such as wearing a button in support of a candidate or making a comment on Bloomberg message greetings.

Journalists shouldn't be mouthpieces for any particular agenda. Reporters and editors shouldn't contribute funds or services to organizations that lobby, disseminate information or otherwise try to shape regulatory, economic or political debate in a way that targets industries that they cover. For example, a reporter covering agriculture should not donate money to a group that campaigns against genetically modified foods. Paying for a subscription to a newsletter published by such an organization to obtain resource material is allowed. Be aware of organizations that treat such subscriptions as memberships.

Journalists may participate in organizations recognized as *tax-exempt* and *nonpolitical charitable corporations*. In the U.S., for instance, these kinds of organizations are typically of a religious, scientific, literary or educational nature and are recognized under section 501(c)(3) of the Internal Revenue Service code.

Journalists who develop a romantic or *close relationship* with a potential newsmaker or source should inform their team leaders and expect to be reassigned. Reporters should also inform their supervisors when spouses or significant others are employed by companies they cover.

Endorsements

Under no circumstances may news staff *endorse any goods or services* other than in a review published by Bloomberg. News staff may contribute jacket copy or cover blurbs for books or periodicals only with advance permission.

Occasionally, companies offer us the opportunity to sample or test new products such as automobiles, telephones, software or hardware to write reviews or provide feedback. The companies may not use that feedback, the Bloomberg trademark or the journalist's name in any advertising or promotional material. Reporters may not keep the product in exchange for the trial.

Bloomberg News *pays its own way* and assumes the cost of travel and meals. Bloomberg News staff may not accept payments, gifts or tokens from people or companies we cover.

News staff may attend public performances, events or conferences without paying only when properly credentialed and only for the purpose of writing or researching a story. Employees may never obtain discounts, food, lodging, preferential treatment or other considerations based solely on their status as journalists.

Memorabilia such as baseball hats, T-shirts or paperweights may be kept if the estimated value is less than $25. Anything exceeding this value should be returned with a letter explaining that accepting the gift violates our editorial policy. Gifts that cannot be returned should be donated to charity.

Bloomberg journalists may not accept *speaking fees* or honoraria. Bloomberg donates all monetary payments received from journalism awards to the Committee to Protect Journalists. Recipients of these awards receive the total value of the award in a separate payment by Bloomberg.

Journalists are permitted to take advantage of offers made to all Bloomberg employees, such as free tickets to museums and theaters or other perks available through the company's Arcade promotional program or VISIT <Go>.

The newsroom staff shouldn't sign any legally binding agreements about gathering or publishing information without review by our lawyer.

Plagiarism

Bloomberg News is legally and ethically obligated to respect the intellectual property of other news organizations and to be honest about our newsgathering.

Plagiarism—the unattributed copying of others' work—is a capital crime in journalism. Bloomberg is proud of the work of its reporters and editors and spends considerable time and resources protecting the integrity of their stories. Always show other news organizations the same respect. Plagiarism is theft. Be prepared to lose your job if you plagiarize.

Always credit original reporting to those who did the legwork, and never reproduce quotes made to others as if we heard them ourselves. Press summaries must cite the publication that did the reporting and explain the attribution used in the original story. While facts are in the public domain, the selection and arrangement of those facts may constitute creative expression, which can be protected by *copyright*. Our press summaries and other work—including graphics, tables and charts—should add value through independent analysis or research when appropriate.

Working for Bloomberg

As journalists often are the most public face of Bloomberg LP, we should be prepared to see anything we say or do available for posterity on the Internet. News staff may not publish websites, Internet blogs or other online journals that:

Discuss companies, people or topics covered by Bloomberg News.

Discuss or disclose internal Bloomberg policies, management or news-gathering decisions.

Direct Internet traffic to media competitors or discuss them.

Imply an endorsement or association with Bloomberg News.

Journalists will always face public scrutiny and should be aware that anything posted on Facebook, MySpace, Twitter, social networks, Web feeds, blogs or other sites can be disseminated by someone seeking to discredit, belittle or embarrass the reporter or the organization. Careless communication that conflicts with Bloomberg best practices may result in termination.

No Bloomberg LP employees may perform work for any other organization during working hours, nor may they accept any employment or compensation that conflicts or directly interferes with work at Bloomberg. (See the *Employee Resource Guide Handbook.*)

Articles written or edited by Bloomberg News employees are the copyrighted property of Bloomberg LP, in accordance with the confidentiality agreement that employees sign as a term of employment.

Bloomberg often allows people or organizations we quote to reproduce or redistribute articles. Requests should be directed to Bloomberg's corporate legal department.

Bloomberg journalists who wish to write a book should make a proposal to the editor-in-chief.

Reporters and freelancers may write articles for professional journalism organizations or educational institutions with the consent of a supervisor. Columnists who freelance for Bloomberg may not grant permission for reprint or redistribution rights for any columns submitted to Bloomberg, whether published or not, without the consent of a supervisor. Columnists must also inform their supervisors on a timely basis about other publications that may publish their work.

Transparency

Bloomberg News encourages *transparency*. We must be free and clear of any potential accusations of manipulating markets, trading on insider news, or profiting from our positions at Bloomberg News. Abide by self-imposed restrictions so that our motives for reporting on markets can never be called into question. Avoid economic relationships that interfere with our ability to make journalistic judgments based on the facts.

Our journalists may not, through a direct buy or sell relationship, acquire any position in any individual equities, bonds or other financial instruments in companies or industries that they cover. Any interests in these companies should be held through mutual funds or through similar arrangements where the decisions to buy, sell or hold the securities are made by an independent money manager or trustee.

Because of the wide range of companies and industries covered by team leaders, bureau chiefs, managing editors, executive editors and the editor-in-chief, we recommend that these people invest only in mutual funds or through similar independently managed arrangements.

In keeping with the obligation of all Bloomberg LP staff, no news employee may profit from news, data or information learned in the course of employment that has yet to be made public.

Bloomberg LP employees are prohibited from *selling short*, or betting that the price of an investment will fall. Securities must be held for a minimum of 30 days from the time of the buy order.

If a journalist is assigned to a new beat in which there is a potential conflict of interest, the team leader must notify a managing editor within 24 hours. Employees may hold, but not increase, stakes in any such investments, or may divest within 90 days of reassignment.

Bloomberg journalists may not discuss or distribute *nonpublic market-moving* information outside of the scope of newsgathering. This prohibition includes providing such information to parents, siblings, spouses, roommates or significant others.

Sometimes we may have to disclose nonpublic and potentially market-moving information to a person from whom we seek comments or verification. Be prudent in sharing.

Journalists who learn about an investment opportunity through working at Bloomberg may take advantage of the information two days after the information becomes public—provided they don't cover that company or industry.

Bloomberg journalists may not, without approval, tout, promote or *recommend any particular investment*, nor may they render financial advice to the public. News staff may not discuss investments, securities or other financial instruments in public or internal venues such as Internet chat rooms, bulletin boards or blogs.

Nonemployee columnists may participate in such discussions so long as they are not identified as Bloomberg columnists and don't attribute their views to Bloomberg News.

Bloomberg News vigorously defends in court the ability of journalists to gather confidential information in the course of reporting. At the same time, if a law enforcement or regulatory body is investigating securities laws violations allegedly committed by a Bloomberg journalist, we will cooperate with lawful and *valid subpoenas for records.*

Never do anything that keeps other news organizations from accomplishing their tasks. It isn't appropriate to ask sources not to talk to other news organizations. In situations in which we are part of a reporting pool, our participation should go beyond what is requested in quality and cooperation.

Covering Bloomberg

Because of the special nature of our company, we should not originate stories about Bloomberg LP. Nevertheless, we will not hesitate to summarize what other news organizations report on the company. A company spokesman should be provided an opportunity to comment on any such story.

There is an obvious conflict of interest when reporting about competitors, so we must disclose any conflict and provide a disclaimer:

> *Bloomberg News competes with Acme News Co. in providing news and information to the financial community.*
> *Bloomberg LP, the parent company of Bloomberg News, competes with Acme News Co. in providing news, information and trading systems to the financial community.*

Avoid any appearance of favoritism in our coverage of Michael Bloomberg. We will report on what he says and does as a government official, philanthropist or candidate. Be especially careful and seek advice from supervisors when summarizing stories from other news organizations that speculate on his future.

Whenever we name Michael Bloomberg in a story, disclose his role as founder and majority owner of Bloomberg LP. When writing about him, we should call him for comment as we would contact any other newsmaker.

Accuracy

The three most important words in journalism are *accuracy, accuracy* and *accuracy*. Anything less than flawless is considered unprofessional. We must guard against inaccuracy, which derives from a variety of failings including bias, carelessness and distortion.

Mistakes can be especially costly because our customers act instantly on information we provide. When we make a mistake, we must fix it as quickly as possible and label the revised story as a correction. No exceptions. Never delay a correction. The longer a mistake remains uncorrected, the more people are likely to come across the error and to question other facts.

Every time we publish a mistake, we chip away at our credibility. That, in turn, can make it difficult to obtain the most credible sources and attract customers.

While mistakes are inevitable, failure to correct the error—and to identify it in the headline and so-called trashline, which explains the changes to the story, as a correction—compromises our integrity.

The only thing worse than making a mistake is failing to correct it. Imagine the trader who notices that facts changed from one update to the next, or the newspaper editor who discovers that we hid the change in an update. Once deceived, they may turn elsewhere for news.

Here are steps we can take to ensure greater accuracy:

Be transparent. Every story should explain how we know what we know, from the one-paragraph first version to the final update. Attribution should be precise, detailed and ubiquitous.

Confirm the name and title of anyone we interview. People in the same company may have similar names or titles. Ask for a business card. Check

Bloomberg profiles for this information. Previous stories may no longer be correct, resulting in an incorrect profile; the person may have a new name or new job.

Check earlier stories. Lifting information from previous stories without verifying each detail is dangerous. Make sure what is asserted as history is consistent with our reporting to date. Never assume we know what happened.

Double-check the spelling of all names and locations. The Bloomberg search engine or Help function can provide references for names, descriptions, locations and brand names.

Confirm the results of Bloomberg functions. Reporters are responsible for the integrity of their reporting, and editors must validate what is published and broadcast. If a reporter puts a stock price in a story, for example, the editor must verify it using <Equity> Q or another function.

Take special care with figures, especially those we calculate. Editors handling merger-and-acquisition stories, for example, need to review with the reporter the math used for valuations. Use HC <Go> when doing calculations or FE11 <Go> for currency conversions. Bloomberg profile entries include birth dates. Verify these details, too.

Know appropriate units of measure. Governments and companies could sell $100 million of bonds; a $100 billion bond sale would be unrealistic. If a currency is worth less than one U.S. dollar, then any conversion into dollars will result in a smaller number, and vice versa. Commodities may be priced in dollars per metric ton, cents per pound or other units.

Print the story. Review the printout and check off each fact, spelling and calculation when verified. Make sure the story's facts are consistent with any related press release, published statement or document.

Have reporters review edited stories. If the lead is changed, the editor must show the reporter, or at least read it to the reporter. Editors should have reporters check stories that have been rewritten or rearranged.

Corrections

We correct misspelled names and words that change the meaning of a sentence (*he pedaled the bonds to Goldman Sachs*), missing first references and incorrect attribution. We also correct errors involving numbers, such as the wrong date, confusing *million, billion* and *trillion,* and inaccurate math or rounding. The online editing system for team leaders should be used to fix dropped words, transposed letters, style violations and faulty grammar or syntax.

Correct any errors as soon as they are found so that the mistakes don't spread to other stories or harm readers.

Any communication asserting that we made an error must be immediately brought to the attention of a team leader and managing editor.

People complaining about a story should always be treated with courtesy. Ask them to identify any error. In cases where the fairness of the story is questioned, be prepared to listen and provide supervisors a summary of the complaints. Deference is sensible and honorable. If the person becomes difficult, forward that complaint to a supervisor. Leave questions about sources, the story's meaning or the editorial process to supervisors.

If a lawyer calls about a story or threatens litigation, forward the call to our newsroom lawyer and inform the team leader, managing editor and executive editor immediately.

Never promise a correction within a certain time or date. Reporters must not negotiate or promise particular language in corrections. Leave it to the editor-in-chief to say, "We stand by our story," when that response is appropriate.

Editors should never send a correction without making every attempt to contact the writer and editor to determine whether the complaint is justified.

Be careful about any written correspondence regarding alleged errors. One columnist was drawn into an exchange that ended up in the hands of lawyers suing the subject company and became part of court pleadings.

If every story meets our standards, there will be fewer threats or complaints that we are unfair. It's hard to complain when the narrative relies solely on anecdotes, examples, nouns and verbs, and omits modifiers. Show, don't tell. Our style paves the way for accurate reporting.

Sending Corrections

Examining and publishing a correction isn't so much about keeping track of personal errors as it is about learning how to make fewer errors by understanding how every mistake happened.

Corrections must include (Correct) at the end of the headline: *Brazil Raises $3 Billion by Selling 10-Year Bonds (Correct)*. Even when the story provides new information, use only (Correct) in the headline. Explain in the trashline at the top of the story what other news was added.

Delete the incorrect versions immediately after sending the corrected story. This ensures that erroneous stories won't become misleading reference material. If the story is in a Top <Go> page, replace it with the corrected article before removing the incorrect version.

A correction doesn't affect the numbering of updates. Continue numbering updates as though no correction occurred and no stories were removed. Once there's a second update, we don't back up and have another second update because of a correction. Corrections are never numbered.

When something is wrong and can't be changed or replaced, remove the information from the story and note that in the trashline: *Removes incorrect reference to 2004 earnings in the fourth paragraph*.

When the mistake is discovered one day or a few days after the story moved, leave the date in the dateline unchanged. Note the original story date in the trashline: *Corrects percentage of stock gain in second paragraph of story published March 8*.

Correct all errors of fact in a stand-alone headline in this style: *CORRECT: IMPERIAL RESULTS ARE FOR FIRST HALF. After the correction moves, remove the incorrect headline immediately.

Typographical errors in stand-alone headlines that don't impart materially wrong information should be fixed and resent, not corrected, and the original headlines deleted.

If we run a headline and make something look like new news and later discover it's a development from earlier than yesterday, publish a correction: *CORRECT: ACME ROSE TO 'NEUTRAL' AT GOLDMAN SACHS. If a headline duplicates news from yesterday, publish another headline that tells readers to disregard the news: *IGNORE: ACME BUYS BACK 30 MILLION SHARES. If a headline is correct but duplicates a head moved earlier in the day, remove the duplicate.

Speed is important. Accuracy is even more important.

Sourcing

As journalists providing the first draft of history, we have an obligation to provide as much of what was said and done as we can. That means we should speak to everyone involved and get people of authority to verify what we're prepared to report. We should be precise about how we know what we report. Did we see it? Do we know someone who did? The best journalism is transparent.

The use of anonymous sources asks readers to accept that we are telling the truth and are accurately citing someone who is in a position to know something important. People who routinely tell reporters something only when their names and positions are withheld may have something to conceal—a situation that should make any reporter or editor suspicious, if not skittish, about justifying the concession to anonymity. We want to be the agent of the reader, not of our sources.

Attribution

The first four paragraphs of a story must disclose how we received the information, such as whether it's from a news release, conference call, interview or government filing.

If the news originated from a company statement, explain the source: *the company said in a statement distributed by PR Newswire* or *the company said on its website*. If we called and couldn't reach anyone, add that as well. Once we get confirmation, change the attribution to something such as *the company said in a statement* or *said Bob Jones, a company spokesman*.

If any of the details in the statement are a surprise, seek verification. If the news or its method of delivery is suspect, such as a facsimile sent at midnight to an out-of-the-way bureau, confirm the news before publishing. If the company doesn't respond and the shares are moving, stories about the stock's movement need to explain that the company didn't return calls.

Include details about the location or circumstances of an interview when they are relevant, such as *said in an interview via e-mail* or *said in a telephone interview from his Shanghai office*.

When possible, avoid the broad attribution of *analysts said* or *traders and analysts say* or *investors said*. Names make news. Some people are more noteworthy than others because of their holdings, track record or reputation and should be identified right away.

Before:

> *Gas trapped between rocks and coal beds will account for 64 percent of total U.S. gas production by 2020, up from 42 percent in 2007, according to analysts.*

After:

> *Gas trapped between rocks and coal beds will account for 64 percent of total U.S. gas production by 2020, up from 42 percent in 2007, according to the American Petroleum Institute, which represents about 400 oil and natural gas companies.*

When writing about politics and policy, name a person or a government agency as a source, rather than a building or city. If information came from the White House, attribute it to the presidential administration or name the person who supplied it. On first reference, cite the U.S. Defense Department. It is even better if we obtain the news from the secretary of defense.

Locations such as the White House, Pentagon and 10 Downing Street should be included as additional detail, such as *an administration official said from the White House; an aide to the prime minister said from 10 Downing Street.* Locations aren't to be confused with the attribution of people and their offices. Washington isn't a synonym for the presidential administration or the U.S. government; Tokyo isn't a synonym for the Japanese government; Brussels isn't a synonym for the Belgian government or for the European Union.

Anonymous Sources

Bloomberg News uses anonymous sources only when necessary to get the news to our readers, viewers and listeners. On-the-record information attributed to people and organizations establishes authority and trust. When we decide to publish information based on unidentified people, we're putting our readers at a disadvantage because the sourcing isn't transparent or credible. It's a rare occasion when an anonymously sourced story rises to the quality of our best work.

In most situations, the editor-in-chief, two executive editors or two managing editors must approve anonymously sourced reporting. When the source is definitive, such as the subject of the piece, there may be an exception. The decision requires the disclosure of names and positions, track records and how the people know the information.

When we decide to use anonymous sourcing, there needs to be a discussion: What did the reporter ask? How was it asked? What was the response? Do all the anonymous sources agree? Why should we trust these people? How do they know what they know? What's their motive? Why don't they want their names used? What are we missing? What we don't know will hurt us.

We don't use direct quotes from anonymous people. Even when we paraphrase, critical comments should include attribution.

A story based on information from anonymous sources should also include on-the-record comment from people who are skeptical of the news or who can give an independent appraisal.

When writing stories based on anonymously obtained documents, seek to verify their authenticity. Referring only to *a memo obtained by Bloomberg News* forces readers to assume the letter is credible. Describe the letter's contents and presentation. How many pages? What was the date? To whom was it addressed? Who signed it? The answers build confidence in our reporting.

These standards shouldn't prevent us from talking to those in the know. Insights of people who insist on anonymity can become fodder for others who are receptive to publicity. After a while, traditionally anonymous people get frustrated when their insights are being trumpeted by less-informed sources.

Once the decision is made to use anonymous attribution, we have an obligation to be as transparent as possible to our audience. We don't want to trivialize the use of an anonymous source by getting in the habit of writing formulaic attribution such as *people familiar* or *a person familiar with the transaction*. Attribution must be as specific as we can make it for the situation:

Describe how the people know what they know.
Explain why the people are willing to share their information.
Explain why the people are insisting on, and are entitled to, anonymity.
Tell readers as much as possible about the people. Describe their credentials as much as possible without jeopardizing their identity. We may be able to identify their departments or positions.

The term *source* is part of our industry jargon. Phrases such as *sources said* or *it is understood* or *Bloomberg has learned* aren't acceptable. It is better to say *person* or *people* with specific attribution.

Some examples of full attribution: *A person present at the meeting; someone who has seen the document; a congressional aide; a department official; a participant and a supporter of the bill; executives who have been briefed on the negotiations.*

Before:

The government has told banks to raise interest rates on third mortgages and demand bigger down payments for such loans, according to a person with knowledge of the matter.

After:

The Chinese government told banks to raise interest rates on third mortgages and demand bigger down payments for such loans, according to a regulator who requested anonymity because the measures haven't been published.

Before:

By mid-2006, according to someone involved in the negotiations, Fox was still concerned that making Avatar would cost too much money.

After:

By mid-2006, Fox was still concerned that making Avatar would cost too much money, according to a person involved in the negotiations who declined to be identified because the talks were private.

Don't mislead readers about a source's identity, even to divert suspicion. For example, don't use *people* when only one person supplied the information.

Don't allow a person to lie on the record while supplying contrary information for anonymous attribution.

Don't say that a person had no comment or declined to comment when we have comment from the person on an anonymous basis.

Conduct

Our work should be invigorating. If we have no time to pause, reflect and feel refreshed, we won't fulfill our potential. It's the quality that matters most. This means the emphasis at Bloomberg News must always be on attaining greater knowledge and skill. It takes informed reporters and editors a fraction of the time to handle news that it does reporters and editors with a limited understanding.

Working long hours day after day isn't a virtue if the consequence is perpetual exhaustion. While it's rare to see people gain without some pain, it's also rare to see people do their best when they are tired.

There are times when Bloomberg journalists must visit offices or attend public events. We must follow the dress code of the place we're visiting and should always be presentable for spontaneous visits by newsmakers, customers and sources. Reporters should behave in a manner appropriate to the events they are covering.

Professionalism dictates that we treat interviewees with respect, even if they are hostile, argumentative or dissembling. While we report the news, we should never create it, such as by arguing with a prime minister during a press conference and then granting interviews to the local press. We can ask questions without Bloomberg becoming part of the story, which compromises our integrity.

The Bloomberg message system is supposed to expedite the communication necessary to produce the best news. Be careful what you write in messages. Reporters and editors are defined by the words they send over the system, as well as the words they choose for stories. Assume that every message can be forwarded or made public.

Keep the potential for libel in mind. Suppose a reporter on a story about company officials under investigation sends a message to another reporter that says, *We are going to get this guy!* That message might become evidence in any libel action and be interpreted as a sign of malicious intent, even if the intention was to say that we should find a way to contact the person.

Even if we don't end up in court, we take a risk when we express our personal judgments, gossip, feelings and desires in messages that could become public. Keep in mind that messages sometimes go to people other than the intended recipients.

Libel

Concentrate on producing the best story possible, one that supplies all the supporting evidence and response, rather than thinking about notions such as actual malice and public figures, which can be misleading and dangerous.

A good journalist is motivated by fairness and has an inner sense for identifying and avoiding defamation. If it makes you think for even the briefest second, "Wow, that's bad," it may be potentially libelous. Stop and ask for guidance.

Bloomberg News, an international organization, can be sued in any jurisdiction where its words are published or broadcast. In some countries, such as the U.S., constitutions protect the press from claims of injured reputation or invaded privacy, assuming certain conditions are met. Other jurisdictions, such as those in Europe and Asia, hold the press to a stricter standard, and errors in reporting can result in monetary damages and even jail sentences.

In many nations, truth is not an absolute defense: The story must serve an important public interest. In other places, a statement need not be defamatory to justify a lawsuit: A factual error that causes monetary loss can be the subject of a suit.

In the U.S., documents obtained from court proceedings usually may be reported with impunity. Many other nations restrict access to such material and may hold a reporter in contempt for publishing court papers.

We don't specify a period for reporters to save notes. Each reporter should set a length of time for keeping and cleaning their files. Some reporters keep neat and chronologically ordered written notes or maintain them on a computer. Others jot information on napkins, and those kinds of notes have a way of getting lost or destroyed. If we had a policy that reporters keep notes for a certain period, the failure to produce notes required in a libel suit—in violation of our own rule—could be introduced to a jury as evidence of bad faith.

These rules change when a story is reviewed for libel. Hold those notes for two years, the statute of limitations in most places. If a story becomes the subject of a libel threat or an autopsy because of libel concerns, save those notes for two years. If space is a concern, send the material to our lawyers.

Red Flags

When a story accuses a person of dishonest, unethical or illegal conduct, it can be said to be defamatory. It doesn't matter whether the statement is true because it still harms the person's reputation.

That doesn't mean the person has enough to win a lawsuit. We might report that Jones has been convicted of fraud because we have a copy of his conviction. The statement hurts his reputation: After all, would you hire him to run your business? Saying that he was found guilty of fraud in the past isn't actionable. Any lawsuit would be defensible because the statement is true.

In many countries, an organization that publishes a libelous statement made in another publication adopts it as its own—and can be held just as liable. Reproducing a defamatory statement merely with attribution to another publication is no defense in court.

Before publishing a press summary or story about another news organization's report that accuses or implies wrongdoing or incompetence, try to obtain comment or denial from the person, company or organization whose reputation is at stake. Note those efforts in the story. Our reputation is at stake as well. We risk perpetuating any sloppiness, inaccuracy, unnamed sourcing or lack of integrity.

Publishing a denial in another news organization's story isn't a substitute for our own attempt to contact the accused. If a subject refused to speak to us or couldn't be reached and has denied the charges elsewhere, include both facts:

Bloomberg News couldn't reach Jones immediately for comment. Jones said the charges were unfounded, the Daily Bugle reported yesterday.

Many jurisdictions restrict what can be quoted from court documents. We fail our readers when we merely quote sensational, defamatory statements made in court papers without putting the news into context and perspective. Be fair, complete and accurate in relying on such materials and exhibit news judgment in deciding what lawsuits to cover.

While libel claims are based on damage to reputation arising from falsehoods, privacy claims cover the sense of intrusion arising from publishing true, but private, facts about people. Bloomberg News doesn't publish home addresses of subjects. Be wary about publishing medical facts, names and photos of juveniles, or financial data that isn't public and directly related to the thrust of a story.

While reporters are encouraged to be enterprising in their pursuit of facts, they are forbidden from breaking laws regarding electronic communications such as e-mails, conference calls or telephone calls. In the U.S., a reporter is allowed to record a call without permission in Alabama, Alaska, Arizona, Arkansas, Colorado, Delaware, the District of Columbia, Georgia, Hawaii, Idaho, Indiana, Iowa, Kansas, Kentucky, Louisiana, Maine, Minnesota, Mississippi, Missouri, Nebraska, New Jersey, New Mexico, New York, North Carolina, North Dakota, Ohio, Oklahoma, Oregon, Rhode Island, South Carolina, South Dakota, Tennessee, Texas, Utah, Vermont, Virginia, West Virginia and Wisconsin.

All other states require the consent of all parties to a phone call before recording.

Unless you and your subject are both in one of these states, you must obtain permission on the telephone before recording. Internationally, Belgium, Canada, France and the Netherlands allow reporters to record telephone interviews without consent. Many jurisdictions have laws that shield a journalist's unpublished notes and outtakes from the hands of investigators. Some of those jurisdictions still allow prosecutors to obtain notes when they show that they need the material for law enforcement and that the notes aren't available anywhere else. It is our policy to challenge such attempts whenever the law and facts allow.

Reporters who interview people with firsthand knowledge or evidence of wrongdoing may become targets of law-enforcement agencies wanting to search those notes for evidence. A court sympathetic to law enforcement will require the reporter to disclose the notes or face a contempt charge.

When a red flag appears in a story, stop and consult with our newsroom lawyer before publication. Bloomberg News always has a lawyer available, including a network of media lawyers around the world who can be called for assistance.

Avoiding Libel

Provide proof. Telling the truth is the surest way to avoid libel. Proving the truth, however, isn't as easy as it seems. Courts demand evidence, or provable truth, not just assurances that you quoted everybody correctly. This means having documents such as court records, prospectuses, proxy statements, tax records and regulatory filings whenever possible. It means taping sensitive interviews with the knowledge of both parties, and even arranging affidavits. It means attributing frequently and completely in stories.

Be humble. Own up to a mistake quickly and completely. Correct completely. Fudging a correction hurts our credibility and reduces libel protection. Don't correct factual mistakes by hiding them in an update. Never delete a story from the Bloomberg system without first moving a correction or getting permission from the editor-in-chief.

Be specific. If ABC Co. Vice President Joe Smith is perceived as a scoundrel, show it with anecdotes and let the reader decide. Be wary of gratuitous statements, such as *By the way, his partner cheats on taxes, too.*

Don't accept facts at face value. Even when talking to usually reliable people, journalists must know fully what the sources are saying. Never be afraid to ask stupid questions.

Who's saying these things? What do they have to gain? What's their ax to grind? Who or what is their source? Does that seem like a reliable source? If you're a reporter, review the people involved and make sure you're not getting used. If you're an editor, start grilling the reporter.

Be meticulous. A typographical error or a misplaced modifier can be grounds for libel if it injures reputation.

Weigh your words. Edit carefully. If you're unsure about something, delete it. A story may be construed as defamatory based on how it arranges some facts and omits others. If we write that a celebrity was accused of something and fail to include that he was acquitted or exonerated, we haven't been fair.

Never let down your libel guard. Be as careful with boilerplate kinds of stories—the formula-based reports we write every day such as movers and summaries—as with any other article. News organizations are as likely to be sued over a brief as an investigative story. Each story deserves full attention.

12

Enterprise

ENTERPRISE is the effort in reporting that produces an exceptional and unique result. Enterprise is difficult to replicate, which is why all stories should be enterprising.

These stories set Bloomberg News apart, surprising readers, listeners and viewers and changing how they perceive the world. Enterprise explains the forces shaping events, reveals the motives and personalities of newsmakers and captures the trends molding the future.

Enterprise begins with reporting. Ideas spring from the work we do every day: talking to people, visiting factories and offices, digging through documents, reading and researching, and observing the world. Curiosity begets ideas. Great reporters are always uncovering something they didn't know or understand.

These stories, whether turned around in a few hours or many months, offer more detail, context, pathos, explanation and perspective than any others we write. Enterprise can pull together isolated facts—often unreported—to show an unknown or global theme.

Enterprise startles. It thrives on counterintuitive ideas and anecdotes that reveal facets of people and events. It supports every assertion with facts, examples and anecdotes.

Great reporters bring enterprise to every story, whether it's a 400-word piece of this-just-in or a 4,000-word magazine story that requires months of reporting.

Idea to Story

An idea alone isn't enough. It needs to be tested before any part of the story is written. Reporters need to hash out the theme with editors and colleagues. Ask many questions to see whether the idea is worth pursuing.

Why this idea now?
What is changing?
What's the surprise?
Does the idea go against common knowledge?
What's the conflict?
Who are the winners and the losers?
Who are the characters in the story?
How will the conflict be resolved?
What does this mean for the future?
What's at stake?
Why should anyone on the other side of the globe care?
What's the big picture?
How will this idea change behavior or perceptions?
Should investors buy or sell these shares, bonds, commodities, currencies, etc.?
Are people talking about this—or should they be?
Has anyone else reported this? If so, what do we know that they don't?
What's another way to tell this story?
What facts are needed to support this idea?
What is the headline?

It may take more research and telephone calls to answer these questions. The time is well spent. Stories with good beginnings have a better chance of achieving good endings. When everyone agrees on the idea at the start, the reporting, writing and editing should be simpler.

Preparing a Pitch

Once the idea is thoroughly considered, write a pitch. Crafting the pitch, which describes the theme in a few sentences or paragraphs, forces the reporter to distill all those questions and answers into the most important themes and facts.

Think of it as a short pitch for a Hollywood movie: What's the story about? Why should anyone care? What's the tension? Who are the actors?

The pitch starts with the headline. If the headline captures the surprise, the newsmakers, the what's-at-stake, the conflict and the resolution, chances are the story will, too. If it doesn't, it's a sign the story idea is flawed.

The first three or four words of the headline should startle:

End-of-Life Warning at $618,616 Makes Me Wonder Was It Worth It
China Builds New Great Wall to Defend Against Mice, Not Mongols
Blankfein Flunks Asset Management as Clark Vows No More Goldman
Ferrari Secret Society Costs Its 29 Members $1.8 Million Each
Lonely Analyst Warns of 2015 Bank Crisis Amid 'Upbeat' Davos
House of Morgan Becomes a Home as Families Move to Wall Street
Trading Pennies Into $7 Billion Drives High-Frequency's Cowboys
Eat-What-You-Kill Brokers Starved as Banks Gorge on Bailout Cash

Spend as much time as needed crafting the headline. "What's the head-line?" is the most important question we can ask ourselves before starting any story. Headlines are the first—and possibly only—words our customers see.

Before:
Click Clack of Metal Spikes, Sign of 'Real Golfer,' Growing Fainter
After:
Another Thing Woods Can Do That You Can't: Wear Metal Spikes

Revise and fine-tune the story pitch, because it will guide the reporting, organizing and writing. Secretly reporting and writing the story first and then crafting the pitch will turn into a time-waster if the proposal is rejected or the theme or direction is revised. If you're having trouble expressing the theme in a headline or a few sentences, you probably don't have a clear concept. Do more reporting and more talking.

A typical pitch will convey four main thoughts:
This is the story of . . .
People should read this story because . . .
We should write this now because . . .
I will report the story by doing . . .

Properly done, the response to the first two points will resemble a lead and a nut paragraph.

In some cases, the pitch may condense the idea into a few sentences. Other stories may require five or six paragraphs, as well as the top four paragraphs of the story.

This pitch explains the theme, the tension and why people should care:

London's Pigeon-Loving Rebels Defy Mayor's Bird Starvation Plan
London's most famous square has become an animal rights battleground as Mayor Ken Livingstone tries to rid it of pigeons. For years, the birds were synonymous with Trafalgar Square and thousands of visitors flocked to buy seed from vendors to feed them. Livingstone, who calls the pigeons "rats with wings," has, over the past six years, removed licenses to sell bird food, made feeding the birds illegal and hired two Harris hawks to patrol the skies around Nelson's Column. Still, an estimated 1,500 pigeons remain, largely thanks to a group of pro-pigeon activists who feed the birds on a section of the square not controlled by the mayor. The pigeons' continued presence may threaten the Nelson monument, renovated last year when years of grime and droppings were removed at a cost of $800,000.

Here is the top of the published story. Notice how it hewed to the themes in the pitch:

Pigeon-Loving Rebels Defy Feed Ban on London's Trafalgar Square
April 24 (Bloomberg) -- As the sun rises over London's Trafalgar Square, hundreds of pigeons huddle under Nelson's Column in a scene from Alfred Hitchcock's "The Birds."
Thirty minutes later, a frenzy of cooing breaks out as a woman approaches wheeling a large suitcase. Inside Shelagh Moorhouse's luggage is 15 pounds of corn. On opening it, she is engulfed by a swarm of flapping wings.

Moorhouse is one of a band of activists dedicated to saving the pigeons of Trafalgar Square. Mayor Ken Livingstone, who calls them "flying rats," has spent the past six years trying to banish the birds, saying they're a health hazard and their droppings cost 140,000 pounds ($280,000) a year to clean up.

"We've got a despot with a pigeon phobia in charge of this city," says Moorhouse, 69, a retired radiographer. "It's cruel and wrong to starve them just because one man doesn't like them. You should be entitled to feed birds anywhere."

Types of Enterprise

Enterprise takes many forms. It can be an overnight story derived from the events of the day or an exclusive interview. It can be about a local event in a far-flung bureau or about markets, companies, economies or governments. It can be a 2,000-word company or personality feature for the magazine that takes six months to prepare.

Here are some of the main types of enterprise we write.

This-just-in. Some enterprise ideas start with breaking news. These are best published within hours or days of the event.

The ideas are vetted as rigorously as less time-sensitive enterprise. Successful stories come from reporters who keep notes—or, as we like to call it, *string*—about the themes on their beats. Those notes collect observations, names, thoughts and research over weeks, months or years, waiting for their useful day. This story stemmed from an interview:

'Rogue Trader' Leeson May Resume Trading After Ruining Barings
     March 7 (Bloomberg) -- Nick Leeson, the rogue trader whose wrong-way bets on Japanese stocks ruined Britain's oldest merchant bank, said he may go back to trading full-time with only his own money at stake.
     Leeson said he trades "when I get the time" and has been buying and selling currencies for the past few months. He is considering "watching screens" for a living when he decides to leave his current job as commercial director of Irish soccer team Galway United FC.

"You wouldn't believe how many people have asked me to manage their money," Leeson, 40, said in an interview in Galway, on Ireland's west coast. "If I make a decision and lose money, fair enough. If I make a decision for somebody else, then I would feel obligated to make it up to them."

Greet the weeks. Each week, we produce stories that examine markets, economies, companies, industries and governments. These stories, called *Greet the Weeks*, help Bloomberg set the agenda.

A story about companies, stocks, bonds, commodities or currencies should tell investors whether to buy, sell or hold. Stories about industries should include an idea that can be used in an investment decision. Articles about the economy must be global in significance and shed light on the economy's direction.

Bernanke, Paulson Were Wrong: Subprime Contagion Is Spreading
    Aug. 10 (Bloomberg) -- Federal Reserve Chairman Ben S. Bernanke was wrong.
    So were U.S. Treasury Secretary Henry Paulson and Merrill Lynch & Co. Chief Executive Officer Stanley O'Neal.
    The subprime mortgage industry's problems were contained, they all said. It turns out that the turmoil was contagious.
    The $2 trillion market for mortgages not backed by government-sponsored agencies is at a standstill. That's just the beginning. Other types of mortgages are suffering. So are firms and banks that package the debt for investors. The ripples were felt in Europe and Asia, where central banks offered cash to banks amid a credit crunch.
    And some corporations, from countertop makers to railroads, are blaming the mortgage meltdown and housing slump for earnings that fell short of analysts' estimates.

Bureaus. Another form of enterprise, called *bureaus stories*, examines the topics people are talking about in the regions where we have offices. The stories seek to convey a sense of that place and the community to readers thousands of miles away.

Kolkata's 'Human Horses' Lose Jobs as Communists Ban Rickshaws
April 18 (Bloomberg) -- Mohammed Jowahar, like his father before him, has pulled rickshaws by hand in the east Indian city of Kolkata for more than three decades. A government ban on the two-wheel carts may leave him destitute.

"This is the only skill I have," said Jowahar, 55, wearing a blue checkered sarong, vest and slippers as he waited outside the Kolkata mayor's office for customers. He supports 11 family members in neighboring Bihar state on less than $3 a day.

Jowahar is among about 18,000 rickshaw pullers in Kolkata, the capital of West Bengal state and the only city in the world still served by so-called human horses. The communist state government says the men have no place in its plans to turn India's old British colonial headquarters into a modern investment destination rivaling Bangalore, Mumbai and New Delhi.

"It's inhuman for a human being to carry another in this day and age," said Mayor Bikash Bhattacharya, 55, a member of West Bengal's ruling Communist Party of India (Marxist). "We have made so much progress. We want rickshaws off the streets."

Profiles. Profiling the people behind every news event helps readers appreciate its significance. The story should include anecdotes and color that reveal character traits and help explain decisions in the news.

Citadel Returns 26 Percent While Breaking Hedge Fund Mold
April 29 (Bloomberg) -- It's a midwinter afternoon in Chicago, and Citadel Investment Group LLC, with $12 billion in assets under management, is wrapping up a typical day—trading almost 2 percent of the daily volume on the Tokyo and New York stock exchanges, or about 70 million shares.

Removed from the trading floor's din in a 36th-floor corner office, Citadel founder and Chief Executive Officer Kenneth Griffin sits at an L-shaped desk devoid of paper.

On his computer screen: an in-box full of messages, not the prices of stocks or bonds. Griffin, 36, no longer trades. "They are better at it than I am," he says, gesturing toward the traders outside his office. Griffin says he has more to think about than the next big trade. He says he wants to build something greater than a simple hedge fund firm: a diversified company that's No. 1 or No. 2 in every investment arena it tackles and that manages tens of billions of dollars. He says he may sell shares in the expanding company to the public, which would make Citadel the first U.S. hedge fund firm listed on a stock exchange.

Magazine and investigations. Other forms of enterprise are investigative or in-depth stories for the Bloomberg or our magazines, *Bloomberg Markets* and *Bloomberg Businessweek*. These stories may take months to prepare.

Drug Industry Human Testing Masks Death, Injury, Compliant FDA
     Nov. 2 (Bloomberg) -- Oscar Cabanerio has been waiting in an experimental-drug testing center in Miami since 7:30 a.m. The 41-year-old undocumented immigrant says he's desperate for cash to send to his wife and four children in Venezuela.
     More than 70 people have crowded into reception rooms furnished with rows of attached blue plastic seats. Cabanerio is one of many regulars who gather at SFBC International Inc.'s test center, which, with 675 beds, is the largest for-profit drug trial site in North America.
     Across the U.S., 3.7 million people have enrolled in drug tests sponsored by the world's largest pharmaceutical companies. The companies have outsourced 75 percent of experimental drug trials to centers like SFBC, a leader in a $14 billion industry.
     At the same time, the U.S. Food and Drug Administration has farmed out much of the responsibility for overseeing safety in these tests to private companies known as institutional review boards. These boards are also financed by pharmaceutical companies.
     So, the drug industry is paying the people who do the tests—and most of the people who regulate those tests. And that combination can be dangerous, and sometimes deadly.

Reporting

Reporting starts with research. Read everything, from stories by other news organizations to academic research to analysts' reports. Run Internet searches and ask Bloomberg's library to collect clips. Listen to old TV and audio interviews.

Only after becoming an expert on the subject is it time to start interviewing and collecting anecdotes. Get out of the office. Nothing produces more anecdotes and details than a face-to-face interview or a visit to the scene. Anecdotes are short and descriptive accounts of something that happened or that illustrate character. Collect as many anecdotes as possible.

Tour the factory floor, the warehouse, a store, a trading room, a data-processing center. Talk to the workers and customers. Look for a moment or an image to convey in a lead. Show what you see, hear and smell. The anecdotes will provide the evidence that the story's theme is true.

Wal-Mart Stores Inc.'s headquarters in Bentonville, Arkansas, used to be furnished with hard, uncomfortable plastic chairs. This was Sam Walton's way of telling visiting manufacturers' representatives that his goal was to get a good deal for customers, not to make them feel comfortable.

Anecdotes rarely fall into reporters' laps. They come from knowing ahead of time what kind of information is needed and probing for it. Then, when the source gives an inkling of a telling example, asking for details: Where were you? When did this happen? What was your reaction? How did you feel about it?

Collect more than one anecdote. What if it falls apart later or the story changes? Get the full names, ages and telephone numbers of the people in the anecdotes, in case we need to check a fact or get more information.

Slaves in Amazon Forced to Make Materials Used by GM, Toyota
Nov. 2 (Bloomberg) -- Labor inspector Benedito Silva Filho and six armed police officers move cautiously through the gray smoke that hugs the ground in the Carvoaria Transcameta work camp near the city of Tucuruí in the Brazilian Amazon. Enveloped in the haze is a solitary man, dressed in soiled red shorts and worn-out plastic sandals.

Alexandre Pereira dos Reis stops shoveling charcoal from a kiln after working for eight hours and, wheezing, walks slowly toward the inspectors. The laborer says malaria, a chronic cough and the 95-degree-Fahrenheit heat have gotten the best of him. "This hits you hard," dos Reis, 32, says. "I would leave if I could, but I need the work."

Like hundreds of thousands of workers in Latin America, dos Reis collects no wages. He toils six days a week and can't afford to leave; he doesn't have enough money to get back to his home in Teresina, 500 miles (800 kilometers) away in northeastern Brazil. Dos Reis lives next to the brick kilns at Transcameta in a shack with no ventilation, running water or electricity.

The charcoal he and the other laborers produce by burning scraps of hardwood will be trucked south to a blast furnace that's six hours away. It will be used there to make pig iron, a basic ingredient of steel.

That pig iron will be purchased by brokers, sold to steelmakers and foundries and then purchased by some of the world's largest companies for use in cars, tractors, sinks and refrigerators made for U.S. consumers.

All this reporting takes time during already busy days. Some reporters make one or two calls a day on the story or spend 30 minutes each day doing research, pulling it together over several weeks. Others arrange days or half-days with their team leaders to allow the reporting.

A Model of Reporting

What distinguishes this *Markets* magazine profile of Bill Gross, who manages the world's biggest bond fund at Pimco Investment Management Co., is its collection of anecdotes. The 4,700-word story is laden with examples that help define Gross, from his childhood to college to military service in Vietnam to management techniques.

Here's how the reporter gathered all this evidence:

Prepare. Before visiting, the reporter read every profile written about Gross as well as the bond manager's two books, *Everything You've Heard About Investing Is Wrong* and *Bill Gross on Investing*. Gross's interest in blackjack was previously reported. In the first interview, the reporter pressed for details about how he became interested in cards (and, by extension, markets). It was a pivotal anecdote: a boy recovering from injury, reading a book about gambling.

Record everything. During her two-day visit at Pimco, the reporter took copious notes, including that Gross snacks on red licorice sticks after lunch, how he failed to become a fighter pilot and how he once ran six marathons in six days.

Follow relentlessly. A lawsuit filed by New Jersey against Pimco came after the reporter's visit. She had to persuade Gross to talk again on the telephone: Where were you when you heard about it? What were you thinking? Who said what to whom? This became the lead anecdote.

When a college buddy told the reporter that Gross had an old car, she asked Gross for the name ("The Blue Lunch") and the make (Oldsmobile).

Collect documents. The reporter asked for and collected every document she could. When Pimco fund manager Mohamed El-Erian said that Gross sends e-mails to deputies, she asked for copies. She also asked for copies of every monthly "outlook" Gross had written since the early 1980s—a knee-high stack.

Here's the result:

Pimco Bond Maestro Gross Battles Regulators as Market Shakes

April 30 (Bloomberg) -- On a Tuesday morning in February, Bill Gross, chief investment officer of Pacific Investment Management Co., was meeting with Chief Executive Officer William Thompson at Pimco's Newport Beach, California, headquarters. Just before 11 a.m., Chief Operating Officer Richard Weil walked into Thompson's third-floor office and shut the door.

"You're not going to believe this," a sullen-faced Weil told them, Gross recalls. New Jersey Attorney General Peter Harvey was suing Pimco, the fifth-largest U.S. mutual fund company, with $394 billion of assets under management, for alleged trading abuses.

"We sat there in total shock and said to ourselves, 'What the hell is going on?'" Gross says.

The New Jersey suit has prompted public pension funds in California, Hawaii and Illinois to review their business with Pimco, a unit of Munich-based Allianz AG, the largest insurance company in Europe. It has also left Gross, Pimco's star fund manager and public face, battling to contain the damage.

From Pimco's trading floor in Newport Beach, 3,000 miles from Wall Street, Gross, 60, manages the world's biggest bond fund. His Pimco Total Return Fund has gained an average of 9.4 percent a year since its inception in 1987, beating the 8.1 percent average return posted by the benchmark Lehman Brothers U.S. Aggregate Bond Index.

Organizing the Story

The first four paragraphs should tell what the story is about, what makes it timely, why the news matters and what is new, different and surprising.

They should convey movement, conflict, tension and challenge. Earnings are soaring or sinking. The stock price is surging or plunging. There is a new chief executive, or the current one is about to be ousted. Shareholders are mad, employees are defecting, regulators are investigating or lawyers are filing class-action lawsuits. There is a new competitor, a new technology, a collapsing foreign market, a big merger in the works, an aging customer base, a new law, a deregulated marketplace. Depending on the subject, other elements may be required on the first screen. For example, a story about a company must provide the information that tells investors whether they should buy, sell or hold that stock.

If anecdotes from the scene capture the essence of the story, use them in the lead. If not, don't force it. Use the best quote first. Aim for a broad one. Convey context, conflict, tension, challenge, strategy or skepticism. Make sure the main points of the pitch show up on the first screen of the story.

Here are some examples of leads that, when reworked, had more appeal and color, or a more compelling message:

Before:

Imported Mercedes Benz and Ford Motor Co. cars are piling up and gathering rust at Chinese ports as the government's crackdown on illegal trading of import licenses cuts the flow of cars into the market.

After:

Thousands of dirt-covered Opel Vectras, Ford Mondeos and Nissan Cefiros sit on a parking lot at China's Tianjin Port, exposed to the corrosive Yellow Sea winds and periodic dust storms blowing from Mongolia.

Before:

Delores Alstodt, 72, calls Canada when she needs refills on her medicines. With a prescription and a major credit card, the Florida retiree can get a 100-day supply of Purdue Pharma LP's Uniphyl lung medication mailed to her home for $33, a 73 percent discount from the $123 she pays at her local drugstore.

After:

Delores Alstodt knows where she can get a 73 percent discount on Purdue Pharma LP's Uniphyl. The Florida retiree buys the lung-muscle relaxant by picking up the phone and ordering from Canada.

The Rest of the Story

After the top is developed, think of the story as a series of sections of three to five paragraphs each, similar to the chapters of a book. The sections should relate to the main point. It helps to print the draft story and label the sections such as background, to be sure, forward spin and kicker.

This helps editors, too. If a story wanders, label each paragraph and group all paragraphs with a similar theme. This will help structure, and probably tighten, the story.

Strive for a narrative flow when organizing. Don't follow a section on how a country's economy is slumping with a series of numbers about how that's dragging down corporate profits. Change the pace by inserting between those sections an example of how one company is affected by the economy with a comment from a relevant executive.

Draw in the reader with a scene, and then step back to look at the issue from a regional or global perspective. Then zoom back in for more anecdotes or examples.

Near the end, sum up the theme, the conflict or the tension. Then push the story into the future, giving a preview of the next challenge or test. That is known as the *kicker*—an apt place to end a discussion of developing, reporting and writing.

13

Chart of the Day

THE CHART OF THE DAY is the exceptional combination of this-just-in reporting and enterprise.

It shows and doesn't just tell. It is the convergence of Bloomberg News, Bloomberg data and Bloomberg analytics. It is a story for the Bloomberg terminal, for Bloomberg.com, for Bloomberg Television, for newspapers publishing Bloomberg News and for Bloomberg's customers to use in their own investing and research.

Drawing on the depth, speed and flexibility of Bloomberg, the Chart of the Day is difficult—if not impossible—to replicate elsewhere. That means we can preempt competitors who may not deliver comparable stories until the next day or later

A chart is a simple and elegant way to present an idea and set fire to the imagination. The Chart of the Day fuses the data points that best tell the story with four to six paragraphs of prose and a quotation.

The aim is to surprise with compelling facts, ideas and perspectives. The inspiration might come from our imagination, an investigation of the data, the day's headlines, an anomaly seen in market prices, or a conversation with an analyst, investor or economist.

We might run one or more Charts of the Day on any day, each no more than 250 words, depending on the news and our creativity. The day after this analyst-inspired piece, the Federal Reserve, European Central Bank, Bank of England and three other central banks lowered interest rates in an unprecedented coordinated effort:

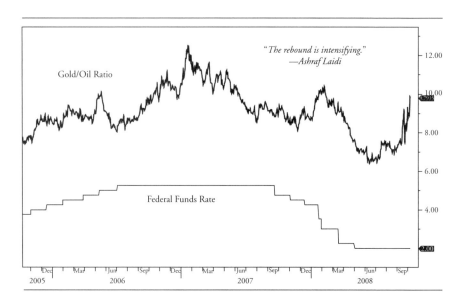

Source: Bloomberg Finance LP.

Gold, Oil Signal 'Coordinated Central Bank' Cuts: Chart of Day
Oct. 7 (Bloomberg) -- Gold and crude oil are signaling investors'
expectations that central banks worldwide may be about to lower interest
rates, according to CMC Markets in New York.
The CHART OF THE DAY compares gold for immediate delivery
with crude-oil futures traded on the New York Mercantile Exchange. The
ratio yesterday rose to the highest in almost eight months as gold jumped
as high as $875.55 an ounce and crude oil dropped below $90 a barrel
for the first time since February. Slower economic growth may sap oil con-
sumption and spur demand for gold as a hedge against financial turmoil.
The ratio reflects increasing pessimism, raising expectations that central
banks will need to cut rates to shore up growth, CMC Chief Currency

Strategist Ashraf Laidi said in a telephone interview from Washington yesterday.

"The rebound in the ratio has been happening for a while but the rebound is intensifying on something extra now," Laidi said. "It is intensifying on increased expectations of coordinated central bank easing."

Goldman Sachs Group Inc. said last week that the U.S. economy, the world's biggest consumer of oil, will enter a recession "significantly deeper" than previously forecast. Australia's central bank cut its benchmark interest rate today by one percentage point, the most since a recession in 1992.

This Chart of the Day was published one day before the price of oil rose to a record and started a decline that continued for the rest of the year.

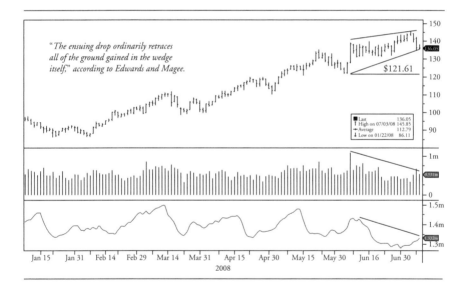

Source: Bloomberg Finance LP.

Oil May Drop to $121.61, Technical Analysis Shows: Chart of Day
  July 10 (Bloomberg) -- Oil may decline after futures prices formed a technical pattern called a wedge formation, a chart arrangement first discovered 60 years ago.

Defined as a narrowing between highest and lowest values in a rising or declining market, the wedge formation was described by Robert D. Edwards and John Magee in "Technical Analysis of Stock Trends," first published in 1948.

"The wedge is a chart formation in which the price fluctuations are confined within converging straight (or practically straight) lines," they wrote. "Both boundary lines either slope up or slope down."

The CHART OF THE DAY illustrates how the price of oil is in a wedge formation. The top section shows the wedge beginning when oil was at $121.61 on June 5, suggesting the price could drop back to that level. The bottom two sections show how both trading volume and open interest have subsided since that date. Crude oil traded at about $136 a barrel today.

"Once prices break out of the wedge on the downside they usually waste little time before declining in earnest," wrote Edwards and Magee. "The ensuing drop ordinarily retraces all of the ground gained in the wedge itself, and sometimes more. "Trading volume in a wedge tends to follow the regular triangle pattern, diminishing gradually as prices move toward the apex of the wedge."

Reporters and editors who would like to contribute a Chart of the Day should first determine whether a graphic would illustrate the point. Then they should ask:

What are investors most worried about or interested in right now?

What do I know about my market that most people don't and would be a surprise to them?

How can I best illustrate the topic with a Bloomberg chart?

Who is the smartest person to illustrate the chart with a pithy quote?

14

How We Work

For Bloomberg News and its reporters, editors, team leaders and bureau chiefs to succeed and prosper, we must pursue precision in language and pay scrupulous attention to detail. We must have a thirst for knowledge, a persistence to get any task accomplished no matter how daunting, the humility to recognize that none of us is infallible and the decency to address anyone and everyone with concern and kindness.

Reporters

Reporters must recognize what's news, deliver the news as fast as they can, explain the news so there isn't any mistaking its importance and be willing to chase any story no matter when or where it breaks. The occupation is a challenging one, full of surprises and occasional epiphanies. Done well, it is invigorating.

Every news beat might be viewed as a rock. It's the job of a reporter to describe the shape, color, weight, texture and size of the rock. The reporter's job is to turn the rock over and examine what's underneath. If there are worms, describe them. If a slug moves, describe that, too. This is writing with anecdotes. It means every statement of fact should be followed by an example, to prove that what we say isn't just the generalization of the reporter but an impartial observation and understanding of the event.

113

Some of this is intuitive. Any reporter with sufficient dedication to the craft can learn to be thorough. The more questions are asked, the more knowledge is gained. The more knowledge is gained, the more authority the reporter accumulates to ask questions, the more intelligent the questions become and so forth. Often the best stories—scoops—are found under rocks.

The best reporters need no supervision because they never wait to be told what to do. They know.

Good reporters start by reading as much as possible about their beat. This provides the opportunity to learn more and to identify people worth knowing.

The best reporters never take no for an answer.

We are only as good as the people we know. The best reporters recognize this and always go to the top. Their stories quote people who are in a position to know something and influence events: chief executive officers, finance ministers, central bankers, senators, parliament members and managing directors.

They look for new people to quote by getting out of the office and by asking others whose opinions or knowledge they value. They visit people on the trading floor, at a trade show, in a restaurant, on a golf course, in an office, on the ski slope and, if the person is a gold mine for scoops, even at the theater.

The more reporters learn about those people—career history, civic activities, education, passions, family—the more they indicate sincerity and commitment. When people have a sense that the reporter won't surprise them in a way that will injure them, they will deem the reporter trustworthy.

Reporters need to be able to reach somebody with knowledge of the beat on occasions when most people aren't at work. That means being prepared enough to have handy the names and telephone numbers of people who can provide instant perspective when the votes are counted at midnight, when the prime minister is assassinated, or when the terrorist attack shuts down the exchange. If we can't reach these people when we need them, we aren't ready to do our best work.

Public-relations departments are the least satisfying sources. Reliance on them is the surest route to mediocrity. Yet, even here, reporters should be polite and creative because we may need help in gaining access.

Reporters should habitually visit the people, places and institutions that constitute their beat. There is no substitute for being there. Reporters who make a practice of visiting their sources and the places where these people work, live and entertain will do a better job of meeting their daily reporting and writing deadlines.

Experience has a way of making the most dedicated reporters the most disciplined reporters: staying that extra hour to get a scoop, getting that fifth anecdote for a feature, or tinkering with that lead yet again. The reward for persistence and preparation is having a story that has never been told or is the best on a subject crowded with competitors' copy.

Interviewing

At the heart of the reporter's job is the interview. A successful interview leads to a good story, a good job and a good reputation. Excellent news organizations are distinguished by their ability to conduct flawless interviews.

Chief executives and others in business often are surprised when they realize they are dealing with someone who has done homework. Many interviewers don't. Executives should come away from an interview impressed by our knowledge, skill and professionalism. There is no better way of ensuring this than by asking intelligent questions.

So much depends on preparation. Not even the smartest people can overcome lack of preparation for an interview. Asking a chief executive officer about widget sales when his company announced a week earlier that it will stop making widgets damages the reporter's reputation and our organization's credibility.

Getting what you want typically depends on manners as well as knowledge. Have you ever heard of a rude salesman being the best salesman? Have you ever heard of a rude or ignorant reporter being the best?

Go into each interview with a strategy for obtaining information and the key quote that supports the theme of the story. The last thing we want to hear is, "It was a quiet day" or "Everything is unchanged."

Listen to what people say. Unexpected ideas can fly by if the reporter isn't paying attention. The best interviewers remain flexible enough to ask follow-up questions based on the live conversation instead of sticking to a preconceived list. Ask follow-ups that will yield details and examples: *How so? How do you know that? Can you give me an example? What was your reaction when that happened? What did you say? Who else was there? What did so-and-so say?*

Ask questions that can't be answered with a yes or no: *What was your reaction when . . . ? What keeps you up at night? How did you come to that decision? Whom do you take the most advice from? Why?*

On the other hand, there are no dumb questions—only dumb answers. Remember Columbo? He's the detective from a U.S. television series of the 1970s. By letting people think he was stupid, he wound up ensnaring the devious. The best reporters admire Columbo because they know that if he were a reporter, he would get the quotes or sound bites.

Suppose a modern-day Columbo went to Microsoft Corp. to interview its chairman, Bill Gates. Gates is used to talking to brilliant journalists who think they know everything about its software. Columbo is different. He asks the questions every journalist doesn't: What's so special about your software? What does it do that the current stuff doesn't do? Why does anybody need it? Gates might think, "Who is this dope?" as he provides answers that are critical to fashioning a better story. Columbo never forgets who he is or where he comes from.

Reporters would be wise to remember that the public isn't an expert and much of the time needs to be reminded of everything. Sometimes it's our job to state the obvious.

Be persistent. E-mails or a visit to the executive's home may succeed when the public-relations staff blocks an interview. One enterprising reporter guessed at the system that Apple used to set up e-mail addresses and reached Chief Executive Officer Steve Jobs, who sent him a response. In other cases, the subjects agreed to talk after the reporter ignored the denied interview request and pursued the person's colleagues, competitors and customers.

The best reporters know how to collect the details and anecdotes that will give their stories color and credibility. When interviewing someone, they note the person's age and at least three other personal characteristics. Chain smoker? Married five times? Rides Harley motorcycles? Wears bow ties? Keeps a watch on each wrist?

It's cause for worry when a reporter ambles back to the newsroom after an interview with a chief executive and says, "He didn't say anything." This is a sure sign the reporter is either inexperienced or not a major leaguer.

Reporters are supposed to get people to say things. That's the challenge of being a reporter.

The more we know about the person, his company and interests, the easier it is for the reporter to ask a question that will yield news. A talented reporter finds a way to challenge the people interviewed, and this requires preparation, poise and vigor.

Accuracy

Reporters are responsible for the accuracy of stories published with their bylines. They have the final say on whether what's about to be published accurately reflects what they've reported.

Reporters should check all facts, including names of people, companies, organizations and locations. They should also check all ages (including birth dates), dates of events, time periods, financial figures, statistics, units of measure (millions, billions, currencies, miles, kilometers, etc.) and physical descriptions of people and places.

For quotes, reporters must check that the comment is accurate, that it was said by the person it's attributed to and that the quote is in context.

Every fact in an anecdote must be checked. The information must come from people who are in a position to know what happened. Wherever possible, physical descriptions of people, places and events should be based on what reporters see with their own eyes and hear with their own ears, buttressed by information from authoritative sources about details like height, weight, width, capacity, temperature and distance.

Reporters should know where every fact in a story comes from and should tell the editor in writing, in person or on the telephone before publication. In stories with multiple reporters, each reporter must vouch for the accuracy of what he or she has reported. It is then the editor's job to make sure that every fact has been vouched for by a reporter.

Whenever possible, reporters should go through a printed copy of the final edit, underline every fact and then note on the paper where each fact came from. The reporter should give this annotated copy to the editor to review before the story is published. When it's not possible to do the checking in writing because of time pressure, the reporter should inform the editor verbally in person or by telephone where the facts came from.

Bloomberg News advocates the use of primary sources. Primary sources include interviews conducted by the reporter who wrote the story; official documents such as financial reports; transcripts of legal proceedings, public meetings and press conferences; and company and organization websites.

Another reporter's story is not a primary source. Facts change. Prices rise and fall. People get older and move to new jobs. Companies go public or go private or get taken over. Even countries can change names. That's why every fact must be checked—every time a reporter writes a story.

Editors

In the same way that the best athletes respond to great coaching, good reporters respond to skillful editing. Editors need to see themselves as the guardians of language and information. They need to make every story clear, logical and accurate.

The challenge at Bloomberg is to be first and fast with the news, remain accurate, and be complete with context and background. An editor who successfully manages a news event will start with a one- or two-sentence story, move it within minutes of the event, and talk with the reporter about how to assemble the writing with facts, quotes and history. This should be done a few paragraphs at a time so that we satisfy readers with the coverage they want at the time they need it the most. A gap of more than 30 minutes between updates in the early stages of breaking news is a failure to serve customers.

The result will be, at the end of the day, a complete story worthy of publication in any medium, with explanatory language that serves the financial-services professional reading on the Bloomberg terminal, the Web browser looking for immediate information, the newspaper reader with a casual interest and the radio and television audience hungry for the latest news.

Editors and reporters ought to be collaborators. That means there is consultation until the work is done and mutual satisfaction when it is. Editors should discuss every story with the reporter before the writing begins, even for as little as a minute. Agreement on the first four paragraphs means the story can be published quickly, and the direction taken by the updates will be unambiguous. An editor who knows what to expect is in a better position to ask questions.

Editors, as Bloomberg's gatekeepers for news judgment and language, can never be too rigorous. Nothing asserted in a story should get by without questions: How do we know this? What are the facts? Are you sure about this? How do you know it's true? What are the examples? Have you seen it? If you haven't seen it, how do you know it's true?

An editor is a reporter's last, best hope. Editors must review all documents. Editors must be on the lookout for libelous allegations and make sure that we have comments from all necessary parties. They must allow no story to pass without confirmation and attribution.

Editors may also have to write short stories that fill out the headlines, update published reports with stock prices or do reporting to keep the story moving in a timely manner.

The best editors enable reporters to be the best reporters. They inspire solutions instead of merely diagnosing problems. They remove the imperfect words, yet allow reporters to write in their own voices. They show reporters a way out through the maze of facts thrown up by news events. Their success is measured by the self-evident improvement brought to any reporter's work.

Editing Checklist

Editors should look over a story a final time before publishing it, just as pilots run down a preflight checklist before taking off. Make sure we haven't missed any of these basic points:

Headline. Does the headline start with the central subject, use an active verb and add context? Does it avoid unnecessary abbreviations? Does it match the lead, especially if the story has been changed?

Size and scope. Is there an appropriate size or scope for the company, person or event in the lead?

Four-paragraph lead. Does the lead establish a theme? Is the theme supported with facts and figures and expanded in the nut paragraph and lead quote?

Where. Is the location of the central event or subject high in the story? Are locations provided for other events or subjects that are introduced lower? Do we say where companies and government agencies are based? Where trading occurred? Do we give locations for the people we quote?

When. Do we give the time element on the first screen, unless it is a market story about today's trading? Do we make the progression of time clear when the news is a reaction to an earlier event? If we use a quote that wasn't obtained today, do we tell when it was said?

How we know what we know. Do we specify on the first screen whether the news comes from a company statement, a government spokesman or an executive interview? If we assert that something or someone is the biggest, best or first, do we explain how we know this?

Clean and concise language. Are word echoes, jargon, cliches and slang removed? Are sentences as precise and concise as they can be? Are there excess clauses and commas that need to be streamlined? Can any dull words be replaced by interesting words?

Accuracy. Have we double-checked percentages and other numbers? Have we checked currency conversions, a common source for errors, by using FE11 <Go>? Have we double-checked spelling of people's names and place names? Have we checked for typographical errors? For dropped words? Have we run the programs that check style and the spelling of names?

Subheadlines. If the story is longer than two full screens, have we added subheadlines to make the pages easier for readers to view?

Links. Does the story include links to the Bloomberg applications that best capture the most important points of our reporting?

Tour. Is the story coded to the tickers of all companies that are central to the news (not just mentioned tangentially)? Is the story coded to all NI categories that are applicable? Have we removed NI codes for subjects that are only indirectly linked to the news?

Team Leaders

Team leaders are the stewards of Bloomberg News. They are responsible for the planning, preparation, communication and collaboration necessary to show that our news isn't a commodity.

News judgment matters seven days a week. No story should be published or revised without the knowledge of our team leaders—especially stories on TOP <Go>. Each of us should insist on being aware of anything that affects our responsibilities.

The team leader is the equivalent of the editor of a section for a magazine or newspaper, so he or she should know—and must insist on knowing—everything published in his or her section. While team leaders don't have to edit each story word for word, line by line, they should always have the opportunity to do so.

Reporters and editors have an obligation to ensure that no story is published without the explicit knowledge of their team leaders.

Team leaders whose reporters and editors are working on a story that spans another beat must speak to their counterpart responsible for that company or industry or market. Failure to communicate and collaborate may result in stories that are incomplete, inaccurate or unfair.

Team leaders should make sure their teams are prepared. When we know something is coming, we should report, write and edit advance stories that cover every possible outcome with background, analysis and quotes.

Covering a central-bank meeting should entail writing one version of the story leading with an interest-rate increase, one for a cut and a third leading with no change. If we are ready for any possibility, we can move a complete story within minutes of an event. In this way, we set the agenda and prove hundreds of times a day that our news is not a commodity.

Just as any classical music composition requires practice to be played without flaws, our best performance is a consequence of how well we prepare. Team leaders should hold weekly meetings with their teams to determine our news judgment and deploy personnel. Such meetings should identify all events on the calendar for the weeks ahead and discuss the elements required to make our reporting exceptional.

The Bloomberg should be the working tool of the weekly meeting. Any event that will be reported by Bloomberg News is important enough to require a specific story agenda so that our dispatch will be complete and timely.

Because names make news, a discussion of the most authoritative newsmakers is appropriate days before the event will be reported. Use the

<Equity> MGMT and <Equity> PHDC functions to select the executives and investors our customers most want to hear, and make arrangements in advance for interviews so we aren't scrambling for comments. We have a better chance of delivering an exceptional report on inflation when we quote Martin Feldstein, the Harvard University economics professor, and the best way to get him is by seeking an appointment weeks in advance.

The weekly team leader meetings also help plug gaps in the Bloomberg profiles of these newsmakers. Are we missing facts we want to see in any profile: date of birth, career history, education, compensation? Are the Reporter's Notes containing information on the people complete? Do they list the phone numbers where we can reach the newsmakers—or their proxies—at work and at home? Whom among these newsmakers do we most want to schedule for broadcast?

The weekly team meeting is an opportunity to discuss what enterprise stories should be assigned. What do our customers need to know about this newsmaker, company, market or economy? What can we anticipate as an outcome? Is the company making acquisitions? Getting rid of businesses? Paying higher interest rates on its debt? Facing a reduction in its credit rating? Cutting jobs? Is the chief executive officer's position on the line?

While all stories have specific editors, team leaders should read all works of enterprise to make sure the theme is consistent with our news judgment.

Team leaders must communicate and coordinate all plans so the requirements for enterprise and broadcast are fulfilled.

Bureau Chiefs

Bureau chiefs fly the flag of Bloomberg News in their offices and communities. They help create an environment that is productive and invigorating. They make sure our news in their cities is competitive and complete. Bureau chiefs should be involved in every aspect of our business, from recruiting staff to making sure the equipment works to keeping people healthy, informed and inspired.

Chiefs should gather their bureaus for regular meetings to keep everyone up-to-date about Bloomberg News and the company as a whole. Review style points and coverage highlights from *Weekly Notes*, honor exemplary work, introduce visitors and new employees, note anniversaries and announce company events or changes in benefits. What are our successes? How can we improve? How are sales? Are there new functions and products?

Bureau chiefs should insist that Bloomberg's coverage meet our goals. Are press summaries completed as quickly as possible? The chiefs should alert the editor-in-chief and executive editors when their bureau summarizes a major story. What is our plan to respond, catch up and get ahead? Are stories from their bureaus or about subjects in their regions meeting the Five Fs and following the four-paragraph lead?

Bureau chiefs should identify and deliver timely and definitive stories about subjects that are the talk of their city, country or region. The idea is to have bureau chiefs exercise their best news judgment and handicap the most important news and issues. If we haven't written the definitive story, the bureau chief should assign it. Even in bureaus with a surplus of stories to choose from, at least we will make a decision about what was most important in the past seven days or what will be in the next seven. This will produce more stories and better stories. Some examples:

> *For Jana Dvorakova, Christmas wouldn't be the same without a carp swimming in her bathtub.*

> *Every year, the 56-year-old pensioner from Prague buys the freshwater fish for dinner from vendors with 800-liter vats parked on street corners. Now the Czech tradition is under threat from the European Union's hygiene laws, animal-rights protesters and competition from supermarkets such as Tesco Plc.*

> *This is the year Kevin Tietjen, a New York City native living in Connecticut, plans to introduce his 5-year-old son to a Christmas tradition from his childhood: opening presents in the glow of a crackling fire beamed into homes by television station WPIX.*

Our bureaus should reflect the best of Bloomberg News. Show off awards, newspaper clippings and photographs so that visitors can see the bureau's best work. Is the office clean and organized? Is the equipment up to standard? What is the plan for taking care of employees in an emergency?

Bureau chiefs should strive to raise our visibility and access. Every bureau should have a list of the top 10 local investors, executives, bankers, educators, politicians, etc. who should be interviewed or be a guest for lunch or breakfast.

Chiefs should visit customers each week. Are they happy? What do they need? Walk around the office and talk to our sales representatives to explain what's happening in news and to hear what clients are saying and doing.

Bureau chiefs are responsible for ensuring that personnel reviews are done on time and that every performance evaluation is coordinated with team leaders. The chiefs should monitor local talent, recruit and push for the hiring of good candidates.

The chiefs need to be aware of who is visiting the office and where people from their bureaus are traveling so all bureaus are informed.

15

Markets

THE BEST WAY to understand perceptions of a country's politics, business and finance is to visit its stock, bond, currency and commodity markets each day. This is where the stakes are the greatest and competing interests receive a specific value. The acuity of our news judgment derives from this fact.

The best stock market reports are a collection of stories about the rise and fall of companies or industries and how national or world affairs affect the price of money in the form of equity.

The bond market is just as much a window on global affairs. There is far more debt in this world than equity. There are far more bondholders than shareholders. Journalism's relative ignorance of debt markets has obscured this fact.

The foreign-exchange market, which surpasses the bond and stock markets in the value of trading every day, provides a minute-by-minute referendum on government policies, outlooks, economies and money flows among types of assets.

A day doesn't pass without a government disclosing economic statistics, issuing a report on industry or proposing a policy initiative—all of which have some effect on money. Yet too often reporters covering governments and their agencies forget that markets are the front line of reaction. The people who buy, sell and analyze investments are the first to react because they have the most at stake: their own money or other people's money. While far from infallible in their judgments, these investors invariably have opinions about the world sooner than the rest of us because their jobs require them to make a judgment whenever there is a turn of events.

This is why it is essential for us to interview as many investors and traders as we can, wherever we are, on whatever beats we cover. This broadens the collective knowledge and self-sufficiency of each reporter.

How to Cover Markets

Our job is to provide coverage that makes markets transparent. Here is how to do that job well for any market.

Answer the basic questions. The first four paragraphs ought to answer the following:

What happened to my investments today? This is the lead.
Why did it happen? This is the theme of the day.
How does today's move compare with the past? This is the perspective.
Who said what? This becomes the main quote.
How will this change your investment behavior?
What does this mean for the future of your investments?

Provide timely updates. Timely reporting is the lifeblood of market coverage. Previews, headlines, quick fills, regular updates, quotes and closers win the confidence of readers and viewers.

The focus of the main market story should shift throughout the day as the benchmarks fluctuate and our reporting offers new perspectives. Keep the writing fresh and obtain new quotes. Send headlines on significant moves such as a market changing direction or reaching a benchmark level. Rewrite the story headline throughout the day to reflect changes in the news and keep the subject fresh.

By reporting, writing and editing templates for multiple scenarios in advance, we can deliver the reaction within seconds.

Avoid jargon. Securities firms have historically tried to make their business opaque because it enabled them to earn more money from commissions and trading. They invented a muddled language to ensure that this opacity prevailed: *profit-taking, range-bound, choppy trading*, and so on. Most journalists never bother to learn the business and instead adopt the firms' language. This is a disservice to investors. When a government says it will raise taxes, we use simple English to explain why the price of that country's bonds rose. If you can't explain it, ask for help.

Explain why. A lead that says prices or yields rose or fell after some report will need to be explained. If the report is released at 8:30 A.M. and prices change at 8:31 A.M., of course they are higher or lower after the report. It's chronology and possibly coincidence.

Instead, ask if and why the report moved the market and explain in the story. What did investors conclude from the report that would lead them to buy or sell? Was a report on economic growth better or worse than expected? What did that suggest about the outlook for interest rates? For corporate earnings? The reporting should identify the companies and any interrelationships.

In many countries, the first and easiest explanation for market movements is to describe them as a reaction to U.S. markets or policies. Explain why what happens in the U.S. influences that country. Is the U.S. its biggest trading partner?

Capture the numbers with Bloomberg data and analytics. It isn't enough to say how prices or yields changed on a given day. Show how that day's trading relates to past performance. Is it the third straight increase? Is today's level the highest in the past six months? Is it the biggest one-day decline in six weeks? At the end of each week, month, quarter, first half and year, include similar numbers and context.

Create links in stories that direct readers to the Bloomberg charts, graphs and other analytical tools that illustrate the market changes.

Customers are always searching for relative value. How does Coca-Cola compare with PepsiCo or with the Standard & Poor's 500 Index? The yen versus the dollar or the euro? What has each returned over different periods of time? What are the forecasts? Is it time to buy or time to sell? Use the Bloomberg to put performance into context.

Be specific about why today. It's not enough to say that bonds fell on concern that the central bank may raise interest rates. What, specifically, is triggering that concern? Did new economic reports or comments from officials lead to that conclusion? If you can't explain, do more reporting.

Handle speculation with care. Markets often rise and fall on speculation about some event—that gold miners will strike, that central banks will sell their currency or that one company will make a takeover offer for another. Be as specific as possible about the speculation, and quote analysts and investors explaining what's triggering the speculating. Make every effort to check the speculation and include those efforts in the story.

Capture the people. Because numbers drive the markets, it's easy to write stories that are glorified price charts. Numbers are better suited to computer monitors, charts and tables than to text. The most valuable part of any market report is the collection of anecdotes showing what people are doing with their money and why.

Who are the buyers? Who are the sellers? What are they buying and selling? What are they saying? Readers, viewers and listeners will seek out reporters who answer these questions daily.

Show what the buy side is doing. Provide the views of money managers, mutual funds, pension funds, hedge funds, insurance companies and other institutions—collectively known as the buy side. Investors have more at stake than the traders, analysts and others working for brokerages and banks—the sell side. When we turn to the buy side for comments and analysis, we also can show how those investors are acting on their views, what they are buying and selling. They will help tell a story within the story that motivates readers to get past the first few paragraphs.

"The economy is slowing, and that makes me very bullish on bonds,"
said Jack Smith, who manages the $40 billion Fixed-Income Fund. Smith
said the fund raised the percentage of 30-year bonds in its portfolio to

80 percent from 50 percent a week ago. "I'd make it 100 percent if the rules of the fund didn't prevent it."

Every investor we talk to and place among the first few paragraphs transforms an otherwise routine piece into a richer story. The Bloomberg terminal, which from its inception has provided information on bondholders and shareholders, is an indispensable tool in this endeavor.

Be transparent. We must make every effort to get investors to tell us whether they hold or are betting against the stocks, bonds, currencies or commodities they mention. Our stories must be transparent about their interests so that readers can judge for themselves whether those quoted are simply "talking their book." When we provide the views of sell-side analysts and strategists, say what their brokerages advise investors to do with their money, whether they own the securities and how good their advice has been in the past.

Focus on the markets, not other news. While the economy, politics and policy can influence market performance, other Bloomberg stories will report on those topics in depth. Market stories don't need to duplicate this coverage. A few sentences, or a paragraph or two, usually will suffice. If the price of oil is affecting the stock market, note how rising or falling petroleum prices will affect corporate profits or the economy.

Provide relative value. How does this investment or country compare with others? This is the context and comparison that makes news from China relevant and understandable in Chicago, Brussels and Sao Paulo. Is it cheap or expensive? Time to buy or sell?

Our customers use yardsticks such as ratios, ratings and performance to compare and contrast investments. So should we. A stock's return becomes more meaningful when we put it in historical perspective or contrast it against peers. Bond reports show more when they mention the creditworthiness of the debt. Currency and commodity stories should show returns over a specific period or rank performance against peers.

Use active verbs. Pick a verb such as *rose* or *fell* that reflects the market's move. If a benchmark stock index rises a lot more than usual, *surged* or *soared* may be appropriate to give a better sense of the magnitude. If it declines more than usual, *tumbled* or *plunged* may work.

Use percentages. Give percentage gains or losses in markets such as currencies and commodities. *Gold rose 1.5 percent last week to a seven-week high* is more meaningful than *Gold rose $3.75 last week.*

Make connections between markets. When commodity prices change, explain the consequences for companies that make, process or use the goods. The story of the pork-belly market is as much about Hormel Foods Corp. as the price of bacon.

Write every story as if it were the last one of the day. Give the big picture of how the market has performed so far for the day. Provide the context and explanation for those reading about the market for the first time.

Connect the dots. Spell out how events can trigger changes in policy and the implications for the market. A narrative about the bond market might connect the dots this way: A government report may set off expectations for faster economic growth and raise concern that inflation may pick up. Inflation erodes the value of the fixed payments from bonds, which would make them less attractive investments and trigger a drop in price. Accelerating inflation may also prompt the central bank to raise interest rates.

Tell a tale that people will want to read. If market prices are little changed and trading is uneventful, write a story that weaves together where people say prices are headed and where they went that day. Or find another theme, such as industry groups that moved the most. Look ahead. A summary of today's markets isn't complete unless at least one pithy sentence provides an outlook for tomorrow's or next week's prices. Stories written at the end of the week should mention this outlook within the first four paragraphs.

Cover biggest movers worldwide. Daily stories about the world's biggest-moving stocks, bonds, currencies and commodities are an opportunity to give customers news they won't get anywhere else. The headline and lead should make clear that this stock, bond, currency or commodity is unlike any other today because its value changed the most.

Poland's zloty rose as much as 0.8 percent, the biggest move of any currency today, after the central bank signaled that it might reduce its benchmark interest rate next month.

Four Pillars of Market Coverage

A market is people brought together by the securities they trade. The essence of market news coverage is to create a narrative about the events that drove these investors to buy or sell. Stories about stocks, bonds, currencies or commodities should approach this task by posing these questions about the four influences on every market:

The market. Each stock, index, bond, currency, commodity, derivative or other security is an anecdote or an example.

What are the benchmark issues, indexes or contracts?

Why are they the benchmarks?

How are the benchmarks moving today? Up or down? Why are they moving? If unchanged, why?

It's the biggest advance or decline since when?

How many days in a row up, down or little changed? Or did the direction reverse?

Highest or lowest level since when?

Narrowest or widest range since when?

Is the benchmark near or past a significant historical or psychological high or low?

Is the event cited as the cause today typical or atypical? When was the last time this happened? What happened the last time?

Which industries, maturities or currencies led the gains or losses?

Put the moves into perspective. What has been the performance over the last week, month, quarter, year or so far this year? From the high or the low?

How has the benchmark performed compared with some other form of investment?

Where is the benchmark likely to go in the future? Why? Says who?

The buy side—investors and traders. The mutual funds, money managers, institutional investors and hedge funds that buy and sell are Bloomberg's customers.

What are they doing? They are paid to get the best returns from investing money, not to sit on their hands and watch the market move.

Are they buying? Betting on a decline? Why?

Changing to different industries in equities, or shifting to company debt from government debt? Why?

Shifting to bonds that are closer to maturing, or have longer maturities? Why?

Moving money from one currency into another? Why?

Hedging in the commodities markets?

What are their forecasts?

What would prompt them to buy more? How about to sell?

Who has the best returns? The worst?

The sell side—securities firms and investment banks. These are our customers, as well.

What are the biggest firms that trade the stocks, bonds, commodities, swaps, currencies and other investments?

Does the firm play a role in the market? Is it a primary dealer, which buys and sells government securities while working directly with the central bank? Or is it a market maker, which buys or sells securities to keep the exchanges running efficiently?

What are the firms buying and selling—and why? They get paid to buy and sell. Even when people say nothing is going on, something is going on.

What do the firm's strategists and analysts say? What are their estimates and ratings? How have their recommendations changed?

Have their forecasts been right or wrong? Which are the most or least successful?

External influences. Politics, global events, natural disasters, regulations, weather and other events outside the market can influence prices.

What does the market's movement say about the world, policies, economies or government finances?

Were any agencies of the government—the central bank, Treasury Department or Ministry of Finance—participating in the market?

Are elections scheduled soon? What are the views of the candidates on markets, policy, government spending and subsidies? What policies might change?

How might the market's price changes affect economic reports or government policies?

What are governments or companies doing? Selling bonds, stocks or currencies? Buying them?

Writing Market Leads

Which prices, yields and rates are moving? Why are they moving? The best market leads answer both these questions.

This lead doesn't work because it lacks specifics:

> *U.S. stocks in Europe fell before the release of U.S. economic reports that could affect the direction of interest rates.*

Which stocks? Why did stocks fall before the economic reports? What were the reports about or what did they show? What is the direction of interest rates: higher or lower? And most important, what about the companies? Any story about the stock market is all about companies and the perception of companies.

This lead works because we know which stocks moved and why:

> *U.S. stocks surged, sending the Dow Jones Industrial Average to its biggest four-day gain in almost 70 years, after Citigroup Inc. and Bank of America Corp. reported higher profits.*

This lead is flawed because it doesn't explain why:

> *The dollar fell against the euro amid concern among many market participants over U.S. congressional plans to spend part of the budget surplus.*

Among many market participants is dry, superfluous and imprecise. *Amid* followed by *over* or *about* doesn't spell out cause and effect. *Plans to spend part of the budget surplus* doesn't explain the pessimism. Leads such as *Stocks fell amid pessimism about corporate earnings* have the same lack of explanation: Why the pessimism?

This rewrite shows the perceived effect of a cut in the budget surplus, increased dependence on foreign capital and its significance for the dollar:

> *The dollar fell against the euro amid concern that congressional plans to spend part of the U.S. budget surplus may lead to increased dependence on foreign capital.*

This lead doesn't work because it says stocks fell because they had risen:

> *Japanese stocks fell as the Nikkei 225 average's 21 percent rebound in the past eight days from a 16-year low convinced investors that recent gains were overdone.*

It needs explanation. Why were prices too high today and not yesterday, or the day before, or the six days before that? What's so special about a 21 percent rise? Did everyone make the same decision at once, as the use of *investors* without a modifier such as *some* implies? Certainly not. Otherwise, there wouldn't be any trading.

This rewrite makes the connection between share prices and profits:

> *Japanese stocks fell as some investors decided corporate profits probably won't increase enough next year to justify the Nikkei 225 average's 21 percent rise during the past eight days.*

Keeping Market Stories Fresh

Stories about markets can have a monotony about them. They follow the same benchmarks day in and day out. Some markets have fewer benchmarks to examine than others. The oil market has few indicators other than the price of a barrel of crude.

Here are points worth considering to make sure we're not writing by the same formula every day and just filling in new numbers or narrative.

Look beyond the benchmark for the story. Other parts of the market may be more interesting. When some benchmark indexes are up and some are down, it is easy to write that the market is mixed. An indicator that moved for the first time in a week or in a different direction may be the most interesting.

It's about the story, not the data. The Bloomberg terminal has so much data and so many functions to dissect those figures that it is easy to think that stories are written to explain the numbers. Not so.

Rather than *What is the price?* a better question would be, *What is the story?* Use the data as evidence to back up the theme.

The more numbers, the harder the story is to read. Customers can already see the numbers. Our job is to give them the story—the explanation, perspective and voices—to show what is going on.

How does each number help tell the story? A good way to focus the story is to use only one price to illustrate what is happening in the market. Does each number at the top help the story? Saying gold is down 75 percent so far this year and has dropped 85 percent in the past 12 months is pretty much the same thing. One can be cut.

Emphasize the new over the old. While the theme may not change day to day, the numbers change every day. Focus on the latest bits of evidence. Does the news today reinforce the trend or work against it? Put newer numbers at the start of a sentence, with history at the end to add perspective. Begin paragraphs with the news. Take today's numbers and put them in the context with last week, last month or last year.

Distinguish one day from another. How extreme is the move? While we prefer not to focus the top of the story on the intraday moves of the market, some days the extent of the swing is the news. The HCPI <Go> function, which shows the ranges of trading, can help show the breadth and drama of a swing:

Crude oil plunged after setting a record high as terrorist bombs killed at least 37 people in London and raised fears of an economic slowdown. The swing in prices was the biggest since the Persian Gulf War 14 years ago.

Weekly Perspective

As each week ends, provide context and perspective on the past week and show where prices and/or yields may be headed. If we apply intelligence and Bloomberg analytics each day, this will be easy to deliver.

This kind of reporting takes two forms: references to weekly performance in market stories each Friday and the weekly review-and-outlook stories that greet the coming week. Both need to address these questions and supply supporting facts and anecdotes:

Biggest weekly gain or loss since when? Most or least trading in components of a stock index since when? Reasons for the fluctuation?

What happened today? The last day of the week shapes perceptions. Don't get so caught up in writing about the week that the daily move is obscured.

What events next week—central bank meeting, economic report, government action, stock or bond sale—may have an impact? What facts or anecdotes explain why the perception is bullish or bearish?

What's the performance of the domestic market versus foreign markets? Are share prices or bond yields higher or lower relative to other countries? Are foreign investors favorable or unfavorable?

When writing the weekly wraps, make a list of themes, facts and anecdotes to help develop and explain the lead. Here are some ideas:

Measure performance. To find end-of-week prices and yields, call up a historical price table by using the HP W <Go> function. Also, HP W <Go> provides cumulative trading totals for stocks in benchmark indexes, permitting week-to-week comparisons. HCP W <Go> shows week-to-week changes in percentage terms or points. That makes comparisons easy:

U.S. stocks rose, sending the Standard & Poor's 500 Index to its longest winning streak since 1997, after a government report showed that employers added almost twice the number of workers forecast in October.

Pay attention to spreads. In the bond market, the difference between two benchmark securities or two yield curves—often called the *spread* or *yield* *premium*—is important because it shows relative value. An investor who is choosing between one bond or another will look at the spread to measure the bonds' relative riskiness, for example.

Look for patterns. Are telephone stocks consistently among the best day-to-day performers? Are the stocks, bonds or currencies of emerging markets such as India, Brazil and Poland moving more than the U.S. markets? Use <Index> MOV and <Index> GMOV, which display the biggest-moving stocks or industry groups, respectively, in an index.

Always ask people for the future word. By looking ahead in every weekly wrap, these stories will become a must-read even for people who know how the market performed. No one expects us to provide tomorrow's or next week's prices. Readers understand that the weekly appraisals explain the current perception of the market and the reasons.

Technical Analysis

Technical analysis refers to the industry of traders, analysts and investors who make judgments and forecasts about the performance of a market, security, commodity or currency on the basis of its value plotted on a graph. Price patterns do matter.

The jargon of the chart watchers is often so opaque that some of us might be deceived into thinking we are encountering some complex world of physics or mathematics. Don't be so impressed. While it's worth writing about the chartists because they are so numerous—a third of our customers use technical analysis—we can explain their work in language that a neophyte can understand.

Seek to understand terms such as *support, resistance, breakout, inverted triangle formation* and *triple bottom*, and translate them. When someone talks about support or resistance, avoid those words by presenting the evidence, such as that the Standard & Poor's 500 has rebounded the past five times it fell to a certain level.

The recent rout in U.S. stocks may be finished, according to a gauge of investor fear that has signaled past market turnarounds.

The Chicago Board Options Exchange Volatility Index, known as the VIX, was above 50 the past two days before falling as U.S. stocks began to rebound. It has topped 50 on just five prior occasions in its 16-year history, including after the Sept. 11 terrorist attacks and the 1987 stock market crash. When the index has reached 50 before, the market set a low within two days.

A VIX above 50 "means you're close to the end" of the selling, said Philip Roth, who charts price and trading patterns as technical analyst at Miller Tabak & Co.

The VIX measures what investors and traders are willing to pay for stock-index options that can protect them against big stock declines.

These are among the most popular gauges used by our customers:

Relative strength index. This indicator attempts to identify turning points by calculating the degree by which the daily losses outpace daily gains, or vice versa, and by putting the measure on a scale of 0 to 100. A drop below 30 suggests to some analysts that a decline in prices is losing momentum and that the market is poised to rise. Above 70, the price may be poised to fall. Use the RSI <Go> function and enter the number of days the source is using.

The euro's three-week rally against the yen, which brought the currency to its highest level since May 1999, may end, according to an index that measures the momentum of the currency's movements.

The euro's relative strength index over a 14-day period reached 74.4 yesterday, before falling back to 69.7 today, leaving it near its highest level since February. Some analysts say that an index above 70 means the currency is poised to fall.

Moving averages. Investors use moving averages to smooth out day-to-day price fluctuations, track trends and predict changes. When a market trades above a moving average, it's interpreted as a signal that the price may rise. Falling below the average suggests a decline. Moving averages can be charted using the functions that run a basic graph, such as GP <Go>, or that are more flexible for examining moving averages, such as MACD <Go>, TE <Go> for trading envelopes and BOLL <Go> for Bollinger bands.

> *Wal-Mart has fallen below its average prices for the past 50 and 200 days, said Charles C. Smith Jr., who manages $5 billion for J. & W. Seligman & Co. The 50-day average is $62.43 and the 200-day average is $52.13. That has triggered selling because it indicates to technical analysts that the stock has further to fall, he said.*
>
> *Wal-Mart makes up 2 percent of Smith's holdings. He said he would consider buying more if it declined to about $40.*

Fibonacci charts. Chartists use *resistance* and *support* to identify a price that a market probably won't exceed (resistance) or fall below (support). One indicator is the Fibonacci sequence, which uses a series of percentages discovered in the 12th century to help calculate levels where the direction in price may reverse. Use the Fibonacci function, GPF <Go>, and enter the period's start date. The chart generates horizontal lines and prices, which are the levels of support or resistance.

> *The euro may fall to 131.7 yen, down almost 4 yen from yesterday's four-year high, a chart designed to predict price movement shows.*
>
> *The chart, known as the Fibonacci sequence, is based on a theory that securities rise or fall by specific percentages after reaching a high or low. One of those levels is 61.8 percent. Some technical analysts said they expect the euro to fall to 131.7 yen because that is 61.8 percent of the difference between its low on March 18 and its high on May 12.*

Functions for Markets

TOP <Go>—Displays the day's biggest stories, enterprise and columns.

<Equity> DES—Description. Contains basic information such as returns, 52-week high and low, and links to other functions related to any security or index.

<Equity> GP—Graph price. Displays closing prices. Useful to find the last time the market closed as high or low.

<Equity> GPO—Displays the range of trading, including the high and low, for each day. Use to find the last time the market traded as high or as low.

<Equity> GIP—Graph intraday price. Shows the course of a day's trading.

<Equity> HP—Historical prices. A table of closing prices and trading volumes. Useful for identifying trends such as rose or fell to the lowest or highest level in a week, month or year. Also shows average trading volume.

<Equity> HCP—Historical change percent. Shows the percentage change for each day, week, month or year. HCPI <Go> provides a percentage change for the high and low price of the day.

<Equity> ROC—Rate of change. Charts the percentage change in a stock's closing. Displays the rate of change, which can show trends such as the biggest one-day rise or decline since a certain date.

<Equity> HRH—Historical return histogram. Shows how often a security has risen or fallen by a certain percentage. Helps determine whether a move is noteworthy.

<Equity> SINS—Since when. Shows size and scope, such as *the biggest daily change since xxx* or *the longest losing streak since xxx*.

Stocks

Nothing explains the performance of the stock market better than the companies that make up the benchmark indexes. If we can report why these companies moved, we can do the best job of explaining why the index moved.

In many cases, changes in the value of shares will reflect changing perceptions about the economy, political situation or industry outlook. We need to make those connections as well. This means the first four paragraphs of our stock-market stories will typically feature the companies and industries that had the biggest effect on benchmark indexes or the market's movement.

Stock Market Leads

Because a stock market is a collection of companies, each company's fluctuating value helps explain the fate of the market as measured by an index. The goal of any lead is to capture the day's theme in a simple sentence or two. Providing a superlative helps readers appreciate why they are reading this now.

The Dow Jones Industrial Average surpassed 13,000 for the first time after profit reports from more than half of its 30 members bolstered speculation that the biggest U.S. companies will weather slower economic growth.

Leads also need to capture changes in people's views and to provide the reason. This lead doesn't hit the mark . . .

U.S. stocks rose, led by computer shares, on optimism about profits after Intel Corp. reported better-than-expected earnings.

. . . because it doesn't explain why computer shares rose, nor does it show that optimism grew or make a connection between Intel's results and the greater optimism. The rewritten version addresses these points:

U.S. stocks rose after earnings at Intel Corp., the world's largest producer of semiconductor chips, exceeded analysts' estimates and spurred speculation that forecasts for computer company profits are too low.

Avoid taking an *on the one hand/on the other hand* approach in leads. Some stocks inevitably will decline as others advance. Using words such as *offset* and *outweigh* to capture both moves makes the story less compelling. Focus on the more telling moves and explain the rest later.

The same applies to the entire market. Benchmark indexes in the same country can move in different directions, making it tempting to write that stocks *were mixed*. Avoid such temptations because they result in leads that have more than one theme, and those competing ideas may exhaust the reader. Focus on the index whose gain or loss was the steepest, the first in some time, or the most newsworthy.

The Nasdaq Composite Index declined, completing its fifth straight losing week. Software stocks slumped after Oracle Corp. said quarterly profit was less than forecast.

Beginning with an index, such as the Nasdaq Composite, rather than a phrase such as *U.S. stocks* is appropriate when it leads to a more compelling story. In this case, the Dow Jones Industrial Average and the Standard & Poor's 500 hadn't fallen for as long.

Themes for Stocks

Identify what's behind the changes in supply and demand that cause share prices to move. If the story focuses on specific companies and industries, provide the reasons for their gains or losses. If the theme is broader, here are some possible reasons:

Earnings reports. Investors use earnings to gauge how much to pay for a company's stock. If a large company's earnings are more or less than analysts estimated, investors may conclude the same will hold true elsewhere in the industry or market. That will affect how much they're willing to pay for shares. When that's the case, name the company and explain the implications of its results.

Economic indicators. Faster economic growth can lead to increased sales and profits at companies, making stocks more attractive. If one or more economic reports caused the outlook for earnings to change, refer to the reports and their implications.

Interest-rate changes. Lower rates can lead to increased corporate sales and profits because they encourage people and companies to borrow more money and to spend more. They also can boost the value of debt securities such as bonds owned by banks and other financial companies.

Relative value. When prices get too high, investors may balk at buying stocks. That can be enough to trigger market moves. The historical comparison needs to show that prices are relatively high or low. Explain why people would see them that way now and include measures such as price-earnings ratios for comparison.

Functions for Stocks

WEI <Go>—World equity indexes. Tracks stock market benchmarks and their recent performance. WEIF <Go> does the same for index futures and WEIS <Go> ranks the best- and worst-performing stock indexes.

MOST <Go>—Most active stocks by shares traded. Also shows stocks with the biggest advances and declines.

<Index> MOV—Movers. Shows which individual stocks are leading or lagging behind an index or are having the biggest impact.

<Index> GMOV—Group movers. Shows which industries are leading and lagging behind the index today. Works only for broader indexes that are broken into smaller sub-groups.

<Index> MRR—Member ranked returns. Shows the best- and worst-performing members of an index.

<Index> GRR—Group ranked returns. Shows the best- and worst-performing industry groups in an index.

LVI90 <Go>—Largest volume increases. Shows surges in trading volume against the 90-day average. Helpful for finding movers.

HILO <Go>—Lists stocks setting 52-week highs and lows.

<Equity> QMC—Quote montage. Displays prices of a company's shares around the world. Prices are adjusted for currencies.

<Equity> COMP—Comparative return graph. Shows price change and total return for a stock or index and for two related benchmarks.

<Equity> RV—Relative value. Compares a stock with rivals in its home country, its region or the world, or against a market or industry group.

TOP STK <Go>—Top stock market news.

Bonds

The bond market is all about the companies, countries and agencies that borrow money and the institutions and individuals that lend money. Any story about U.S. Treasury borrowing can be as much a political story as a profile of the nation's Treasury secretary. Any story about Intel Corp. selling debt can be as much a profile of the company as can an interview with the chief executive officer.

In the U.S. alone, about $1 trillion in bonds changes hands every day, helping determine the health of governments and companies. About $165 billion in company bonds trades daily, double the value of stocks and roughly equal to the economy of Singapore or the United Arab Emirates. Few journalists recognize the importance of these comparisons. The bond market is the most precise measure of domestic and international prosperity. That creates an opportunity for news organizations whose reporters and editors understand and cover the story of debt.

Our job is to make the subject transparent. Daily debt coverage ought to spotlight borrowers in the same way that coverage of the stock market provides perspective about companies. It needs to examine borrowers' capacity to pay their debts, along with the perception of that capacity among investors and credit-rating companies.

Any story about Sweden, Denmark or Qantas Airways selling bonds, for instance, should mention the Swedish and Danish economies and the performance of Qantas Airways. It should identify probable investors and detractors, by name and by institution. The story should introduce the borrower. It should examine the bonds' relative value, based on price, yield, market history and credit quality.

Bond stories need to acknowledge that relative value helps drive price and yield. Currency and interest rates often determine whether bonds are poised to gain or fall. A currency perceived as strong may boost the value of that country's bonds. A weakening currency can erode the value of the bonds for investors who plan to convert the proceeds to another currency. Rising interest rates in one part of the world may prevent yields from falling in others. The difference in yields between the bonds of different countries may widen or narrow.

Reporters covering bond markets need to get comfortable with the mechanics of the market and write narratives that explain the movements in terms that any reader can understand.

Most bonds are debt instruments that pay interest—called a *coupon*—at regular intervals. The bond represents an agreement to borrow a certain amount—called a *face amount*—for a period of time that ends when the bond matures. Identify individual bonds by coupon and maturity date. A U.S. Treasury bond with a face amount of $1,000 may pay a fixed coupon of 4 percent until February 2015.

Bond prices are typically close to 100. The price represents the current value of the bond as a percentage of the bond's face amount. So a Treasury bond with a price of 105 means the buyer must pay $1,050.

The yield represents the investor's return on the bond at the current price. It is calculated by adding up the cash flows from the bond over time and the repayment of the face amount. The yield moves inversely to price.

Government Bonds

Bond stories ought to do the following:

Lead with the benchmark. The first market-related numbers in any story ought to show how at least one benchmark security performed. Typically it's the security with the longest maturity that is sold regularly, which is 10 years in most countries. Include other maturities—even make them the lead—when their moves are significant. The details in the price paragraph should reflect the maturities cited in the lead.

Highlight yield. Yields reflect investor expectations for interest rates. They also determine other rates, such as those on adjustable-rate mortgages. The yield on a market's benchmark issue must be prominently cited in every story, preferably by the fourth paragraph.

Provide comparisons. After explaining the direction of interest rates, government bond stories ought to be about changes in the difference in yield between securities of different maturities, typically the most-traded short and long maturities. The news is found in the widening and narrowing of spreads and what that says about expectations for the country's interest rates and economy.

Show how government debt markets affect everyone. Anyone who needs money to buy a house, car, boat or other durable goods stands to benefit by knowing what is happening in the government bond market. Those rates can affect what consumers pay for mortgages, loans and credit cards.

Add economic perspective. In stories that focus on economic indicators, add details about the reports and explain their relevance to the bond market. Keep the background to a minimum.

Themes for Government Bonds

Changes in economic outlook. Indicators that point toward faster or slower economic growth or inflation can cause bonds to fall or rise, respectively, because the rate of growth influences:

The rate of inflation, because inflation erodes the value of the fixed payments on bonds.

The amount of borrowing done to finance a government budget, which affects the supply of government securities.

The growth of corporate profits, which affects the attractiveness of stocks and company bonds relative to government bonds.

Changes in the outlook for central bank policy. Central banks typically raise benchmark interest rates to slow economic growth and to prevent inflation from accelerating, and they cut rates when the economy is slumping and inflation is dormant. Even speculation that a central bank is leaning toward a policy change may push bonds higher or lower. Point out the prevailing view, the reason for it and its significance.

Sales of new bonds. Bonds may rise and fall because governments and companies raise a lot of money by selling new securities. Sales increase the supply of bonds. Firms that buy the new bonds for resale to investors typically sell existing securities.

Relative value. When yields get low, investors may balk at buying bonds because other investments such as dividend-paying stocks may offer better returns. The historical comparison needs to show whether prices are relatively high or low and explain why people see them that way. Fixed-income securities may also be seen as a haven when the outlook for returns from other investments becomes clouded.

Moves in other markets. Changes in currency values can influence people's willingness to own securities denominated in a given currency. Changes in stock prices can affect their relative value when compared with bonds. When another market influences bond prices, explain what the other market's performance has to do with fixed-income securities.

Risk. Political developments may move the prices of a country's bonds as investors have more or less confidence in the government's ability to repay its debts. Every government bond story ought to find a way to say whether the latest move signals that the state of Denmark, or any other, is rotten or not. The more likely it is that a government may default on its debt, the more return—or yield—investors will demand to compensate them for the risk of holding the debt.

Government Bond Leads

Government bonds are as much about economies and the direction of interest rates as they are about politics and the latest legislation. If yields are higher today than yesterday, that may indicate people have less confidence in the government's ability to manage its affairs. Lower yields signal that people have more confidence in the government. It's our job to explain and interpret the results.

Here is an example of a U.S. bond story that accomplishes the goal by noting how an economic report, which triggered a market decline, might affect central-bank policy:

> *U.S. 10-year Treasuries fell for the fourth straight day, the longest slump since the start of November, after government reports signaled that the economy may be rebounding from a fourth-quarter slowdown.*
>
> *The declines pushed yields on 10-year notes above 4.5 percent for the first time since Dec. 15 and less than a week before the Federal Reserve is likely to increase its interest-rate target by a quarter percentage point from 4.25 percent. Evidence that economic growth is holding up may bolster speculation that the central bank will raise rates again in March.*
>
> *"We'll probably keep going higher in yield," said Dan Shackelford, who manages $7 billion of bonds at T. Rowe Price Group Inc. in Baltimore. Shackelford said he hasn't made any changes in his government debt holdings this week.*
>
> *The yield on the benchmark 10-year note rose 4 basis points, or 0.04 percentage point, to 4.52 percent at 5:15 p.m. in New York, according to Bloomberg Bond Trader prices. The yield, which moves inversely to the note's price, is the highest since Dec. 14. The price of the 4 1/2 percent note due in November 2015 dropped 5/16, or $3.13 per $1,000 face amount, to 99 27/32.*

Here is an example that focuses on the impact of political developments:

> *Turkish government bonds rose for a fourth straight day in Istanbul on speculation that talks on reunifying the island of Cyprus will resume after an election next month, helping Turkey's bid for membership in the European Union.*

Corporate Bonds

Debt can tell stories about companies that stocks cannot. Because a bond is a loan to the company, any hint or perception that investors may not get their money back will send the price lower and the cost of borrowing higher. Holders of Enron Corp. and Xerox Corp. debt caught the scent of trouble before investors in the stocks. Reporters who followed the debt got the scoops.

Company reporters should cultivate debt investors and analysts as avidly as those who own and follow the stocks. Too often, stories concentrate on a company's assets and revenue and not on its expenses and liabilities. The latter are of great interest to debt holders, who are among the first in line to be paid when a company goes bust at bankruptcy court.

Companies generally pay more to borrow than governments do, because they are more likely to default. They don't have the ability to tax citizens or print money the way a state can. Government bond yields provide a benchmark for corporate borrowing costs. How much Greek companies must pay to borrow will largely be driven by how much the Greek government pays.

When covering corporate bonds, write about how much more companies must pay than the government. That difference in yield between the corporate bond and the government bond is known as the *spread*, or *yield premium*.

Companies that are more risky (and carry a lower credit rating from international rating companies such as Standard & Poor's) pay a wider yield premium over a benchmark. Companies whose fortunes are improving will see the difference in the yields narrow. The companies with the highest risk carry a credit rating known as *junk*, or *non-investment grade*, which is below BBB– by Standard & Poor's and Baa3 by Moody's.

It's also possible to compare corporate bonds of the same rating. Checking the spread on a company's bonds can offer different clues than the company's stock price about how investors view its prospects. Bondholders are focused on the company's ability to repay its debt, or the risk of owning this particular company's credit. They are less concerned about short-term trends such as quarterly earnings reports.

Themes for Corporate Bonds

Spreads. Focus on the spread, or the difference in the yield against the benchmark, rather than price or yield. Yields may rise or fall along with the country's prevailing interest rates. The spread shows how investors are viewing the company's prospects.

Events. When a company says it plans to make an acquisition, sell a division or buy a new license, follow the money. Ask: *How are you going to pay for this?* or *What will you do with the proceeds?* Answers to these questions may affect the company's bonds even more than the stock price.

Ability to repay. Trends that make the company more likely to keep its commitments to bondholders—rising market share, a hot new product or currency changes that boost earnings—will make bondholders feel more comfortable. A slump in sales or a new management team may make bondholders nervous about the company's ability to return their money.

Increasing or decreasing debt. Companies may say they are repaying bondholders more rapidly or more slowly than expected. They may also issue new debt at lower rates to cut their interest payments. Companies that are spending more on investments in factories or equipment may need to borrow more, which may result in lower market prices for the bonds as investors become more concerned about the companies' ability to manage the debt burden.

Swaps

The swaps market is where investors, companies and institutions exchange one kind of payment for another, such as a fixed interest rate for a floating rate or from one currency to another. Some use swaps to hedge borrowing costs or as protection from changes in interest rates. Swaps also can be used to speculate on market direction or to replicate the return on specific investments. Size alone makes this market important. With $450 trillion in notional value outstanding, the swaps market is larger than the global stock and bond markets combined.

There are many different kinds of swaps. In an interest-rate swap, a company or country can exchange its fixed-interest payments on a specific amount of debt to end up making floating-rate payments, which change on agreed-upon dates, typically daily or every three months. The swap helps to add some certainty to the amount of interest the parties will pay or receive in the future.

Currency swaps involve the exchange of the principal and interest in one currency, such as euros, for the same in another currency, perhaps dollars.

Equity swaps allow fund managers to receive the return on a foreign stock index in exchange for the return on the domestic index.

Credit-default swaps, once the fastest-growing segment of the market, provide protection if a borrower fails to live up to its obligations and defaults on its debt. Investors also use them to speculate on the ability of a company, a government or a group of borrowers to repay its debt. Unlike stocks and bonds, these are not securities issued by the companies.

Here's an example of how an interest-rate swap, the most common form of exchange, would work.

Widget Inc.'s chief financial officer prefers to pay a floating rate on the company's debt, perhaps because the expense of its debt would increase when interest rates rise with a booming economy and the company could better afford the higher cost, or vice versa. The problem is that Widget's investors want to buy fixed-rate debt so that they can count on a constant stream of interest income.

So, Widget sells fixed-rate bonds to investors. It then enters into an agreement with a swap dealer, such as a commercial bank or investment firm, that will pay Widget the fixed rate it needs to pay the fixed payments on the bonds. In return, Widget pays the bank a floating rate usually tied to the London interbank offered rate (Libor). The principal amount of money is never exchanged; only the interest-rate payments are swapped.

The company gets the flexibility it wants with floating rates and the investors get their fixed payments.

Perhaps potential investors in another country want to buy Widget's debt because of the company's relatively high credit rating. The investors, though, don't want to own bonds that are issued in dollars because fluctuations in their own currency may reduce their investment's value and increase their risk. If the bonds were denominated in the local currency, these investors might be willing to lend to Widget at a lower interest rate than U.S. investors are.

In this case, Widget sells the bonds in euros and enters into a swap with a dealer in which the company exchanges the bond proceeds for dollars. Widget then agrees to pay interest in dollars to the dealer in exchange for receiving interest payments in euros, which the company passes on to the bondholders. When the bond matures, Widget and the dealer will swap the original sums of money at the initial exchange rate.

Money Markets

The way to understand the outlook for a country is to know its money market—the interest rates on Treasury bills, overnight loans between banks or commercial paper. The London interbank offered rate, or Libor, is a benchmark for money borrowed in a wide array of currencies.

The slightest move in rates can signal a change in the outlook for a country, its economy and the stock, bond and currency markets. It can also affect financial institutions and the earnings and financing of companies.

There are many reasons why rates change. Some signals are strong, such as shifts in inflation rates and currency values, changes in demand for the country's debt, or comments from officials, such as when Federal Reserve Board Chairman Alan Greenspan characterized the U.S. stock markets at the time as showing "irrational exuberance." Others carry less significance, such as the need for cash to do holiday shopping or withdrawals to make tax payments or to buy securities. Our stories have to be able to show the reasons that apply and to explain their importance.

Focus on overnight rates or the one-, three-, six- and 12-month deposit rates from banks, corporate borrowers and the central bank. Compare and contrast today's rates with yesterday's, last week's and last year's, and explain the difference and the outlook if the rates are little changed.

The European Central Bank, in an unprecedented response to a sudden demand for cash from banks roiled by the subprime mortgage collapse in the U.S., loaned 94.8 billion euros ($130 billion) to assuage a shortage of credit.

The overnight rates banks charge each other to lend in dollars soared to the highest in six years after the biggest French bank halted withdrawals from funds linked to U.S. subprime mortgages. The London interbank offered rate rose to 5.86 percent today from 5.35 percent and in euros jumped to 4.31 percent from 4.11 percent.

The ECB said it would provide unlimited cash as the biggest increase in overnight Libor since June 2004 signaled banks are reducing the supply of money just as investors retreat because of losses from the U.S. real-estate slump. Paris-based BNP Paribas SA halted withdrawals from three investment funds today because the French bank couldn't value its holdings.

Functions for Bonds

<Corp> GY or <Govt> GY—Graph yield. These functions track the yield on a bond.

WB <Go>—World bond monitor. Displays market prices and yields for benchmark government securities, along with historical yield changes.

WBIS <Go> and EBIS <Go>—Compares total-return indexes for international bond markets.

GGR <Go>—Generic rates for government benchmark bonds.

TRACE <Go> or TACT <Go>—Monitors for the most-active U.S. company bonds.

FIT <Go>—A live bond market monitor for Treasuries, Fannie Mae and Freddie Mac bonds, mortgage bonds and other debt.

<Equity> DDIS—Debt distribution. Shows the principal amount of a company's bonds that will mature each year.

<Equity> CRPR—Credit profiles. Displays a company's current ratings and provides historical ratings.

RATD <Go>—Rating definitions. Includes tables that compare the credit ratings used by companies such as Standard & Poor's and Moody's Investors Service. RATC <Go> tracks changes in ratings.

NIM <Go>—New issue monitor. The easiest way to find out which borrowers sold bonds and how much they raised.

GCDS <Go>—Credit-default swap rates by industry, company and country.

TOP BON <Go>—Top bond news.

Currencies

Currency markets, like bond markets, provide a daily referendum on governments, including those that don't sell bonds regularly. If one currency rises in value against others, it suggests that investors are more confident in a country's economy and political system. If it falls, the opposite may be true. A currency also rises or falls because of traders' perceptions about how much they may make on their investments.

These moves matter to people who make their living from foreign-exchange trading and to companies that sell goods and services internationally.

Currency values can have economic implications because of their link to interest rates. Higher rates make it more attractive for people to own assets denominated in a currency; lower rates make it less attractive. Central banks seeking to lift currencies will often increase interest rates.

Here is an example of a currency story that captures the latest market moves, along with their implications:

> *The dollar fell against the euro after U.S. consumer confidence plunged the most in 11 years, adding to concern that the economy's slowdown will worsen.*
>
> *The dollar dropped 0.06 percent to 92.29 U.S. cents per euro at 3 p.m. London time, from 91.71 late yesterday in New York. The Conference Board said its consumer confidence index fell to 97.6 this month, the lowest level since January 1996. Economists polled by Bloomberg had forecast a reading of 105.*
>
> *"There will be a lot more data like that in the next few months," along with disappointing earnings reports, said Dirk Morris, who helps manage about $50 billion as head of global currencies at Putnam Investments in Boston.*

Currencies *rise* or *fall, weaken* or *strengthen, appreciate* or *depreciate.* These are all acceptable verbs. Currencies aren't *weak* or *strong,* in keeping with Bloomberg style that limits the use of modifiers. Be specific: *The dollar, which has fallen to a three-year low against the yen, . . .*

Currencies don't move in a vacuum, so we must note a second currency in the comparison: *The yen strengthened against the dollar* or *The euro rose against the dollar.*

Covering Currency Markets

Currency stories ought to do the following:

Lead with the currency. The first paragraph should begin with the currency that's the subject of the main action, such as the dollar, the euro or the yen.

> *The dollar surged to a four-month high against the euro and advanced versus the yen in New York after sales at U.S. retailers rose the most in a year.*

Quote currencies according to market convention. Most currencies are quoted per U.S. dollar, so the number we use in our story is the number of South African rand or Japanese yen it takes to buy one U.S. dollar. Some currencies, including the euro and the British pound, are more commonly quoted as the number of U.S. dollars per euro or pound. Follow the market conventions in each case.

Calculate percentage change. Note that when calculating the percentage change in a currency, the way the currency is expressed will determine how the change is calculated. For example, when calculating the yen/dollar rate over a quarter or year, the amount the yen has gained will not be the same number as the amount the dollar has weakened, because the two figures will be calculated from a different base.

Show what big traders and big money are doing. There must be a quote in the first four paragraphs. Ideally, this is a comment from a money manager who discloses what he is doing and the role of currencies in his decisions.

In the event we quote a trader or strategist at a bank, include the person's predictions for the market. Did the strategist just raise or cut his forecast for the currency? Is this bank one of the biggest traders in the foreign-exchange market? Does it have a history of accurate predictions on exchange rates? All of these are valuable insights.

Beware of too many numbers in the first four paragraphs. The story is about currencies, not an economic indicator. Readers can go to the economy story if they want complete details of the economic report.

The currency prices are ideally in the fourth paragraph. It's best to avoid too many numbers too soon, which may interrupt the flow of the story.

Be clear about comparisons. When citing prices, be mindful of making the proper comparison. For the dollar, euro and yen, use 5 p.m. prices in New York the previous day. For other currencies, such as the British pound, Canadian dollar or South African rand, use the 5 p.m. price the previous day in the place where it is most actively traded. Other comparisons can be included to explain reaction to an event that occurred outside business hours.

Add perspective on other markets. It may be relevant to refer to what's happening in the bond, stock or commodity markets to put currency trading into perspective.

Name the winners and losers. Which companies are benefiting from swings in an exchange rate and how? During earnings season, this may add valuable context and perspective.

> *The U.S. currency has dropped 9 percent in the past year against the euro, boosting revenue at companies. International Business Machines Corp. said yesterday that currency gains added 3 percent to sales in the first quarter.*

Make careful comparisons. Avoid writing that the yen *fell* to a bigger number from a smaller one; use *weakened* instead.

> *The yen weakened 0.05 percent to 109.86 per dollar at 7:08 a.m. in New York, the lowest since Oct. 14, from 109.26 late yesterday.*

Themes for Currencies

Public statements. Comments by central-bank officers, finance ministers and other government officials that provide insight into a country's policy toward interest rates or the value of its currency can be a catalyst for market moves.

The dollar rose the most in 2 1/2 months against the euro after Hong Kong Monetary Authority Chief Executive Joseph Yam suggested that Asian central banks shouldn't rush to boost euro holdings at the expense of the U.S. currency.

Economic reports. Currencies can reflect differences between countries, such as their interest rates, flows of capital, current account balances and relative economic growth rates. Any statistics such as measures of economic growth and inflation that change people's expectations for rates can push currencies higher or lower.

Political events. Some countries print money and back it with foreign-exchange reserves, so events affecting perceptions of their political stability can affect currency values. Political instability creates uncertainty. Will the government print money to help quell the situation? Will the government confiscate property? When a major conflict occurs, for instance, people may prefer to have their assets in dollars and other currencies perceived to be relatively stable.

Trade reports. Purchases of imported goods and services typically lead to an exchange of one currency for another, as do export sales. Statistics on imports and exports can influence the value of one currency against another.

Other markets. Rallies in a country's stock and bond markets can boost a currency's value because they signal that people are investing more money there and need the currency to make their investments. Similarly, market declines can lead to a lower currency as international investors convert the proceeds of their sales.

Company comments. Statements by chief executives, treasurers, chief financial officers and corporate economists about currencies are news that traders can use. An increase in a company's home currency can make its goods more expensive abroad and reduce sales. What exchange rate is the company forecasting? How will a change in the currency affect profit or sales? Is the company hedged against a swing in the currency?

Functions for Currencies

WCR <Go>—World currency rates. Displays the value of a currency against a table of others. Shows change for today and over time. A related function, WCRS <Go>, ranks the best- and worst-performing currencies.

<Curncy> GX24—Graphs 24 hours of a currency's trading in the New York, London and Tokyo markets.

WFX <Go>—A monitor for currencies.

FXC <Go>—Cross-currency rates. Monitors the value of currencies against each other.

FE11 <Go>—Converts one currency into another.

TOP FRX <Go>—Top currency news.

Commodities

Our goal is to give commodities the same insightful and well-written coverage that we provide for stocks, bonds and currencies, because commodities have a direct effect on people's wealth. If the price of oil rises, consumers may pay more for gasoline. Higher coffee, orange juice or pork-belly prices can make their breakfast more expensive.

Commodity prices can also affect the profitability of companies, drive investment decisions and influence the performance of stocks and bonds. Higher prices tend to increase the profit of companies producing these commodities and boost expenses for firms using them as raw materials.

Because commodity prices can fuel inflation, an increase may cause a central bank to raise interest rates, causing bond prices to decline. Higher interest rates would tend to reduce economic growth and corporate profits, causing stock prices to decline.

Copper futures rose the most in more than two years on signs that Chile's Codelco, the world's largest producer, may follow the lead of other mining companies and reduce output.

The state-run company may curtail production next year as it switches to mining ore with lower copper content, President Juan Villarzu said. Phelps Dodge Corp., the second-largest producer, and BHP Billiton Ltd. had announced cuts aimed at boosting prices from 14-year lows.

"Production cuts are turning this market around," said Vincent Rego, president and chief executive officer of Encore Wire Corp. in McKinney, Texas, which uses about 25 million pounds of copper a month to make electrical wiring for homes, schools and office buildings. "Now all we need is for demand to come back."

Copper for December delivery rose 4.2 percent to 64.1 cents a pound on the Comex division of the New York Mercantile Exchange. The gain was the biggest for a most active contract since June 30, 1999, and led to the highest closing price since Oct. 16.

As the quote in this example suggests, covering commodities means following the latest price changes and the companies that use the raw materials. Reporters need to develop sources at companies that produce and use commodities, especially the companies that can cause market prices to move by changing their retail prices, orders and factory operations.

Likewise, company reporters on beats from consumer products to paper to automobiles must understand commodity markets. Price changes may affect a company's profits a lot or a little, depending on whether it locks in prices ahead of time. Reporters who marry companies and commodities in their stories will be far more influential than their competitors. The same is true for economy and policy reporters who tie commodity price movements to the data from their beats.

Market coverage ought to include a few paragraphs explaining commodity price charts, or technical analysis, because commodity traders follow them closely.

Many commodities are traded around the world, so it's important to specify in the lead where the commodity is being traded.

Gold futures in New York fell for the first time in three days on speculation that U.S. job growth is improving, increasing the likelihood that the Federal Reserve will boost interest rates from a 46-year low.

Pay attention to groups of commodities. Drought or other adverse weather may cause grains—including soybeans, wheat and corn—to rise. An OPEC decision to boost production might send the price of energy—including oil, gasoline and natural gas—lower.

Themes for Commodities

Global news events. In oil-producing regions and commodities-producing nations elsewhere, anything that may signal increased risk to supplies is important. Political unrest can affect prices. In many countries, the governments own the natural resources and rely on their sale for budget revenue. Changes in the supply, demand or price of a critical commodity could affect that nation's economy as well as its bonds, equity markets and currency.

Supply reports. Industry groups and government agencies report on current and future supplies of many commodities. If the reports show that supplies are higher or lower than expected, prices change. Commodity exchanges periodically report the amount of inventory available in their warehouses, where people can take delivery under the terms of their contracts. Changes in the available stockpiles can influence prices.

Supply or demand changes. The shutdown or resumption of operations at a mine, production facility or processing plant can indicate whether supplies will rise or fall, causing prices to move. So can changes in production costs, such as feed for livestock. Refinery closings, pipeline disruptions, grounded tankers, fires, floods and earthquakes may disrupt supply or spur demand. Changes in demand such as grain tenders or adverse weather can make a country an importer instead of an exporter.

Economic reports. Demand for some commodities rises and falls along with economic growth, so reports on the economy's performance can influence prices. Statistics on housing starts can lead to a change in the price of copper because the metal is used in electrical wires and plumbing. They also can affect the price of lumber because it's used to build homes.

Governmental actions. Regulatory or policy changes made in countries that are major producers or consumers of a commodity can affect supply or demand, leading to price changes. Even the expectation that a government will—or won't—make changes can move prices.

Supplier actions. Policy changes or other actions carried out by suppliers such as the Organization of Petroleum Exporting Countries or Codelco,

Chile's state-owned copper company and the world's largest supplier of copper, can lead to price changes.

Weather. If the weather's just right, crops will grow in abundance. If it's too hot, cold, wet or dry, they won't. Prices often rise and fall because the actual temperature or rainfall differs from forecasts, or because the forecasts change.

Seasonal patterns. Demand for some commodities changes from one season to the next. U.S. demand for heating oil peaks during the winter. Deviation from this pattern can push prices higher or lower.

Regulation. News related to regulation of utilities and environmental rules is essential because it affects decisions about investments, production and supply. A utility spending millions on new pollution-control devices at a power plant will need to shut down during the installation, meaning others can step in as suppliers.

Functions for Commodities

CTM <Go>—Contract table menu. Displays a list of commodities sorted by subject.

CEM <Go>—Table of contracts by exchange.

OIL <Go>—Global oil markets menu. Provides links to petroleum menus.

LME <Go>—London Metal Exchange monitor. Has prices for aluminum, copper, zinc and other metals.

MINE <Go>—Metals, minerals and mining menu. Has links to market monitors and industry statistics.

NRG <Go>—Energy-related menu.

CRR <GO>—Commodity rankings. Tracks performance of different commodities and indexes.

CMCX <Go>—UBS/Bloomberg commodity indexes, with charts showing performance attribution.

16

Companies

W HEN COMPANIES MAKE news, we must provide the detail and perspective of the daily newspapers with the real-time speed of a news service.

Technology helps us fulfill part of that obligation. We publish thousands of press releases each day from companies that arrive on electronic feeds from public-relations wires and stock exchanges, by facsimile, by Internet downloads or by e-mail.

Technology can't judge the importance of the news in the release. It can't discern what was left out of the release that people need to know. It can't uncover the news buried in annual reports, regulatory filings, lawsuits and other documents. It can't talk with executives, investors, analysts and other stakeholders to break news or examine the implications. It can't explain the links between companies, markets and policies or offer speculation on what happens next.

Those duties are left to reporters and editors, who must be aware of the ways that companies make news, possible approaches to covering the news, and questions that have to be answered: What are the key pieces of information that anyone needs to know about a company right now? Every company story ought to have that background and context in summary form to give a clear sense of what is happening at any time.

People often know more about products and services than they do about the companies that make or provide them. Weave a few of the company's best-known brands high in the story. Europeans and Americans will be more inclined to pay attention to SABMiller Plc if we tell them that its beers include Pilsner Urquell and Miller Lite.

Market Perspective

Events often have an immediate effect on a company's shares and bonds. When that happens, highlight the movement in the first few paragraphs—sometimes in the lead. The bigger the change, the bigger the news.

Look beyond the day's performance for comparisons that put the move into context or show how it's out of the ordinary. Consider a stock that falls 20 percent to $10.50. If the shares had tripled during a 12-month period, the event that triggered the loss might be a break with the company's past. If the shares had plunged 80 percent the past year, the news is likely to be in keeping with earlier events.

Every time we cite a stock, run <Equity> GP D or <Equity> GP W to see how it has performed the past year or several years. Use <Equity> COMP to compare the stock's returns against competitors or a benchmark index. If it's part of a major index, run <Index> MRR to see how the stock's performance ranks among the companies in the index.

Stories are more informative when we include a company's valuation after its shares have made a substantial move. Measures such as the total value of the shares or price-earnings ratio (the price divided by earnings per share for a 12-month period) can provide perspective. Find such figures by using the <Equity> DES and <Equity> GE functions.

Show how analysts perceive the company by using the ratings function <Equity> ANR. Do they rate the stock a buy, a sell or a hold? Our customers ask this question every time they evaluate a company, the outcome of an event or the chief executive officer. So should we.

Shares Up and Down

Focusing on market performance is a sure way to fashion the lead of any story about a company or an industry because the increase or decline in value is a measure of a change in perception. The approach works best when a stock rises or falls in response to information disclosed at the end of the previous day or when the change in price is more newsworthy than the event.

During the trading day, refer to the extent of the move only in general terms in story headlines. Being specific isn't appropriate because the price is fluctuating and we'd have to keep changing the headlines. *AIG Tumbles on Accounting Probe* is fine. *AIG Falls as Much as 9.5% on Accounting Probe* isn't as helpful because the percentage may change by the time the reader sees the story. Once the day ends, rewrite to add the final percentage change: *AIG Falls 8% on Accounting Probe Concerns.*

Refer to percentage changes in leads in order to keep numbers to a minimum. Weave the price change and the latest price into the first screen:

> *Tokyo Electron Ltd., the world's second-largest maker of semiconductor equipment, rose as much as 6 percent in Japanese trading on optimism that rising demand for chips will spur demand for the company's tools.*
>
> *Worldwide computer-chip sales will rise 20 percent next year to the highest level since 2000, market researcher Gartner Inc. said yesterday. Also, Applied Materials Inc., the world's biggest maker of computer-chip production equipment, reported its first quarterly profit in a year yesterday as orders climbed.*
>
> *Tokyo Electron rose 4.6 percent to 8,140 as of 11:18 a.m. in Tokyo Stock Exchange trading and earlier reached 8,250. The stock has gained 52 percent this year.*

Putting the movement into perspective can tell a more interesting story:

> *Google Inc. plunged as much as 10 percent in New York trading, the biggest decline since the Internet search-engine operator sold shares to the public in 2004, after profit rose less than analysts estimated.*

Debt

Debt provides the most precise depiction of a company's health and prospects. If the debtor can't pay interest and principal on time, default and liquidation may be the outcome. Even if a share price declines to 5 cents from $50, the company may remain viable if its debts are paid.

Any story about the fortunes of a company—earnings, acquisitions, bankruptcy, executive changes, regulatory investigations, a change in its bond rating or a change in capital structure such as a share or debt sale—needs to include at least one paragraph about debt.

Evaluating debt helps us understand whether a company is becoming a safer or more risky investment. Bond investors often sniff out bad news about a company before stock investors do.

The debt paragraph should include how much the company has borrowed. It should also show whether the company is becoming more or less risky to investors. One way is to show the difference, or spread, between the yield on a company's bond and a U.S. Treasury or other benchmark bond that has a comparable maturity. The riskier the company, the bigger the premium that investors will demand to own the debt. Another way is to include the ratings from Moody's Investors Service, Standard & Poor's or another service and how that evaluation has changed:

General Motors is the third-biggest corporate debtor in the U.S. Fitch Ratings reduced its rating on GM today to BBB- from BBB, one step above non-investment grade, and said it may cut the rating further.

Credit-Default Swaps

Credit-default swaps are similar to insurance policies. An owner of corporate (or government) debt can purchase a swap as protection against a loss of value when the debtor fails to pay the obligation on time. The credit-default swap seller acts as the insurer, agreeing to cover the debt owed in case of default.

Although there are guidelines investors agree to follow, the market lacks regulation. Trading is dominated by a handful of the world's largest banks, which created the credit-default swaps a decade ago. For all these reasons, there is little transparency.

Banks may purchase credit-default swaps to limit their risk of losses from credit changes such as a decline in a company's credit rating. Investors such as hedge funds also buy them to speculate on changes in the creditworthiness of individual companies or on the corporate debt market in general.

Most pension funds and government investment funds are excluded from this market because of the lack of regulation and transparency.

Hedge funds and banks trade credit derivatives based on the debt of more than 3,000 companies, in part because it's cheaper and easier to use the contracts than buying or selling the underlying debt. Credit-default swaps are quoted in basis points. An increase in price indicates that investors are more wary of the company's creditworthiness; a drop means the opposite.

> *Credit-default swaps linked to AT&T's debt rose 11.6 basis points to 87.4 in New York, according to CMA prices. A basis point on a swap protecting $10 million of debt from default for five years is equivalent to $1,000 a year.*

Earnings

News judgment determines the scope of earnings coverage, with the focus always on the surprise.

Important companies and industries require complete reporting, beginning with curtain-raisers that include relative value analysis. Other companies, with no surprises, merit minimal attention.

The process begins by deciding each quarter (or half) which companies deserve exceptional reporting. That determination is based on trends within companies and industries.

Before a company discloses results to shareholders, teams should review the earnings history and any news that may have an impact on revenue and profit, such as commodity prices, acquisitions, personnel changes and economic trends.

The first headlines and story typically compare profit and sales with the estimates or provide other numbers that clients need urgently, such as forecasts. Share movement may be an early indicator of whether an earnings report is perceived as positive or negative.

For updates, company teams should dig deeper for the news most significant to investors. Scrutinize announcements for surprises, both in the text and in the numbers on the income statement. Then scour the balance sheet, cash-flow statement and disclosures for longer-term trends not yet showing in earnings.

News we may find in earnings releases, executive interviews or conference calls includes:

A forecast for earnings or sales or margins. These are often more useful to investors than the profit/loss.

Comments on acquisition intentions, industry trends, the economy's impact and the direction of commodity prices.

Numbers other than profit/loss that show how the company is performing. Many are standard for particular industries, such as cash flow for biotechnology startups, occupancy rates for hotel companies and backlogs for defense contractors.

On the income statement, assess numbers such as additions to loan-loss reserves.

Look at more than one financial statement. U.S. companies must file their balance sheet and cash flow quarterly with the Securities and Exchange Commission, and many countries have similar requirements. Sometimes these are made available with earnings, or we can request them. The balance sheet shows a company's liquidity, shortages or surpluses in inventory or supply, whether liabilities are in line with assets, how much cash is on hand. The cash-flow statement shows cash generation or deterioration, and if the company is investing in its own stock, other companies or capital such as factories and warehouses.

No matter the angle of the lead, updates must include net income or net loss. When starting with a profit measure that backs out some items, reconcile it to the bottom line. This ensures that investors aren't subjected to manipulated numbers in ways that don't meet accounting standards. Net income/net loss measures all companies by the same parameters, giving our global audience a uniform scale for comparison.

Read company releases with skepticism to ensure that the information is transparent. The bull market of the 1990s and its dot-com bubble bequeathed a legacy of imprecise earnings reports. So-called cash earnings and Ebitda, or earnings before interest, taxes, depreciation and amortization, are among measures of financial performance that confuse more than clarify.

Beware of the labels *pro forma, special, one-time* and *adjusted*. All are warning flags that the earnings numbers have been massaged to look better than they would under a standard presentation. Companies often try to disguise costs or expenses that are a regular part of doing business.

When the earnings aren't consistent with the curtain-raiser, explain why.

Use appropriate language. Numbers and terminology must follow Bloomberg style.

Compare profit, per-share results and revenue with the year-earlier period, and give the percentage change for profit and revenue. Use the most complete numbers available for rounding and for calculating percentages.

It's acceptable to use a general term such as *earnings, profit* or *loss* in the lead. In later paragraphs, provide a specific definition that makes the reference clear, such as *net income* or *profit from continuing operations*.

Use active verbs such as *rose, increased, fell* or *decreased* when comparing profits, and *widened, narrowed, deepened* or *shrank* when comparing losses. When comparing a profit in one period with a loss in another, use *compared with*.

Charge is acceptable only in the first story. For updates, find out what the company is writing down or writing off. Is it a cost, expense, investment loss, or something else?

Profit/loss from continuing operations should be used only when a company exits a business dissimilar from its main activity.

Profit/loss from operations is reserved for the rare instance when a gain or loss is so extraordinary that it's justified to present results excluding the item before giving net income/loss. No additional results should be lumped with the item for backing out. *Pro forma, special, one-time* and *adjusted* are warning signs of this situation.

Operating income/profit/loss is acceptable only in the first story. For updates, obtain the company's definition of what is included and excluded in this measure and provide that in the story.

Look for the net income or net loss that is before payment of preferred stock dividends and after results of minority or non-controlling interests. There may be several numbers labeled "net" at the bottom of the income statement, and we may have to do the math to figure out which is this bottom line.

Avoid suggesting that we are comparing profit in a quarter with full-year profit. Rather than writing *Widgets Inc. said first-quarter earnings increased 12 percent from last year*, write *Widgets Inc. said first-quarter earnings rose 12 percent from a year earlier.*

When writing about losses, it's better to say *Widgets had a $4 million loss* than *Widgets lost $4 million.* The latter implies that the company misplaced some cash and can't find it.

Avoid the jargon of writing that a company or executive is *comfortable* with estimates. Of course they are comfortable—they gave out the figures. Paraphrase.

Compute implied earnings when necessary. Companies outside the U.S. often omit the latest quarter's results and instead give figures for the first-half, nine-month and full-year periods.

Because the figures for the just-ended period are often the most newsworthy, calculate the profit by subtracting the amount in one period from the amount in another. Typically, we headline and lead the story with the figures the company announced. Once we calculate the most recent results and call the company to confirm the calculations, switch to the implied results.

Compare this assessment of a company's nine-month results . . .

Isuzu Motors Ltd., Japan's biggest maker of trucks and commercial vehicles, said profit in the first nine months fell 16 percent after it spent more for research and development. Net income dropped to 42.9 billion yen ($366 million), or 22.89 yen a share, in the period ended Dec. 31, from 51.1 billion yen, or 21.48 yen, a year earlier. Sales rose 4.8 percent to 1.13 trillion yen, the Tokyo-based company said in a statement today.

. . . with how it performed in the most recent quarter . . .

Isuzu Motors Ltd., Japan's biggest maker of trucks and commercial vehicles, posted an 11 percent increase in third-quarter profit on higher sales in Japan and overseas.

Net income rose to 16.8 billion yen ($143 million) in the quarter ended Dec. 31, from 15.2 billion yen a year earlier. Sales rose 14 percent to 396.4 billion yen.

The stories tell different tales, because the nine-month figures are influenced by what happened in the first six months of the year. Make our calculations transparent. Explain how we arrived at the numbers and that they are based on figures provided by the company.

Third-quarter net income was derived by subtracting the company's first-half earnings from the nine-month results published today.

Analysts and investors in some nations concentrate on cumulative results on a pretax basis, with no concern for per-share figures or net income. To accommodate these local preferences, insert the cumulative pretax earnings after the four-paragraph lead.

Use numbers sparingly. It is easy to overwhelm readers with figures. Keep them to a minimum. Stories usually begin by showing how much earnings changed from the year-earlier period and why:

Microsoft Corp., the world's biggest software maker, said second-quarter profit rose 5.5 percent on the release of new software for server computers.

Putting a percentage change in the lead keeps numbers to a minimum and provides instant perspective. Actual figures can't be read easily and don't by themselves answer the central question of any earnings story: Did the company do better or worse, and why?

There are times when the earnings number helps illuminate the story:

Exxon Mobil Corp., the world's biggest oil company, said fourth-quarter net income rose 27 percent to a record $10.7 billion, capping the most profitable year for a U.S. company.

Put the numbers into perspective. Context about earnings or sales— biggest increase in 10 years, first loss as a public company, 10th straight quarter of declining sales—explains why the news is unique.

> *Lehman Brothers Holdings Inc. posted the biggest quarterly profit in its 156-year history as revenue from trading stocks and investment banking set records and complemented its traditional strength in bonds.*

Provide the stock price. This will illustrate how investors view the results. They will clamor to buy the stock if the report is a good one, and they will sell if it's bad. How high to put the share price depends on the relative size of the move. A 5 percent change is small for some companies, large for others. Use the <Equity> HCP and <Equity> SINS functions to find when the shares last moved that much.

Include company and industry perspective. What is happening to the industry? What is notable about this company or its performance? If it sells or buys a commodity such as oil or gold, describe how much the price rose or fell during the period. If competitors' results were better than expected, say so, because that will affect the interpretation of the company's results.

> *Fixed-income revenue, which typically accounts for half of Bear Stearns's total, fell 21 percent as delinquencies on subprime home loans surged. Bigger competitors Goldman Sachs Group Inc. and Lehman Brothers Holdings Inc. reported profit gains for the quarter as investment-banking and equity-trading revenue helped compensate for the slump in selling bonds, currencies and commodities.*

Make it personal. Ask the great writers of fiction or nonfiction what makes a good story, and their answers will be characters and plot. Earnings stories that focus on the chief executive officer and the biggest shareholders are more complete and more interesting than a formulaic recitation of numbers. Even if profit and sales are unchanged, there's a plot: Why has the executive failed to improve performance? Or, how has the person managed to keep the company from falling further?

> *The results mark the third consecutive year of record earnings for Goldman Sachs, the world's biggest securities firm by market value. While trading remained the dominant source of profit, Chief Executive Officer*

Lloyd Blankfein, who took over from Henry Paulson in June, reaped gains from bigger investments in leveraged buyouts and paid a smaller percentage of revenue in compensation.

Focus on after-tax figures for special items. If after-tax amounts aren't available, use pretax dollar amounts and be sure they are clearly labeled.

Mergers and Acquisitions

Mergers and acquisitions are among the most important events in a company's history, whether it's a $90 billion transaction that spans the globe or a $500 million sale of a minority stake. They affect employees, suppliers, competitors, customers and investors.

The question that determines how we write about these kinds of transactions is the nature of the change. If Company A will be in control of a combined company, for instance, we would write that Company A will buy Company B, regardless of whether the companies call it a merger. If the two companies will become equal partners, we would write that Company A and Company B will merge. Most transactions are purchases.

The value of any merger or acquisition is determined by asking: What do the shareholders of the company to be acquired get? If Company A acquires Company B, the value of the acquisition will be the monetary sum Company B's shareholders receive, denominated in shares, cash, some combination of the two, or any other form of payment. If the companies merge, they typically exchange shares at a ratio determined by several criteria including market capitalization, earnings and cash flow.

Write about a pending transaction from every angle. What is happening and why? How much will it cost? How will it be financed? What does it mean for the buyer? The seller? What does this tell us about the success, failure or ambitions of the chief executives? What will it do to the competition and how will they react to the changes? Will there be more consolidation? Will regulators approve? Will jobs be lost? Gained? Most of all, what does it mean for our customers?

Use conditional language until the transaction is completed. There isn't any assurance that regulators, shareholders, banks, company managements and others that must agree to a merger or acquisition will do so. Write: *The combined company would be the biggest*, not *will be the biggest*.

> *Mittal Steel Co., attempting to control 10 percent of worldwide steel production, offered 18.6 billion euros ($22.5 billion) for Arcelor SA in a hostile bid that would be the industry's biggest takeover.*
>
> *Billionaire Lakshmi Mittal, who built his Rotterdam-based company into the world's largest steelmaker through three of the industry's 10 largest takeovers since 1990, wants to increase bargaining power with customers including Ford Motor Co. and suppliers such as Cia. Vale do Rio Doce. Arcelor supplies the steel used in half the cars made in Europe and has mills in Europe as well as Latin America.*
>
> *"It makes enormous industrial sense," said Samir Essafri, a fund manager at Richelieu Finance in Paris who oversees about $3.6 billion of assets, including Arcelor shares. "The industry is very fragmented."*
>
> *Mittal bid 28.21 euros a share for Arcelor, 27 percent more than yesterday's closing price. Arcelor shares jumped as high as 31.29 euros, signaling that investors expect a higher offer.*

When companies suddenly become targets or would-be acquirers, the moment begs for the quick, everything-you-should-know-about-this-company feature. This is the point when our customers have the strongest desire to know whatever we can produce that informs and enlightens their perspective. Keep the story simple: performance, successes, failures, etc. What will shareholders get? What will the chief executive officer be paid, and will it reflect or belie performance?

Weave the action of investment bankers and lawyers advising the companies into the narrative. The adviser and the chief executive have a symbiotic relationship because acquisitions are as much about the bankers who arrange the deals. Who are the bankers? What did they do? How did the acquisition succeed? How long did it take? How much will the bankers be paid? These questions must be answered with context instead of paying lip service to Wall Street's part with a list of names in the last paragraph.

Gillette said it approached Procter & Gamble about the acquisition, the biggest in the industry since at least 1999. Merrill Lynch & Co., UBS AG and Goldman Sachs Group Inc. probably will split fees of more than $75 million for arranging the acquisition, according to data compiled by Bloomberg from acquisitions last year of a similar size. Merrill, the largest securities firm by equity capital, is advising P&G. UBS, Europe's largest bank, and Goldman Sachs, the third-largest securities firm, is advising Gillette.

Valuation

When valuing merger and acquisition offers, start with the assumption that one company will buy the other. Otherwise, customers won't be able to make meaningful comparisons between transactions.

To determine the buyer in a merger, bear in mind that one company will either survive afterward or have its shareholders exchange stock on a 1-for-1 basis for shares of a new company. Either way, holders won't be compensated for agreeing to the merger. Their company is *effectively* buying the other. The value of the offer made to the other company's shareholders becomes the basis for determining the transaction's value. In other words, the only complication in merger valuation is determining which company is the *buyer* and which is the *seller*.

After making that judgment, take the terms of the offer into account. There are a number of alternatives from which companies can choose.

Cash transaction. A relatively simple calculation: *(Offer price per share) × (Seller shares outstanding)*

It's best to obtain the figure for shares outstanding from the company so it's up-to-date. If it's unavailable, use the most recent number found in the company's press releases or regulatory filings or what appears under <Equity> DES.

Stock transaction. Acquisitions can involve an exchange of stock instead of cash. Mergers always do. The terms of any transaction will include an exchange ratio. In an acquisition, Company A may offer to swap 1.5 shares for each Company B share. In a merger, Company B's shareholders may receive 1.5 shares of the newly formed company for each of their shares, while Company A's holders may be entitled to a 1-for-1 exchange.

In both examples, Company A is the buyer and Company B is the seller. Here is the formula for calculating the value of the transaction: *(Exchange ratio)* × *(Buyer share price)* × *(Seller shares and equivalents)*

Press releases on stock-swap transactions will typically include the ratio. If it isn't part of a release, ask for it immediately. Ask for the total number of shares and share equivalents that need to be exchanged as well. For companies that use stock options to compensate employees, this figure can be much larger than the number of shares outstanding.

In some cases, the companies establish limits on the value of the stock it will exchange. Use the cash formula to calculate the maximum amount. Use the figure, preceded by *as much as*, in the lead. Describe the limits later in the story.

Cash and stock transaction. Use the first formula to calculate the value of the cash portion of the offer, and the second to determine the value of the stock portion. Add the two numbers for the total value.

Other securities. Sometimes an acquirer's offer will include preferred stock, warrants or other equity securities. These types of securities can be difficult to value precisely because appropriate figures aren't readily available. Use the cash and/or stock formula to calculate as much of the value as possible. Call people evaluating the offer, such as shareholders and analysts, and rely on their estimates of its total value.

Debt and cash on hand. Lower in the story, provide an alternative value that includes the base value, the amount of debt being assumed and the amount of cash on hand that the buyer will receive in the purchase. This is the enterprise value, which many investors and analysts use. It helps address the future cost of the acquisition. While the buyer may be taking on more debt, it may get cash that can be used to pay the debt. Debt often is refinanced, so the current amount owed isn't a stable number that can be added to the basic price.

Companies don't always disclose the assumed debt and cash on hand when announcing an acquisition, so reporters should ask.

When a company is the target of takeover speculation, include an estimate from analysts or investors of the potential price or the current market value of the target's shares.

Value Comparisons

Show whether investors expect the offer to succeed or fail. Comparisons between the market value of a target company's shares and the value of a would-be buyer's offer can provide the evidence. There are three possible outcomes:

The market price of the target company substantially exceeds the offer. This indicates that investors anticipate a higher bid, either from the acquirer or someone else. Ask people which scenario is more likely. If it's the latter, determine who might submit offers.

The market price is equal to or less than the offer. This indicates that investors expect the bid to succeed. The target company's stock will typically trade at a little less than the offer price for two reasons: Buyers would receive little or no return if they paid the offer price, and the market price will reflect any perceived risk that the transaction won't be completed. Find out which is the case and whether there are any strenuous objections among the target's or buyer's largest shareholders.

The market price is substantially less than the offer. This shows that investors expect the bid to fail because of objections from the target company or a key shareholder, regulatory obstacles such as potential antitrust violations or financing delays. Explain the issues and whether investors' expectations are justified.

Any story about a merger or acquisition is incomplete unless it shows the relative value of the companies, compares the amount paid against historical examples, identifies companies that also may be considered targets and includes the returns for shareholders of similar takeovers.

The answers to these questions will help provide context and perspective.

Is the acquisition cheap or expensive? Compare the offer against purchases by the company or in the industry to determine whether the price is cheap or expensive for both sets of shareholders. Comparing the price against measures such as sales, profit or cash flow of other transactions will also help determine whether the buyer is paying a lot or a little. The MA <Go> database will show relative value and historical comparisons.

What has the buyer done before? This will help put the deal into historical context. Show whether past purchases have helped or hurt the company's performance and investors. Use the CACS screen to find past corporate actions.

> *The deal is the largest for AT&T since the acquisition of BellSouth Corp. in 2006 for about $83 billion, according to data compiled by Bloomberg. It's the largest takeover to be announced in the wireless industry worldwide since 2004, when Sprint agreed to merge with Nextel Communications Inc., and the sixth-largest mobile-phone deal of all time.*

Can the buyer afford the purchase? Check to see how much cash and short-term investments are on the company's balance sheet, either through a regulatory filing or the FA <Go> function. Ask whether the buyer will need to raise cash by selling stock, which would dilute the holdings of other investors, or take on debt by selling bonds or getting a loan, both of which would raise interest costs.

What other companies are potential targets? One purchase often leads to investor speculation that companies making or selling similar products and services may be bought. To find a company's competitors, use the PPC <Go> function. Calculate the relative value of their shares as multiples of profit or sales to determine which companies are cheap or expensive in comparison.

> *Marathon Oil is valued at 4.2 times estimated Ebitda, the second-lowest level behind Chevron among U.S. integrated oil producers.*

Marathon Oil has a cheaper valuation than any of the U.S. refiners that don't drill oil wells, according to Bloomberg data.

Financing

Securities sales and bank loans are among the most ignored events in financial journalism. Whenever a company sells equity or debt or raises money through a loan, we have an obligation to write a story about its performance and prospects.

The easiest way to meet these obligations is to write a curtain-raiser. When the day of the sale finally arrives or the loan agreement is completed, the reporter is prepared to deliver a detailed and polished piece on deadline by adding how much money the company raised and whether the price or yield was more or less than expected.

This type of story ought to answer the following questions within the first four paragraphs:

What are the size and amount of the transaction? For bond sales, these two numbers will generally be about the same. An exception: zero-coupon bonds, sold at a deep discount to face value. For stock sales, include the number of shares to be sold and the amount that the company will raise.

Why is the company raising money now? Many companies sell bonds or seek loans when interest rates are dropping and they can borrow relatively cheaply. Sometimes this is done to pay off more expensive debt. So if lower rates are an issue, find out how much the company is going to save. A company may sell shares at an opportune moment. Perhaps its industry is booming or its stock is at a record high.

What is the company going to do with the money? What separates an in-depth story from a shorter, breaking news item on a bond or stock sale is an examination of the company's strategy and details on how the new money will be used to pursue that course.

NRG Energy Inc., the owner of power plants in 14 U.S. states, sold $3.6 billion of debt, the biggest sale of junk bonds since 1989, to help finance its purchase of electricity producer Texas Genco Holdings LLC.

Why do investors want the securities? It's one thing for companies and their underwriters to put bonds and stocks up for sale, or for companies to pursue bank financing. It's quite another for investors to buy them, or for banks to provide money. Make this distinction clear by showing how investors view the company's finances and business prospects.

Will the transaction succeed? This is the bottom line. If the company is able to raise all the funds it wants, it's in a better position to pursue its strategy, and its underwriters make a profit. If not, both can lose. Add investors' comments by the fourth or fifth paragraph to show whether they expect the sale will be successful or a flop, in which underwriters get stuck owning many of the securities.

Goldman Sachs Group Inc., JPMorgan Chase & Co. and the rest of Wall Street are stuck with at least $11 billion of loans and bonds they can't readily sell.

The banks have had to dig into their own pockets to finance parts of at least five leveraged buyouts during the past month because of the worst bear market in high-yield debt in more than two years, data compiled by Bloomberg show.

Initial Public Offerings

Equity markets provide a way for companies to raise funds from a broader range of investors. Companies may choose to sell stock to any interested investors through initial public offerings.

Stories about these companies need to include the percentage of the stake up for sale. Writing that Widgets Corp. sold 10 million shares at $8 a share doesn't mean much without saying whether the sale represented a 50 percent stake, a 10 percent stake, or some other figure. Include the market value of how much was raised and of the entire company.

Google Inc., the owner of the most-used search engine, raised $1.67 billion in its initial public offering, selling shares at the bottom of the company's price range after cutting the size by half.

Google and its investors sold 19.6 million shares yesterday at $85 each in the biggest auction-style IPO. The company cut the price to a range of $85 to $95 and reduced the number of shares offered. Google's failure to *get the $108 to $135 initially sought came after statements by executives that prompted investigations by the Securities and Exchange Commission.*

The sale, the biggest IPO for an Internet company in four years, gave Mountain View, California–based Google a market value of $23 billion, more than Gannett Co., the largest U.S. newspaper publisher. At least 18 other companies canceled stock sales this month amid a drop in computer-related stocks.

"Investors may have been scared off because the initial pricing range was so outrageously high," said Jim Lyon, a portfolio manager Oakwood Capital Management in Los Angeles. Oakwood Capital Management oversees about $400 million.

Aside from the price, the most important question we can answer about initial sales is whether the stock is cheap, expensive or fairly valued. Reporters who help investors make that judgment provide a service beyond the scope of most competitors. It's possible using the Bloomberg.

First get the price-earnings multiple for the company, using the proposed share price and per-share earnings cited in the company's prospectus. Then compare that with the multiples of the whole industry and competitors. A number higher than those of rivals means the IPO is expensive. A lower number means the offering is inexpensive. For companies that don't have earnings, use an alternative measure that's followed in that industry, such as comparing the stock's price as a multiple of sales, cash flow or enterprise value, which is the value of a company's equity, minority interests and preferred shares minus its cash and cash equivalents.

At $33 a share, GM is valued at 7.8 times annual earnings, based on its net income in the first nine months of 2010. Ford Motor Co. trades at 8.1 times analysts' estimates for 2010 profit. Ford has been the world's most profitable automaker this year through September.

Identify the banks that led the offering:

Morgan Stanley, JPMorgan Chase & Co., Bank of America Corp. and Citigroup Inc. led the IPO, which includes 35 underwriters, according to a GM filing with the Securities and Exchange Commission. Barclays

Plc, Credit Suisse Group AG, Deutsche Bank AG, Goldman Sachs Group Inc. and Royal Bank of Canada were also listed in the prospectus.

Bond Sales

When writing about bond sales, include details from the prospectus on the company's performance such as products, finances, profits, strategy and risks. They may help explain why investors like or dislike the company. Here are some questions worth answering:

How much debt is the company carrying now? After the sale? Use ratios to show what the debt load means to the company's health, performance and prospects. Long-term debt to shareholders' equity is a good ratio to use. In general, a company with a ratio above 50 percent may be too leveraged. Always compare the percentage with other ratios in that company's industry to show whether it's high or not.

How much will the company's interest expense rise (or fall)? Compare the interest expense with information that can be found in cash flow statements, which will indicate ability to pay. If funds from operations are dropping, interest expense is rising and the two are getting close to each other, that could indicate trouble ahead. What happens if the company loses a key customer or sales of its main product decline?

What do the ratings tell us? What is the company's rating from Moody's, Standard & Poor's and Fitch? How do the ratings compare with those of similar-sized companies in the industry? Why is the rating higher or lower than the industry average? Analysts who follow bonds are knowledgeable about debt and balance sheets.

How does the yield compare with the average for similar companies? Find the appropriate fair-market yield curve based on the type of company, its bond ratings and the market where it will raise the money. FMC <Go> provides the current fair-market yields, while FMCH <Go> provides historical yields. Both are based on Bloomberg calculations.

Then look for the benchmark government yield curve and run the function. Note the fair-market yield for comparable bonds and subtract it from the yield on comparable government bonds to determine the spread.

Analysts at rating companies can explain why a particular company might have to pay more or less than the average yield or spread to borrow. What are the terms for converting the bond into stock, if any? For instance, if a bond is convertible into common stock at a rate of 10 shares for each $1,000 face amount, the story needs to say so and to mention when the conversion can be done. Calculate the value of 10 shares of common and compare it with the $1,000 face amount to see how attractive conversion could be to bondholders.

Some of these questions are applicable when writing about bank loans. Details about a company's debt burden and credit ratings, for instance, are essential.

Repurchases and Dividends

Companies can choose to reward investors by buying their shares or paying dividends. The purchases reduce the amount of available stock and may boost earnings per share. Stories about repurchases ought to spotlight the percentage of shares a company will buy back. The news in a buyback usually isn't the absolute number or dollar value of shares to be purchased. When a company has 120 million shares outstanding and decides to buy back 30 million to thwart a takeover bid, the story should note on first reference that the company plans to buy 25 percent of its shares.

If a company says how many shares it plans to buy back, include the percentage of shares outstanding the company may purchase. If a company says how much it plans to spend on the buyback, figure out how many shares that amount would buy at the current price. Then figure the percentage of shares outstanding that the buyback represents.

> *Chevron Corp., the second-largest U.S. oil company, said it plans to buy as much as $15 billion of its stock as record crude prices increase earnings. The three-year program follows repurchases of $5 billion each completed in 2005, 2006 and 2007, Chevron said today in a statement. At yesterday's closing price, $15 billion would buy more than 163 million shares, or about 7.6 percent of the San Ramon, California–based company's stock.*

Companies that make a profit can either pay that money to shareholders as a dividend or invest the earnings in their business by making acquisitions, buying equipment, expanding research, etc. Many companies do both. Publicly traded companies usually pay dividends on a fixed schedule, such as annually, twice a year or each quarter. Sometimes they pay a special, one-time dividend or pay the dividend in the form of new stock.

Cutting or omitting the dividend is a signal of change, and it typically happens when the company needs to conserve cash. The top of the story should focus on the percentage increase or decrease of the dividend and explain why. Then provide the amount of the new and old dividends and note when shareholders will be paid. Use <Equity> DVD for context on how many times the company has increased or cut its payout.

Microsoft Corp., awash with more cash than any U.S. company outside the financial industry, will return more than $75 billion to shareholders during the next four years through a special payout, stock buybacks and an increased dividend.

Microsoft will buy back as much as $30 billion in stock, pay $32 billion, or $3 a share, in a one-time dividend, and increase its regular payout to 32 cents a year, the company said in a statement today.

The payout, the largest return of capital for a U.S. company, is Chief Executive Officer Steve Ballmer's response to investor pressure to return some of the company's $56.4 billion in cash. The Redmond, Washington–based company's plan is bigger than the market value of all but 24 other companies in the Standard & Poor's 500 index.

Functions for Companies

<Equity> CN—Company news. Displays the headlines, stories, press releases and analysts' reports about a company.

<Equity> CF—Company filings. Lists the filings made by the company to regulators.

<Equity> DVD—History of dividends and stock splits.

<Equity> CACS—Corporate action calendar. Shows a company's actions, such as dividends, mergers and meetings.

<Equity> PHDC and <Equity> HDS—These list the company's investors.

<Equity> MGMT—Lists the company's executives and directors.

<Equity> ANR—Analyst ratings. Lists how analysts rate the company.

<Equity> ERN—A chart of the company's earnings history.

<Equity> EEB—Earnings estimates. Gives the average estimates of analysts.

<Equity> GE—Tracks ratios—including price-earnings, price-to-sales and others—over time.

<Equity> EM—Earnings matrix. Compares percentage changes in sales and earnings from the year-earlier period.

<Equity> RV—Relative value. Shows how the security has performed by different measures against its peers.

<Equity> FA—Fundamental analysis. Historical records of company-specific figures such as sales, earnings, ratios and debt.

MA <Go>—Mergers and acquisitions database. Ranks the biggest acquisitions and the top investment banking and legal advisers.

LEAG <Go>—League tables containing underwriter rankings for stocks and bonds.

17

Economies

THE STORY OF an economy is more than a dry recitation of numbers released by governments and the study of those facts and figures by economists. It's about people making, selling and buying goods and services, and that's always a compelling tale to tell.

Whenever we write about an economy, we ought to consider these five elements: inflation, interest rates, jobs, sales and production. We measure an economy's growth by how much wealth and how many jobs it creates and the value of goods, services and food produced, bought and sold.

A growing economy prompts investors in financial and commodity markets to wonder whether the government or its central bank will raise interest rates to maintain the current value of money and to prevent sudden increases in prices and wages, known as inflation. A declining rate of inflation helps increase the value of money and other financial assets. A rising inflation rate helps boost prices for commodities, services and wages.

A shrinking economy prompts investors to wonder if the government or its central bank will lower interest rates to make money cheaper to borrow and, in the process, encourage people to buy and sell more goods and services and to create more jobs and wealth.

When governments report economic indicators, the number can be more than, less than or the same as economists had forecast. The only way we can deliver the story our readers want most is to prepare all three stories in advance, use one and discard the other two. There isn't any waste when customers reap the benefit of preparation.

Curtain-raisers are a must. Before writing, produce a median forecast by surveying economists. Try for a minimum of five estimates. Explain what those numbers imply about prospects for economic growth, inflation, employment, the trade balance, etc.

Include quotes from companies in the preview and push for information that will move the story forward. In writing about monthly retail sales, what does the largest department-store chain say about its recent sales?

Once the preview is published, templates replete with details, context and quotes make for winning coverage. Start by looking at a chart of the recent series of numbers. For investors, it's often the trend that matters. Then begin building top news sections for at least three alternatives—beating, missing or matching forecasts—with appropriate setup quotes from company officials, money managers or economists.

That way, the first story published will probably have more detail, context and background than the final version from competitors.

Covering Economies

The goal is to explain what the raw numbers mean. Write it as a narrative to draw people into the story, especially if it includes anecdotes that capture and support the story's theme. Here are some tips:

Economy stories ought to be company stories writ large. The economy is all about companies, and the story of companies is the economy. Economy stories speak with more authority when they include comments from chief executives and anecdotes about the fortunes (and misfortunes) of companies. Such voices and examples complement the dry and pseudo-scientific jargon that comes from many economists. A story about a rising employment rate has more credibility when it includes captains of business talking about jobs, productivity, wages or benefits, the movement of plants to less-expensive nations, reduced capital spending, etc.

German business confidence fell to an 11-month low, the latest sign that Europe's economy may contract in the first quarter.

The Ifo economic institute, which surveys 7,000 companies, said its index of western German business confidence declined to 87.1 from 87.3 in November. Economists had expected a drop to 87.

"Business conditions in Germany are a catastrophe," said Burkhard Schuchmann, chief executive officer of Vossloh AG, a maker of rail equipment for customers including Deutsche Bahn AG, Europe's biggest rail operator. "Customers are thinking twice about investing."

Back up stories with charts. Search the relevant charts for trends that support the theme, such as whether sales peaked several months ago or are still rising. This helps provide the context and background to make the story authoritative: What's the trend? The figure is the highest or lowest since when? How does it compare with other economies?

Setup quotes are a must. When preparing templates, talk to people of authority and ask them for the implications of each possible outcome. Assure them the quotes will be used only as appropriate.

Have a clearly identified theme. A well-constructed template goes a long way toward making sure the story tracks the theme. That usually means highlighting the tension in the lead or nut paragraph. Will the central bank raise or cut interest rates? Will the report put added pressure on the dollar, the yen or the euro? Think it through ahead of time and the story will set the agenda for that day's coverage by the currency, bond and equity teams at Bloomberg—as well as for our competitors and customers.

Watch the titles. Avoid referring to an indicator by name on first reference, and instead refer to the information it provides. *Prices paid to factories, farmers and other producers* is easier to grasp and more conversational than *producer prices*, even if it is longer.

Start headlines by naming the country. Because we are a global news service and cover the economies of dozens of nations, minimize confusion by starting with the country: *India's Economy Grows at Fastest Pace in Two Decades.*

Present comparative figures in the first four paragraphs. What do we know today that we didn't know yesterday? That means we usually focus on the change from the prior month or quarter, not the year-earlier period (which means most of the change was already known).

Some countries release only year-to-year changes. If so, work with the government agencies and economists to find a simple formula for calculating month-to-month changes. Because this requires seasonal adjustments, which some countries don't calculate, the request may not be easily granted.

If all numbers are released on a year-to-year basis, mention near the top of a story how the latest number compares with other recent weekly, monthly or quarterly numbers in the series. If the number for the latest month or quarter is available, compare it to at least the previous month's or quarter's number.

Use the headline number in the first paragraph if it is easy to understand: *China's economy grew 11.3 percent in the second quarter, the fastest pace in more than a decade.*

Include the market's reaction. The movements of bond, stock and currency markets help explain the meaning of the number and the surprise of the news. Where is the economy headed? Are interest rates more likely to rise, fall or remain the same? Who are the winners? The losers? The sooner we deliver this reaction and explanation, the better. In this story, the reaction comes in the second paragraph.

Employers in the U.S. cut more jobs than forecast in June and unemployment rose to the highest rate in almost 26 years, offering little evidence that the Obama administration's stimulus package is putting Americans back to work.

Stocks tumbled and bond yields fell as investors bet that the 18th straight month of job losses will further sap consumer spending, weakening a recovery from the deepest recession in half a century. The economy has lost about 6.5 million jobs since December 2007 as companies from General Motors Corp. to Kimberly-Clark Corp. reduce costs.

Begin the search for reaction quotes once the story is published. When our reporting gathers live quotes, take out the comments collected before the news was released.

Keep growth and inflation in mind. Make connections between economic news and central bank policy. Explain the connection between growth, inflation and interest-rate decisions. If the economy is growing too fast, that often leads to inflation, which central banks try to damp by boosting borrowing costs. Sluggish growth in a low-inflation environment often prompts interest-rate cuts. Stock and bond prices and quotes from money managers or economists can illustrate this point.

Package the news as a daily roundup story. The story, called a *wrap*, doesn't have to be a complete rewrite. What does add value is a demonstration that we take the time early each day to repackage the economy story to include the best quotes, the best market analysis, and the best forward look— what today's numbers tell us about where we are going.

Functions for Economies

ECO <Go> and WECO <Go>—Calendars of world economic events.

ECST <Go>—Economic statistics from around the globe.

ESNP <Go>—Snapshot of a nation's major economic statistics.

ECOR <Go>—A complete menu of all the different U.S. economic releases.

GEW <Go>—Global Economy Watch. Comparison of economic statistics by country.

IECO <Go> Compares economies worldwide by type, such as by unemployment or inflation.

ECOF <Go>—Finds economic statistics worldwide.

18

Politics and Policy

REPORTING ON GOVERNMENT becomes especially meaningful when it assesses the impact of legislation, policymaking and regulation on companies, markets, economies, consumers and taxpayers.

Bloomberg News covers governments because their decisions influence the price and trading of bonds, stocks, currencies and commodities, and because they raise billions of dollars by selling bonds to finance spending. We follow regulations and the people who influence the decisions because they determine the fate of corporate profits and whether investors will make or lose money. Politics and policy are covered to the extent that they help explain an economy and the people and institutions that shape it, including financial and commodity markets.

Reporting on government is defined by answering these questions:

Which companies or industries will be probable winners or losers?
Governments regulate society primarily by legislating business, so our stories should identify which companies and industries will be helped or hurt by new laws and regulations.

MF Global Holdings Ltd., Jefferies Group Inc. and dozens of smaller banks and brokers may win entree to the market for derivatives clearinghouses dominated by Wall Street's biggest banks under a U.S. regulatory proposal.

191

The Commodity Futures Trading Commission has proposed a rule that would require clearinghouses in the $583 trillion global swaps market to open membership to companies with at least $50 million in capital. ICE Trust LLC, the largest U.S. clearinghouse for credit-default swaps, and LCH.Clearnet Group Ltd., the world's largest interest-rate swaps clearinghouse, require members to have at least $5 billion in capital.

What is the likely impact of the government's decision on revenue for companies and industries? The shares of the companies identified in this story moved after the scoop:

Dialysis companies led by DaVita Inc. and Fresenius Medical Care AG may be on the verge of reversing a Medicare payment rule that's projected to cost the providers almost $250 million in revenue this year.

What is the likely impact on costs? Higher costs may reduce profits and force companies to fire workers or find other ways to reduce expenses.

The explosion at a Massey Energy Co. mine that killed 29 people last year is exacting a price for competitors International Coal Group Inc. and Patriot Coal Corp., as the Obama administration steps up safety inspections and penalties.

What is the impact on profitability?

Pfizer Inc., the world's largest drugmaker, leads pharmaceutical companies that have grown more reliant on U.S. government purchases following the recession, making the industry more vulnerable to price-cutting by Medicare and Medicaid.

What is the impact on market share? Legislation and regulation may benefit some companies or industries at the expense of others.

The biggest U.S. banks, facing tighter scrutiny and higher capital requirements, are pressing regulators to force hedge funds, money managers and insurers to share the pain.

What is the likely impact on company and industry strategies? How are they changing? How are they lobbying to change the rules?

Three years after collateralized debt obligations helped trigger the worst financial crisis in 70 years, Wall Street is exploring how to use them to deflect rules intended to prevent the next crisis.

What is the potential for acquisitions or sales of assets? The expenses of new regulation or changes in antitrust rules may result in mergers or asset sales.

Almost 5 percent of the nation's hospitals, those owned by physicians, may soon have "For Sale" signs.

A clause in legislation changing U.S. health care bars Medicare or Medicaid funds from being spent at new facilities getting patients referred by the doctor-owners. The number of such hospitals has quadrupled to about 270 in the last decade.

What is the probability of passage of the legislation? Hospital and insurance stocks rose or fell during President Obama's push to change the laws governing health-care coverage and costs.

Top executives from UnitedHealth Group Inc. and WellPoint Inc. are meeting almost monthly with their counterparts from Aetna Inc., Cigna Corp. and Humana Inc. in an informal lobbying alliance aimed at blunting parts of the health-care law, say people with knowledge of the sessions.

Every Bloomberg story about legislation before Congress or a parliament or another ruling body should identify in the first four paragraphs which commercial entities will be enriched or will be hurt.

The Republican victories in Congress mean U.S. companies from Goldman Sachs Group Inc. to WellPoint Inc. may be able to weaken or block what they consider President Barack Obama's anti-business policies on health care, the environment, taxes and financial reform.

Follow the Money

Industry teams should know how legislation and regulations in the works would affect their industries, identify potential winners and losers and collaborate with the government teams. Lobbyists, for example, are the representatives of companies and belong in every industry reporter's source list. Lobbyists hold more sway than the average citizen.

When we follow the money, we'll understand the politics as well. Reporters covering governments and their agencies ought to remember that markets are the front line of reaction to an economic statistic, policy initiative, budget, election, change in leadership or other action. The people who buy, sell, trade, invest and analyze money are the first to react to news because they have the most at stake: their own money or other people's money.

It isn't a coincidence that stock, bond and currency investors widely assumed that the North American Free Trade Agreement would receive congressional approval. Yet the most experienced political writers in Washington continued to write dueling vote-count stories until the day Congress voted, without mentioning the assumptions of investors and traders who had already made their bets. Bloomberg News reported the outcome before votes were counted because our reporters went to the people with the most at stake, an old-fashioned concept in journalism.

Never forget to follow the money.

We can use this approach to cover war and natural disasters, too. Our responsibility includes reporting the cost of devastation and the cost of rebuilding. Bloomberg goes wherever industry is marshaled and markets are made. World War II was the most important story of the 20th century because it was the biggest economic, financial and business story as well as the biggest political and social story.

At the start of the 21st century, the biggest story has been the cause and effects of the deepest recession since the Great Depression, the spending (or not) of governments to stimulate their economies and markets, and how institutions and individuals recover from their accumulated debt.

Financing Government

Following the money means providing coverage of government bond sales that goes beyond recitation of numbers. When governments sell bonds, we have an opportunity—and an obligation—to provide the latest scoop on a country's financial and economic health, recent history and prospects. Provide the following information in the first four paragraphs:

What's the size and amount of the transaction?

Why is the government selling securities?

Why do investors want them?

Will the transaction succeed?

By the fourth or fifth paragraph, add investors' comments to show whether the sale will be a success or a flop. The easiest way to meet this obligation is to write a curtain-raiser that includes most of these elements. When the day of the sale arrives, the reporter is in a position to deliver a detailed and polished piece on deadline.

> *Brazil sold $1.5 billion of bonds, locking in its lowest borrowing rates after a two-month rally in the nation's benchmark security.*
>
> *The 9.25 percent bonds due in 2010 were priced to yield 9.45 percent, the central bank said today in a statement. Merrill Lynch & Co. and Credit Suisse First Boston managed the sale for Brazil, which is South America's largest economy.*
>
> *The sale is Brazil's biggest this year and comes a day after the 8 percent bond due 2014 climbed to a record on speculation that the nation's credit rating will be upgraded. The bond has more than doubled in price in the past year on confidence that President Luiz Inacio Lula da Silva's government will repay debt after it cut spending, trimmed the budget deficit and brought down inflation.*

Opinion Polls

Surveys of public opinion, also known as polls, make news. Ephemeral and often misleading, polls nevertheless tell us what we think, and that explains their headline appeal. For journalists, the temptation to rely on polls grows in direct proportion to the complexity of the event and the difficulty of providing in-depth reporting.

Keep in mind that polls are a snapshot of opinion at a particular time and don't predict behavior. Instead of *A Gallup Organization poll predicts Smith will beat Jones by 12 percentage points,* write *A Gallup Organization poll shows Smith leading Jones by 12 percentage points.*

Any story that cites surveys of public opinion, whether about political candidates or issues, should include these pieces of information:

Size of the survey sample. National polls in the United States typically have a sample size of 1,000 to 1,200 adults; state polls often run between 500 and 800. Every story should note whether some answers are applicable only to particular groups, such as registered voters or likely voters. This is important in political polls, because the margin of error for such groups will be larger than for the entire survey.

Who was polled. There are three common groups surveyed: adults, registered voters and likely voters. Be specific.

Adults are those 18 and older who reside in the U.S. and may include people who aren't eligible to vote because they aren't citizens or are otherwise restricted under state election laws. Typically, general questions about the state of the country, the economy or support for a war are asked of the largest sample, such as all adults.

Registered voters are adults who say they are registered to vote in their local jurisdiction. While all registered voters are eligible to vote, not all eligible voters are registered and not all adults are eligible.

Likely voters are often identified by polling firms through a set of questions including whether the respondent voted in past elections and intends to vote this year.

The survey of 1,004 adults nationwide, including those who may not be eligible to vote, showed that 54 percent said the nation is heading in the wrong direction.

The margin of error. This shows whether the point spread is statistically significant. It is always expressed as *plus or minus x.x percentage points.*

Say a poll shows one candidate leading by 23 percent to 20 percent. If the margin of error was 4.4 percentage points, the leader could become the laggard in a random sample the next day. This helps put the results in perspective.

Some surveys may report samples only from likely voters. In that case, use the total margin.

When the poll was conducted. Stories should define the period when questions were posed to indicate whether the figures are current or have been overtaken by events. Were they just before or after a major speech or news event? What was the result when the same question was asked last month? Results more than a week or two old are usually worthless except when compared with recent results.

Is the result a change from the earlier survey from the same polling organization or from another polling firm? Call the polling firm or an outside expert who can explain the difference. Points that may help explain the difference include the size of the samples for each poll, the days of the week when the polls were taken—workdays or weekends—and the number of days the polls spanned. The margin of error also may be a factor. Two polls showing a 6-point difference for one candidate or the other are not significantly divergent if both surveys have an error margin of plus or minus 3 percentage points.

Where the poll was conducted. In the early stages of a political campaign, for instance, national preference polls about a party's candidates say little, and national polls about a president's performance may say a lot.

How the poll was conducted. Telephone is the most common and statistically accurate method of getting a random sample. There are occasional exceptions, such as exit polls on election day.

Any Internet survey—sometimes called an *interactive* poll—or poll in which the respondents send in a questionnaire, click choices on a website or call a toll-free telephone number should be ignored. The results aren't coming from a random sample and can't give an accurate indicator.

Identify the poll. Instead of a lead that says *according to a poll,* use the organization's name: *according to an Annenberg poll.*

If we are summarizing a story from another organization that fails to mention any of the background data, note that in our story. Check the website of the polling firm or ask the polling group. If the information isn't available, regard the survey as suspect.

We should only write about legitimate random surveys sponsored by independent entities, such as reputable news organizations or nonpartisan public-interest research groups and university-affiliated policy institutes. Beware of polls from political parties, campaigns and advocacy groups. Some polls paid for by advocacy groups don't transparently describe the relationship. Polling is as much art as science, and it isn't difficult to frame questions or interpret results with a specific outcome in mind.

19

People

STORIES ABOUT MONEY are, ultimately, stories about people: portfolio managers, investors, analysts, traders, investment bankers, commercial bankers, company officials and the like.

If we don't know the people on our beats, what they do, where they're doing it, when they're doing it and how they do it, we don't know our beats. If we cover stocks, bonds, currencies or commodities, we need to know the answers to these questions:

Who's the most successful trader? Why?

Who was the most successful and isn't now? Why?

What do they get paid?

Whose prediction was the most accurate? The least accurate?

Which firm pays the most? The least?

Who changed firms the most in the past five years? Who stayed put?

Which firm had the best earnings record in the past five years? The worst record?

Each answer is a story about people.

Reporters who cover markets, for instance, are in the best position to break news about the people in those markets. People love to read about people. Our customers love to read about themselves. Stories without people won't have many people reading them.

We have to know what questions will get people talking. If you called someone, identified yourself as a reporter for Bloomberg News and asked *So what's the outlook today?* that person would conclude that you probably didn't have any idea. If you asked whether the dollar's climb to more than 100 yen means the so-called dollar crisis is over, that person might want to engage you in conversation.

Include the age, education, work history and biographical anecdotes of the story's protagonists. *Rupert Murdoch, the 80-year-old chairman of News Corp., said he has no plans to retire.* Readers are curious to know everything they can about newsmakers. These anecdotes demonstrate our passion for detail and make the reporting more credible.

Because we appreciate that most events aren't newsworthy without people, we should also appreciate that our recipe for news is incomplete without a daily dose of profiles. There is no good story without people, and there is no coverage of a big event that shouldn't include a profile.

Profiling the people behind an event helps readers appreciate the significance of the news. Every time there's a major change at a company, it helps to provide a quick profile of the person behind the news, typically the chief executive. Same-day or overnight delivery is a winner, as a profile becomes a must-read because of timeliness.

Follow the example of details and collect just the facts and anecdotes: ages; physical characteristics such as height, weight and eye color; parents' occupations; siblings; education; employment history; achievements; failures; hobbies; notable quotes—these are some of the details that help build the story. Even if we never talk to the person, we can tell his or her story without compromising accuracy.

Anecdotes are especially important. A one-sentence anecdote such as, *He hasn't driven a car since he crashed his father's Buick LeSabre in 1972* or *She stopped eating meat after her sophomore year at Pleasantville High School* can be more informative than three paragraphs of quotations.

Compare the draft and published versions of this passage from a profile of former Brazilian President Luiz Inacio Lula da Silva. Which is more memorable?

Before:

The former union chief, who's missing a finger from a lathe accident, made failed bids for the presidency in 1989, 1994 and 1998, pledging to boost state control of the economy and break up big landholdings.

After:

He quit school at 14 and worked in a warehouse, then a screw factory. When he was 19, he got a job at a metalworking shop. In his authorized biography, he explains how he lost the little finger of his left hand there: One night a part on the arm of a press broke, causing the stamper to fall. He had to wait for the shift to end at 6 a.m., when the shop owner arrived, before he could go to a doctor, who amputated the crushed finger.

In 1969, he started organizing Sao Paulo auto workers, leading strikes against military rulers in the 1970s. He served a month in prison in 1980 and created the Workers' Party later the same year. The former union chief made failed bids for the presidency in 1989, 1994 and 1998, pledging to boost state control of the economy and break up big landholdings.

Executives speak in platitudes. They speak in jargon. They are big-picture people. They are politicians. They are used to talking to people who hang on their every word. Collecting two pithy quotes from an hourlong interview with an executive is doing well.

Be ready to ask follow-up questions. Here are four of the most important:

How?

This leads to the anecdotes and examples that provide the proof.

EXECUTIVE: *We're changing our culture to be more customer-centric and open.*

REPORTER: *How are you doing that?*

EXECUTIVE: *We've removed all the portraits of past chairmen from the head-quarters lobby and carted them off to the boardroom.*

Can you give me an example?

REPORTER: *Can you give me an example?*

EXECUTIVE: *We dropped the coat-and-tie dress code in favor of casual dress.*

REPORTER: *Anything more?*
EXECUTIVE: *No one gets a job in the executive suite without putting in a week at a store.*

Why?

EXECUTIVE: *We are opening a new plant in China next month.*
REPORTER: *Why are you expanding in China now?*
How have you prepared for the possibility of an economic slowdown there?
Are you concerned that your suppliers may be using prison labor?
Can you give me an example of how you have managed to expand in a similar market?

Which companies have you learned from? Good executives are always learning. When Jack Welch ran General Electric Co., he shamelessly adopted ideas from other companies.

20

Stories

Headlines allow readers to decide whether a story is worthy of their attention. Subheadlines make longer stories easier to read by breaking up blocks of text. Trashlines explain why stories are updated and corrected. Datelines let readers know the date of the event. Bylines show who did the writing, reporting and editing, and provide telephone numbers and e-mail addresses in case readers want to contact those people.

Bloomberg News stories also include links that connect the text to functions and information, lending credibility and authority by showing that which words can often only tell.

Story Headlines

Writing headlines must be as much an exercise of skill and judgment as any four-paragraph lead. The best are graceful, precise and specific, and depend on nouns and verbs. They make it easy to understand the story by providing as much detail as possible. The headline must surprise.

Headlines often begin with the name of the subject: the company, firm, country, agency or person central to the story. A headline without a name, or with the name buried in the middle or at the end, is as easy to dismiss as a headline without news.

Obama Names Former Shuttle Commander Bolden as New NASA Chief obscures the news by featuring President Obama. *Shuttle Commander Charles Bolden Named NASA Head by Obama* puts the news out front.

Be as specific as needed with names. Walt Disney Co. doesn't need Walt or Co. in the headline. There is only one Disney. Dow may refer to Dow Chemical Co. or Dow Corning Corp., as well as the stock indexes that start with Dow Jones. Include enough of the name to distinguish the subject from others with similar names.

Define the news and action. *U.S. Criticizes China Statement on Use of Force Against Taiwan* characterizes the news and doesn't explain what the U.S. said. *U.S. Says China's Statement on Taiwan Force Is 'Unhelpful'* tells more.

Include a verb, preferably an active verb: *Lufthansa Pilots Threaten Strike After Talks Collapse*.

Abbreviations such as *Govt, CEO, CFO, CIO, Intl, Ops, Cont Ops, Qtr, Yr, Mln, Bln* and *Tln* should be avoided because they are difficult to understand and aesthetically inferior.

Add a *why* or a *so what* to entice readers. *Australian Mortgage Approvals Rise by Most in Two Years* explains why the reader should care more than *Australian November Home-Loan Approvals Rise 2.7%*.

Use context and perspective instead of reeling off numbers. *New York City Purchasers February Index Reaches 69.8* isn't as enlightening as *New York City Business Expansion Is Fastest in a Decade*.

Some newsmakers need no introduction. Instead of beginning the headline with the obvious identity in *ECB's Trichet Says Rates Still 'Low' After Increase*, start with the newsmaker and weave in the context: *Trichet Says ECB's Rates Still 'Low' After Increase*.

Include the country name, when appropriate, to avoid confusion. U.S. FTC distinguishes the U.S. Federal Trade Commission from Japan's Fair Trade Commission.

Select words that tantalize the reader and advertise the story's theme, such as *nuclear, terror, China, salary, cancer, billionaire, Harvard* and *hedge fund*. Consider dropping numbers, time periods and attribution to make way for words that will sell the story. *NYC Says Debris Near Blast Site Positive for Asbestos* doesn't capture the imagination as much as *Asbestos Is Found in Debris Near New York Blast Site.*

Consider our global audience. Will anyone in Mumbai, London or Bogota know that *Undecided Voters Are Pessimistic on Economy, Poll Shows* is about the U.S. election? More precise: *Undecided U.S. Voters Are Gloomy on Economy, Poll Shows.*

Headlines should match the story. Retain the local currency in the headline, not the conversion to U.S. dollars.

Use as much of the space allowed as possible because the headline is prime real estate for selling the story.

Capitalize the first letter of all words except two- or three-letter prepositions and conjunctions that aren't part of a phrase: *and, in, of, on, to, Tie Up, If Only.* For comments, enclose within single quotation marks rather than the double quote marks used in story text.

Style and Punctuation

When a time period—week, month, quarter, year, etc.—isn't specified or is used as a modifier, use the present tense:

U.S. Housing Starts Plunge 17% to Lowest Level on Record
Acme Manufacturing's Net Increases 6% as Sales Gain
Japan's Trade Surplus Widens as Car Exports Surge

When the time period appears after the verb, use the past tense for the verb:

U.S. Housing Starts Fell to Record Low in January
Acme Manufacturing's Profit Increased 6% in 2002
Japan's Trade Surplus Widened in February on Car Exports

When *says* is the first verb, we usually follow with a verb that uses the past tense:

King Says U.K. Economy Grew in First Quarter
Fed Minutes Show Policymakers Said Growth Was Accelerating

Before a merger or acquisition is completed, use the infinitive form of the verb:

Ambition Software to Acquire Zebra Tech for $200 Million
Liz Claiborne Agrees to Buy Clothes Designer Juicy Couture

After the merger or acquisition is completed, switch to the present tense:

Ambition Software Buys Zebra Tech for $200 Million
Liz Claiborne Buys Clothing Designer Juicy Couture

Use semicolons only in headlines that have two subjects and two verbs. Otherwise, use commas. Think of the semicolon as acting as a period; a comma as the word *and*:

GM Plans to Close Three Plants, Fire 800 Workers
GM Plans to Close Three Plants; Union Vows Strike

The fewer punctuation marks, abbreviations and conjunctions such as "and," the easier the headline will read.

When writing about securities or indexes as they fluctuate, use the appropriate verb without a specific percentage change: *Wal-Mart Tumbles on Reduced Profit Forecast*. Once a closing price is available, add the change: *Wal-Mart Falls 11% on Lower Profit Forecast*.

Stand-Alone Headlines

Nothing is more crucial to the success of Bloomberg News than being the First Word. Most often, that's accomplished through the stand-alone headlines that editors publish when news breaks. Customers often say their survival depends on the timeliness and content of these headlines.

Editors should send as many headlines as needed to give customers the depth, breadth and context of the news:

*JP MORGAN TO BOOST DIVIDEND TO 25 CENTS A SHARE
*JP MORGAN TO BUY BACK $15 BILLION COMMON STOCK
*JP MORGAN QUARTERLY DIVIDEND WAS 5 CENTS
*JP MORGAN SAYS $8 BILLION BUYBACK APPROVED FOR '11
*JP MORGAN COMMENTS IN E-MAILED STATEMENT

*JP MORGAN SHARES EXTEND GAIN TO 1.8%
*S&P 500 BANKS INDEX EXTENDS GAIN TO 2%

Notice that these headlines start with an asterisk, which indicates that no story accompanies this news. The headlines should be in all capital letters and at least one headline in a group about company news should include the stock's ticker at the end. The software that editors use to send the headlines automatically takes care of these chores.

Stand-alone headlines need not fill an entire line like story headlines. It's faster and often clearer to publish two short headlines rather than one long one.

While stand-alone headlines have more leeway in using abbreviations, they should conform in other ways.

Be aware of our global audience. Identify the subject and locate the news to prevent confusion. GlaxoSmithKline's stock declined after we published this headline: *GLAXOSMITHKLINE SAYS 1Q SALES GROWTH WILL NOT BE SUSTAINABLE. The headline was corrected because the news was about the company's Indian unit. Better: *GLAXOSMITHKLINE INDIA SAYS 1Q SALES GROWTH NOT SUSTAINABLE.

Subheadlines

The purpose of a subheadline is visual: to break up a block of type so it is easier on the eye.

A subheadline is required on any full screen of text except for the first screen, with the byline, or the last screen, with the reporter and editor contact information. Use one subheadline for each screen.

Subheadlines should be two or three words. Consider aesthetics: Two short words will look skimpy, and three long words will look crowded. Follow the style for story headlines, such as using single quotation marks around direct quotes.

The subheadline should refer to information in the paragraph that immediately follows. It should be a label or express a complete thought. Avoid phrases such as *Well Above* that don't make sense on their own. If the paragraph after the subheadline refers to a pending stock sale, for instance, *Pending Sale* will do just fine.

Here's how a subheadline would appear in text:

The theft would be the largest embezzlement from a major U.S. financial institution since OpVantage, a unit of Fitch Risk, began tracking control breakdowns at financial firms a decade ago, said Penny Cagan, senior vice president of OpVantage.

Handwriting Doesn't Match

Ashok Kashyap, a handwriting expert in New Delhi with 40 years of experience, said Gilhotra's actual signature doesn't match the signature on the document accepted by Merrill.

Place the subheadlines toward the middle of the screen, anywhere from one-third to two-thirds of the way down the page. To see where the text breaks should be placed, click on the Preview Lite button in the Bloomberg's customized version of Microsoft Word. Center the words horizontally.

In breaking news stories, the subhead's content is less important than its placement, especially under deadline pressure. In feature stories, use the luxury of extra time to compose subheads that entice the reader to continue through the story.

Trashlines

All updated and corrected stories require brief explanations of the changes of content in the new versions.

Place the trashline between the headline and byline, with one blank line above and below. Indent and enclose in parentheses. Explain what new content was added, and in which paragraphs. Be concise and specific. Consider a reader who, having read an earlier story, has to sift through the paragraphs to figure out what's new. Cite the two or three biggest changes and identify the affected paragraphs. A broad reference such as *Adds details d*oesn't tell the reader what details were added or where they appear. Better: *(Adds consumer confidence report in fifth paragraph and bond yields in sixth paragraph.)*

Style guidelines for abbreviations, capitalization, punctuation and grammar apply. Changes such as moving a paragraph, style fixes, subhead placement or changes to coding don't need to be addressed.

Journalism descriptions such as *edits, revise, rewrites* or *recasts* lack precision. *Correcting typo* isn't acceptable because some readers wouldn't know that *typo* is short for typographical error. Make the action in the trashline clear to all readers worldwide.

Before:

> *(Closes shares.)*

After:

> *(Updates with closing share prices in seventh paragraph.)*

Use ordinal numbers when referring to the paragraphs. Spell out first through ninth, and use numerals for 10th and higher. Not paragraph 5, paragraph 17. Phrases such as *second section, third section a*nd so on are meaningless. Instead, use paragraph numbers. In long stories such as magazine pieces, use the subheadline as a marker.

Before:

> *(Rewrites. Updates with CEO comment in paragraph 2. Adds details throughout.)*

After:

> *(Adds comment from Chief Executive Officer John Smith in second paragraph, details on venture in fourth paragraph.)*

When stories are corrected, always note what was fixed and where it was located.

> *(Corrects name of law firm to Winken, Blinken & Nod in third paragraph.)*

If erroneous information was provided by a person, company, government or other organization, indicate the source of the mistake.

> *(Company corrects date when John Smith became chairman in third paragraph of story published June 3.)*

Datelines

Bloomberg News uses only the date and Bloomberg name in datelines, not a city.

Sept. 15 (Bloomberg) -- Lehman Brothers Holdings Inc., the fourth-largest U.S. investment bank, succumbed to the subprime mortgage crisis it helped create in the biggest bankruptcy filing in history.

Provide locations for where the news is unfolding in the first four paragraphs. That means specifying where a company is located, where a government official spoke, where trading occurred, where an investor is based, where a battle happened or where a conference took place.

Often we need to use multiple locations for different subjects or elements in a story: The company is based in London, the chief executive officer is speaking at a conference in Montreal, the main shareholder is in Dubai and the shares are moving in U.S. trading.

Market stories should give the location of trading in the lead. If we say U.S. stocks rose or U.K. stocks rose, that's clear enough for the top, unless we're talking about a country's stocks trading in another region, such as Japanese shares trading in the U.S. Many commodities, securities and currencies are traded around the world, so it's important to specify the city in the lead: *Gold futures rose in New York trading* or *Crude oil fell in London.*

Be as specific as possible with locations. Saying a company is German or Malaysian or India's biggest retailer isn't enough. Include the headquarters city.

Give the location of government agencies, and specify which country when applicable. The U.S. Central Intelligence Agency, for example, has its headquarters in McLean, Virginia, not Washington. For example: *according to Statistics Canada in Ottawa.*

Say where government officials are speaking from: *said Governor Jerry Brown in Sacramento, California,* or *Federal Reserve Chairman Ben S. Bernanke told reporters after a speech at a Tokyo conference hosted by the Japanese Association of Monetary Economics.*

The date in the dateline should reflect when and where the news in the lead occurred. For example, a reporter in New York is summarizing a story about events in Japan, where it is past midnight. While it may be June 3 in New York, the dateline should be June 4. Match the date to where the action happened. If a Japanese news service is reporting June 4 on something that happened June 3, use June 4 as the dateline.

If it's an anecdotal lead, use the date that is today for the location of that anecdote.

In press summaries, say when the news happened. The date when the news was published or broadcast isn't necessary unless it's relevant. If we're summarizing a story that doesn't contain a time element, don't insert one. We can't assume that the time element is indicated by the date in the dateline. It could have been days before.

Bylines

The byline should name the one or two reporters who contributed the most to the story. Consider who broke the news as well as who wrote the story. That includes broadcast staff. The names and their order in the byline may change as information is added in updates. Bylines with three names require an executive editor's approval. The byline is placed between the headline and text. The story should look like this:

Intel Profit Rises 44% on First Sales Gain in Six Quarters

By Ian King
  July 17 (Bloomberg) -- Intel Corp., the world's largest computer-chip maker, said second-quarter profit rose 44 percent after sales gained for the first time in six periods on improving demand for laptops.
  Net income increased to $1.28 billion, or 22 cents a share, from $885 million, or 15 cents, a year earlier, the Santa Clara, California–based company said today in a statement distributed by Business Wire.

For Related News and Information:
Intel earnings news: {INTC US <Equity> TCNI ERN <GO>}
Intel earnings history: {INTC US <Equity> ERN <GO>}
Intel's earnings forecasts: {INTC US <Equity> GUID <GO>}
Earnings analysis: {EA <GO>}
To compare Intel with peers: {INTC US <Equity> PPC <GO>}

With assistance from Monica Bertran in New York. Editors: Cesca Antonelli, Jonathan Thaw.

To contact the reporter on this story:
Ian King in San Francisco at +1-415-743-3548 or lanking@bloomberg.net.

To contact the editor responsible for this story:
Cesca Antonelli at +1-202-654-4305 or
fantonelli@bloomberg.net.

Deviating from this style can disrupt the formatting of stories sent to newspapers. For that reason, use the specialized macro for the newsroom that's built into the Microsoft Word software. Hitting the Alt and Y keys activates the macro, which is faster than typing out the byline, reduces typographical errors and ensures style consistency. Leave one line between the headline and the byline. There is no space between the byline and the text.

At the end of the story, leave one line of space before the *with assistance from* tagline. The tagline must start with a double hyphen, flush left, immediately followed by the name and location of any additional reporters who contributed material to the story. Don't leave a space between the end of the double hyphen and the start of the tagline.

The editor credits at the end of a story should list a maximum of two names: the person primarily responsible for editing the story and the one who proofed it. Use full names.

The tagline is followed by information on how to contact the reporters and team leaders. After *To contact the reporters on this story:*, skip to the next line and include the reporter's name, location, telephone number and e-mail address. Use the country code and city code for all telephone numbers, separated by hyphens. When there are two reporters listed in the byline, include locations and contact information for both of them.

The reporter's location should reflect where the reporter was physically when gathering information for the main action of the story. This is important to help newspapers that want to use a city in their datelines. We want to disclose where the reporter visited, while we don't want to imply that a reporter was on-site when reporting was done by telephone. Even when the reporter has returned from the field, use that location, for both news and feature stories.

After *To contact the editors responsible for this story:*, go to the next line and add the team leader's telephone number and e-mail address. The location isn't needed. If more than one team worked on a story, or a team has more than one leader, use all the team leaders' names in the contact line. If a story is being updated and it is nighttime where it originated, only use the name of the team leader who can still be reached at the office telephone number.

If the team leader has the day off, use the deputy's name. On weekends and holidays, name the supervising editor. When the reporter's team leader and deputy live in a far-removed time zone, list the bureau chief as the editor contact. In some regional features, cite the bureau chief instead of the team leader as the editor responsible for the story.

If an editor both writes and sends a two-paragraph story to fill headlines, use that name for the byline, the editor list and the reporter contact.

Links

There is no better way for Bloomberg users to appreciate the scope of the terminal than through the clickable blue links we embed throughout each story and the For Related News and Information tour at the end that connect to functions, news, data, media clips, graphics, photographs and Internet sites. These connections make our news more useful by integrating Bloomberg's stories, data and analytical tools and by providing a way for customers to interact with our services and learn what's on the terminal.

The first screen of any story should include clickable links that highlight the Bloomberg applications that best capture the most important point of the article.

Link the names of newsmakers to their profiles or archived interviews on the Bloomberg. Company names should direct readers to functions that help explain or support the news, such as a list of executives or descriptive information. Securities such as stocks, bonds and indexes can point to charts of prices or analytical programs.

We can also link to the original sources of information, helping make the news transparent. These would include press releases, court documents, regulatory documents or the Internet version of a story we are summarizing. Too many links will distract readers and make the story difficult to read. Too few links won't help highlight all that's available on the Bloomberg.

Highlight words that suggest the link, such as names, information or attributions. Links on descriptive words such as *high* or *slow* aren't intuitive. Linking a company's name to the front page of its website, such as connecting General Motors Co. to http://www.gm.com, can create the impression that the company has sponsored the link or paid for advertising, especially in stories that aren't critical of the company. If the information isn't available on the Bloomberg, link to pertinent documents or informational or investor-relations pages such as biographies on the company's website.

At the end of the story, insert a section that points readers to news searches, functions and information related to the topic. It should contain a link to the ticker of the main company mentioned:

> *For Related News and Information:*
> *Citigroup earnings stories: {C US <Equity> TCNI ERN <GO>}*
> *Banking earnings stories: {TNI BNK ERN <GO>}*
> *Citigroup earnings history: {C US <Equity> EM <GO>}*
> *Citigroup's sales by segment: {C US <Equity> PGEO <GO>}*
> *Comparison with peers: {C US <Equity> PPC <GO>}*
> *Relative value comparison: {C US <Equity> RVC <GO>}*
> *Earnings analysis: {EA <GO>}*
> *Top stories about finance: {FTOP <GO>}*

When writing multiple stories about a news event, add a paragraph after the subheadline on the second screen that refers and links to the related articles. Enclose the paragraph in parentheses.

> *(For a related story on the Supreme Court ruling's impact on class action litigation, click here. To read a story on how it may affect defenses against employee claims, click here. For a story on how the decision may affect company bias policies, click here.)*

Coding

Customers can only appreciate our efforts to report, write and edit authoritatively if they can find our stories. It's up to reporters and editors to ensure that stories are coded for the appropriate news menus.

These menus come in three main categories: companies, news subjects and people. We also add codes for economic indexes and currencies.

Think about adding at least a few codes from each of these general categories:

Geographic codes that point to the countries or states where the action took place or where companies are located.

Industry codes that identify what industries are involved.

Market codes for stocks, bonds, currencies, commodities, etc.

Action codes for particular types of company actions, such as mergers and acquisitions, stock purchases, initial stock sales.

Security codes for types of securities, such as convertible bonds, options or warrants.

Reporters and editors are responsible for knowing codes or finding the right ones to use. Adding too many or too few codes can confuse customers, who will wonder why some codes are overflowing with unrelated stories or why they can't find a story under an obvious code.

Codes for companies and subjects must be added manually. They go at the bottom of the story and are positioned flush left. The codes for people are usually attached by editors when they publish the story.

Include each company's equity ticker and exchange code, followed by <Equity>. This will make the story available in the news section of a company's ticker. Tickers can also be added for economic indexes.

For each subject, include NI, a space and its code. To check for the latter, type a word or phrase describing the subject at the top of a Bloomberg terminal screen and search the pop-up window for the closest match. Or enter NI <Go> and type your best guess in the search box. Or use the search engine, NSE <Go>.

Here is an example of how the coding section might look for an earnings story on Qualcomm Inc., which licenses patents for mobile phones and makes semiconductors:

QCOM US <Equity>
MOT US <Equity>
NOK1V FH <Equity>
ERICB SS <Equity>

NI COS
NI TEL
NI WRLS
NI SEM
NI TEC
NI ERN
NI US

NI CA
NI IL
NI FINLAND
NI SWEDE
NI PATENT

QCOM is Qualcomm's ticker. The other companies are the tickers for three mobile-phone makers—Motorola Inc., Nokia Oyj and Ericsson AB—mentioned in the story. The *US* designates that Qualcomm's and Motorola's stocks are trading in the United States. The *FH* symbol following the Nokia ticker notes that it trades on the Helsinki exchange in Finland while the *SS* indicates the Stockholm exchange in Sweden.

NI COS belongs on all stories about companies. The next four NI codes are for industries: *TEL* for telecommunications equipment, W*RLS* for wireless phones, *SEM* for semiconductors and *TEC* for technology. *NI ERN* goes on all earnings stories.

The last five codes are for the U.S. and California, Qualcomm's home country and state; Illinois, the home state of Motorola; Finland, home to Nokia; and Sweden, home to Ericsson. The regional codes are popular with customers and newspaper editors. Be sure to include them so that stories will get their attention.

Updates

Any story that contains new information and doesn't correct the previous version must be identified as an update. All updates have a numbered label—(1), (2), etc.—at the end of the headline.

Here are how headlines would appear with updates and corrections.

Ackman's Greatest Short Ever Told Began With Handshake Refused
Bear Stearns Thrives in Diaspora Giving to Sheryl Crow Tune (1)
Japan Uses Helicopters, Water Cannons to Quell Meltdown (2)
All Clear Sounded as Markets Shrug Off Multiple Black Swans (3)
Bini Smaghi Says Euro-Area Rates Are 'Expansionist' (Correct)

Update the story when we have details, context or quotes to add that enhance the understanding of the news. Obtaining more facts doesn't mean they're worth adding, or that they can't wait until a later version. Too many updates will exasperate readers and waste the reporters' and editors' time.

Corrections don't have any effect on numbering. If a newly published story gets corrected and then updated, for example, the updated version would still have the (1) label in the headline.

When the main news in a lead changes, publish a new story with a fresh headline rather than an update, even when much of the material stays the same.

Limit stories to three updates to spare readers the confusion created by multiple updates. If there is more to say beyond the third update, start a new story with a new headline.

If the previous version of the story appeared in any TOP <Go> menu, make sure the updated version takes its place. If the lead is rewritten, alert the editors who manage the TOP menus because the headline should be changed.

Repeat stories only for formatting or transmission errors. All repeats require a (Repeat) label at the end of the headline: *Brazil Raises $3 Billion by Selling 10-Year Bonds (Repeat)*

Summaries

Bloomberg News doesn't subscribe to the *not invented here* school of journalism. If another news organization—a competing news service or broadcast outlet, a local newspaper, a reputable Web site, etc.—breaks news that our customers need because it may move markets or is of public interest, we should publish that news as soon as possible.

Strive to deliver a comprehensive and consistent package of news so that Bloomberg is a complete source of information, either as reported by Bloomberg News or as summarized by Bloomberg News. Accurate and timely delivery is important because markets are sensitive to all kinds of events, whether a man-made or natural disaster, terrorist attack or political scandal.

As we've insisted since the beginning of Bloomberg News in 1990, our readers don't care who reports the news as long as it's correct. Here's a sample:

Buffett Marries Longtime Companion Menks, World-Herald Says

By Catherine Larkin

Aug. 31 (Bloomberg) -- Billionaire Warren Buffett married his longtime companion, Astrid Menks, yesterday in a private ceremony on his 76th birthday, the Omaha World-Herald reported.

Buffett, chief executive officer of Berkshire Hathaway Inc., and Menks, 60, were wed by Douglas County District Judge Patricia Lamberty at about 5 p.m. at the home of Buffett's daughter, Susan A. Buffett, in Omaha, Nebraska, the World-Herald reported. Susan Buffett said the couple had been considering marriage for a while and don't have plans to take a honeymoon, the newspaper reported.

Buffett got married before, to Susan Thompson Buffett, in 1952, the World-Herald said. His first wife moved out of their house in 1977 and arranged for her husband to meet Menks before she died in July 2004 of a stroke, the newspaper said.

When another organization breaks news that's available on the Internet or terminal, editors should first publish a headline that links to the article or website. That's the fastest way to give customers access to the news. Once that's done, we should write a summary for any important or market-moving reports, even if we plan to write our own story or could match it with a telephone call or two. Think of it this way: headline, link, summarize, match, advance.

Always consider the credibility of the news organization and the sources it is citing. Some stories, such as those about idle speculation, may not be worth a summary. When in doubt, ask your team leader.

Summaries rarely should be longer than one Bloomberg screen. They can be one paragraph or even one sentence. Use your own words. Pick up quotes from the original report only when they're central and compelling to the story.

Attribute the information and quotations in the headline and each paragraph. Never use *news reports said*. Be specific: *the Financial Times said*.

News from different organizations should get its own summary. If more than one publication is reporting the same details, such as the Boston Globe and the Boston Herald, summarize the better story. If news organizations are providing different details, write separate summaries.

Before summing, search the Bloomberg to see whether we have the news. If another publication's story contains major elements that we lack—a fact, a development or a significant voice—summarize those.

A paragraph that adds information not in the report may be included when we need to clarify or enhance the information from the original story. Attribute so there is no risk that readers ascribe it to the original news source. Information from the Bloomberg, such as size and scope, should be added in a paragraph at the end with appropriate attribution.

Press summaries shouldn't be updated, except to add comment sought by Bloomberg for balance and fairness. If the comment is contrary to what we have summarized, it should become a new story, leading with the denial of information included in our original summary. If there's a denial, call the news organization for a response.

Include a link to the original story in the text of the summary.

Use a dateline that reflects the date when the action occurred, instead of the date the publication ran the story.

When the identity of the source isn't clear, be as specific as possible: *the Associated Press said, citing unidentified people close to the situation;* or *the Washington Post reported, without saying where it obtained the information.*

It's acceptable to use globally recognizable abbreviations for media organizations in headlines, including: *ABC, AP, BBC, CBS, CNBC, CNN, FT, NYT, WSJ.* Abbreviations for regional news outlets such as *SCMP* for the South China Morning Post or *F&M* for Finanza & Mercati are vague.

Fairness for Summaries

When a story being summarized includes an accusation or information that may be considered defamatory or unfair, or is based on information from an unidentified person, call the subject of the story for a response and include that in the summary. Don't rely on the original report's response.

Calling a switchboard or voicemail, leaving a message, and then writing that no one could be reached or someone didn't return a call isn't sufficient. Call as many numbers as are available. Seek help from other teams.

We must be satisfied that our attempt to seek comment was thorough enough that writing *Smith didn't return a telephone call seeking comment* is accurate and fair. We try to be transparent even to the point of counting the number of calls placed. *Acme's public relations department didn't return two telephone calls and an e-mail seeking comment.*

Hold off publishing the summary until we're satisfied that our effort has been fair. That doesn't mean delay publication until we get a response. Weigh the seriousness of the allegation against how much we do to seek comment. For more serious allegations, make more calls and wait longer. When in doubt, discuss with a team leader, who may want to consult with our lawyers or the legal-news team.

Voices

Bloomberg News uses a format called Voices to send quotes as soon as possible after getting off the telephone with a trader or investor, a company executive, an economist, a government official or anyone else whose remarks are worth reporting promptly. Many derive from our television and radio interviews.

These items don't replace or delay stories. Instead, they give readers a flavor of what is happening before a more complete story is available. The key is speed, so the Voices stories are stripped of all but the bare essentials.

They are not meant to be complete transcripts and should be no more than one or two screens long. Reporters should select only the best quotes and put them in context. As always, avoid jargon.

If the speaker didn't identify the companies, markets, industries or people likely to be affected by the topic of the comments, add a paragraph that provides context. The reader shouldn't be forced to connect the dots.

Headlines for Voices should summarize the speaker's most interesting point. This will help draw readers.

Here's a sample:

Jim Rogers Says Agriculture Commodities Will Outperform Gold

By Mike McKee and Millie Munshi
June 11 (Bloomberg) -- Jim Rogers, chairman of Beeland Interests Inc., comments on commodity investments. Rogers predicted the start of the commodities rally in 1999.

On agriculture:
"Agriculture is depressed and it has been for a year. The fundamentals are changing radically and positively. That is the only thing I would put money into."

"Everybody is raising corn. If everybody plants corn, that means less soybeans, less cotton, less of everything else, and so all agricultural prices will be going up."

On gold:
"I would not tie gold and the dollar together. I own gold. I own all precious metals. I think you're going to make more money in agriculture than in gold. I would worry about gold."

Send all of these comments to NI VOICES and code them to the named person, companies and topics. After they are published, we can weave the best quotes into stories.

Sending to Newspapers

During the sending process, editors must designate whether to make the story available to Bloomberg's media clients. This usually takes one step: selecting the transmission code that will simultaneously send the story to the Bloomberg terminal as well as media subscribers.

Editors should send stories on general-interest topics outside of business, finance and economy subjects to the relevant departments at our newspaper customers. Stories about topics such as disasters, drug approvals, politics, obituaries, medical studies and product recalls require special coding to direct them to the correct departments.

Newspaper clients receive budgets during the day to alert them to published and scheduled stories. All budget items begin with a slug, which Bloomberg News editors attach to the story when sending. The slug sums up the story's topic in a few words to inform and entice newspaper editors.

Newspaper editors can wade through thousands of stories each day from Bloomberg News and other sources, and the slug line is often all they see.

Here are some guidelines for writing and attaching slugs:

Be concise. Provide just enough words to identify a story. Use no more than three words for the first version. (Later versions will need to include the word CORRECT or the number of the update as the last part of the slug.) Longer slugs may not display correctly at some newspapers, diminishing the chances that our story will be opened by an editor and selected for publication: CANADA-BUDGET-2, GLOBAL-MARKETS-CORRECT.

Be compelling. Use recognizable names, issues and keywords that will draw an editor's attention: SONY-JOBS, SIEMENS-CLOSINGS, BUFFETT-CURRENCY, AIR-CANADA-UNION.

Use action verbs. Tell the story in brief: SAMSUNG-DENIED-PERMIT, MONY-AXA-APPROVED, SHELL-NAMES-CEO.

Avoid punctuation. Except for hyphens between words, don't use periods, commas or parentheses in slugs. Use *US* and *UK*, for example, rather than *U.S.* and *U.K.* Ampersands are fine: *AT&T* is preferable to *ATT*.

Omit company identifiers. Avoid *Inc., Co., Corp., SA* and similar descriptions unless they are necessary for newspapers to tell the difference between two companies.

Think globally. Slugs are viewed by editors around the globe. Stories about economies, markets and governments should start with the country name: ARGENTINA-OUTPUT, FRANCE-HIRINGS, GREECE-STOCKS.

Be consistent. Stories edited by more than one bureau as they develop need to keep the same slug. If Tokyo files a story slugged US-JAPAN-TRADE, for example, then Washington must use that same slug in handling any updates.

Slugs for a package of stories must start with the same words. If the main lead is slugged ROYAL-BANK-ABN, then the slugs for all related sidebars must start with those three words: ROYAL-BANK-ABN-TIMELINE, ROYAL-BANK-ABN-SHARES, etc. This will enable editors searching for slugs that start ROYAL-BANK-ABN to retrieve all our stories.

Acquisitions. Use the company names. Most stories lead with the acquiring company, so to be consistent it's usually better to have the purchaser followed by the company being bought: ACQUIRER-ACQUIREE, BLACKSTONE-EQUITY-OFFICE.

Earnings. Start with the company name and end with -EARNS, as in IBM-EARNS.

Other company stories. Use the company name and a one-word description in most cases: SONY-SHARES, GM-PRODUCTION. Abbreviate the company name only when it will be recognizable worldwide. When there is more than one story on a company, add another word to describe the subject more exactly: GM-SALESFORECAST.

Election stories. Start with ELECT- followed by the state or country holding the elections, as in ELECT-HUNGARY.

Closing market stories. Start with the country, then the market, and end with -CLOSE, as in CANADA-BONDS-CLOSE.

Standing features. Regular items should bear the same root slug. For columns, use the writer's last name followed by the word COLUMN, as in BAUM-COLUMN.

Tables. Use -TABLE at the end of the slug: CPI-TABLE.

AV

Print, television and radio reporters should all be part of each story. By providing audio, video and print renditions of the news, we deliver the final word—spoken, seen and written—on any subject.

Sometimes this takes the form of a recording of an interview meant to produce quotes for a print story. This can be from the desk or in the field. Ask for training on technology that records telephone calls.

Reporters also have access to a voice recorder or handheld video camera for remote assignments such as news conferences or interviews, and the audio and video can be stored on the system. Company conference calls can also be recorded and archived.

Bloomberg Radio may use this audio for on-air sound bites. Bloomberg Television may produce the story for broadcast, often adding its own interviews.

The Bloomberg AV department will produce the audio and video into files that appear as stand-alone news content and as attachments to the print story. They will contain *index points* that highlight what was said and provide fast access to selected sections. You can find these on AV <Go> or NI AV <Go>.

An ideal Bloomberg News package includes a story, an audio recording of the conference call, a video or audio interview with a guest on television or radio, photographs, charts and a copy of the news release.

Inform the AV staff in advance about teleconferences, Webcasts, satellite feeds or other opportunities for gathering audio and video news. Include the date and time of the event and the call-in number, Web address or satellite coordinates.

AV also can arrange to record speeches, panel discussions and other events and feed them to a news bureau, freeing the reporter to pursue opportunities such as one-on-one interviews in the field. The sooner the AV staff is alerted, the better. It takes time to set up coverage and to order telephone lines if the event isn't available via telephone or Webcast.

The consent to record an interview is not the same as the consent to broadcast. Often, both are needed. In U.S. states and countries where the law allows journalists to record a telephone call without the other parties' consent, it's not a given that the conversation or conference call can be broadcast. AV and Multimedia should always ask the reporter whether broadcast consent was given before putting tapes on the system or putting them on air.

21

Questions

To WIN THE trust of readers, listeners and viewers, we must provide all the information they need as fast as we can. Here are some questions that will help reporters and editors give them that information.

Stock Activity

For the company:

Do you know what is causing the movement in your stock today?

Do you know who the big buyers or sellers are?

Are there any corporate developments to be announced, or is there any news pending?

Is the company planning to make any public announcements?

Have any analysts issued reports on your company today?

Have you held any meetings with analysts or investors recently? When is the next one?

For rumors and news reports:

Have you heard this rumor or report? What is the source?

What is your response? Is there an official response? If not, when will there be one?

What has the company said about the subject in the past?

For speculation involving another company:

Do you have any current business relationship with this company?
Is there an official response? If not, when will there be?
Which part of this report is true? False?

For stock activity between reporting periods:

How is the quarter/half going so far? Can you comment about sales and earnings trends?
Do you expect to meet, exceed or fall short of analysts' estimates?

For analysts, investors and traders:

Why are the shares moving? Are you aware of any news, rumors or actions by investors or brokers that may be moving the shares?
Can you confirm or deny the information?
If not, what has the company told you about this issue?
Do you agree or disagree with the latest information?
Are you investing in this stock or changing your recommendation?
What do you think about the company?
Has the information changed your view of the company's strategy? Its competitive position? Trends within the industry?
What are your earnings and sales estimates? Have you changed them recently? If so, why? If not, are you considering changing them?
What is your investment rating on the stock? Have you changed it recently? If so, why? If not, are you considering a change?
How much better or worse do you think the stock will perform than the market's benchmark index? During what time period?
Do you have a target price for the stock? Is there a price at which you would change your investment rating?
How recently have you spoken with the company? Was the contact a regular analysts' meeting, an individual visit or a telephone conversation?
When is your next visit scheduled?

For analysts:

Does your firm act as the company's broker or financial adviser?
Does your firm have a position in the company?

For investors:

Do you invest personally in the company?
Does your firm provide any other services to this company?
Do you manage any of the company's pension funds or other assets?
Can you suggest anyone else to speak with who has a strong opinion on this subject?

Equity and Debt Sales

How much will be sold? At what price?
Why now? What's different today from yesterday or tomorrow?
How does the price compare with forecasts? With other recent sales by similar sellers?
When was the company's most recent sale? How much was sold? At what price?
Why is the company borrowing or selling shares?
What will the seller do with the money?
Why would investors want the securities?
How does the company justify to investors an offering at this price and at this time?
What are the biggest risks before the sale?
Who is underwriting the sale? How much will the managers receive in fees? How do the fees compare with those of similar offerings?

For stock sales:

Who is selling: the company, shareholders, or both? In what proportions?
What percentage of the total shares does this represent?
By how much will this dilute current shares outstanding?
How does the price compare with similar companies?

For bond sales:

What type of bonds is the company selling?
When must the borrowings be repaid?
Is the company financing today because it expects interest rates to climb tomorrow? What do you expect borrowing costs to do this year?

What will you do with the proceeds?

Are you refinancing existing debt or borrowing additional funds?

Will this affect the ratings from Moody's Investors Service, Standard & Poor's or Fitch Ratings?

What currency will you be borrowing?

Will you be reaching the same investors who hold your existing debt? New ones?

Depending on the type of debt: Why with fixed-rate bonds instead of floating-rate notes? Why bonds that convert into shares?

What's your current debt-to-equity ratio and what's your target?

What sort of yield/spread will you have to pay? How does that compare with your other borrowings? Are you paying more or less this time? Why?

Are there any new restrictive covenants that investors would be concerned about?

Why borrow instead of using alternatives such as selling shares or financing internally?

Loans and Lines of Credit

Why the need for short-term money?

How much will the company receive?

What type of financing is being provided?

What are the terms? What is the interest rate? Repayment schedule?

What kind of collateral has been pledged?

What will the company do with the proceeds?

How will debt ratios change as a result of the financing?

Is there some advantage to arranging loans and lines of credit now?

Management Changes

Who is leaving? Who is his or her replacement?

How old is the person leaving?

How long has he or she been with the company?

What positions has this person held?

If a replacement is named, what is the new executive's background? Age?

If not, who are the candidates and what are their backgrounds?

What is the official explanation for the change?

Were there specific events leading to the change?

Did the executive jump or was he or she pushed out?

What will the departing executive do now?

How much will the new executive be paid?

How has the company performed during this executive's tenure?

What were the executive's accomplishments?

How much money will the executive get in a separation agreement?

What does the change mean for the company's strategy?

Stock Buybacks

Why is this the best use of shareholders' money?

Why not invest internally in plants, equipment or research and development?

What does this do to offset previous option grants?

Why be a buyer at this valuation?

Where will the money for the buyback come from? New debt issues or cash on hand?

How many shares will be repurchased, or how much will the company spend?

What percentage of the shares outstanding will be repurchased?

How long does the company have to buy them back?

Is this a new or an expanded program?

When was the last time the company bought back shares?

Dividend Payments

How much is the company paying now?

How much has it paid?

What is the dividend yield? How does it compare with the yield on similar stocks?

What is the dividend payout ratio? How has it changed over time?

How and why has the company's financial position changed?

Why is this the best use of shareholders' money?

Does this come at the sacrifice of investments elsewhere? Will the company have to forgo investments?

Interest and Principal Payments

How much is due? On what date?

What is the total principal amount?

At what price and yield are the issues currently trading?

Has the company talked with lenders about restructuring its debt?

How and why has the company's financial position changed?

Mergers and Acquisitions

What is the value of the bid?

Are there any potential regulatory hurdles?

What justifies this price?

Will the bidder pay cash, stock or a combination of both? If both, what percentage will be in cash or in stock?

Does the purchase price include the assumption of debt? How much?

How much of the business is being acquired? Does the acquirer plan to sell parts of the business? If so, which parts?

Has the target company been receptive to the overtures?

Is there a good fit between the target company's operations and the bidder's in terms of products and services? Geography? Technology?

Have you been in touch with institutional shareholders of the target company to discuss their views on the transaction?

When will the transaction be completed?

Which investment banking firms are advising the bidder? The target company?

How much will the investment bankers make if the transaction is completed?

Is there a breakup fee in case the transaction fails?

What is the impact on earnings? When will it be recognized?

Will you cut jobs or close plants in any consolidation? How many? Where?

How much will the consolidation cost? When will it begin to produce cost savings? How much will the merged company save annually?

How will the merged company retain key employees of the target company?

Who will run the merged company?

What name will it use?

Where will it be based?

What are the expectations for the merged company's earnings?
For sales or revenue? Market share? Stock price?
How will it affect the competitive balance of the industry? Who is threatened?

Bankruptcies

What business units filed for bankruptcy?
Where was the filing submitted?
What prompted the company to file?
How has it performed recently?
What had it done to avoid filing?
How much in assets does it have? Liabilities?
Who are the largest creditors? What are the creditor classes?
What is the total amount owed to creditors? How much will they get?
Who are the company's competitors? How will they benefit?
Who are the company's suppliers? How much do they stand to lose?
How will they account for the losses?
Will the filing result in firings? Plant shutdowns? Asset sales?
How long will the proceedings last? When will the company file a reorganization plan? When will it emerge from bankruptcy?
What law firms are handling the case?

Litigation

Who are the parties in the lawsuit?
Where was it filed?
What is the basis for the claims, issues or accusations?
What are the charges?
What does the plaintiff want?
Has there been previous litigation between the parties?
Has the plaintiff filed similar suits against others?
Who is representing the plaintiff? The defendant?
When will the case be heard?
How is the court expected to rule? How would a decision affect each of the parties?
Are the parties prepared for any losses that may result?

Regulation

For all cases:

Which agency? Which country?

What action is being taken? What prompted the action?

If the company asked the agency to act, is the decision in keeping with that request? If not, how does it differ?

How will the decision affect the company's operations? Earnings?

How will it affect other companies' operations? Earnings?

What kind of relationship has the company had with the agency? Other regulators?

Is the agency taking similar actions against any other companies?

If not, are there other companies that could become targets?

For product approvals:

What are the terms of the approval?

How much did the company spend to develop the product?

What other companies have similar products on the market or in development? How will the decision affect them?

When is a decision expected?

Products and Services

For all cases:

How do the products/services fit with the company's other lines?

How do they compare with similar ones offered by other companies?

Who are the company's potential customers? Why would they be interested in buying?

For introduction:

When will they be introduced?

How will they be delivered? Marketed?

How much has the company spent on development?

How much will it spend on the introduction?

What is the company's sales target?

What are the chances that the target will be met?
How will earnings be affected if the target is met? Or if it isn't met?

For discontinuance:

How much will it cost to drop the lines?
How will it dispose of them: sale, shutdown or a spinoff to shareholders?
Does the company expect a gain or loss from the decision?
When will the gain or loss be recorded?
How will the discontinuance affect earnings?

Property, Plant and Equipment

For all cases:

Check capital expenditures. If they're increasing: When can investors expect to see a return on this investment? If they're decreasing: Should investors be concerned that the company is pulling back on spending?

For purchases:

Who is the seller?
What is the purchase price?
How much will production capacity increase?
How will the company finance the purchase?
What kind of tax breaks, if any, are involved in the transaction?

For sales:

Who is the buyer?
What is the sale price?
Will there be a gain or loss on the transaction?
When will it be recorded in the financial statements?

For natural disasters:

How did the damage occur?
How extensive was the damage?
How will the company compensate for the lost capacity?

How much will it cost to repair the damage?
Will the company suffer a financial loss?
Who is the company's insurance carrier?
Will the government pay some of the repair costs?
When will operations return to normal?

Contracts and Agreements

Who are the parties?
What does the agreement cover?
How long will it remain in effect?
Is it exclusive or nonexclusive?
What quantities, payments and other terms are involved?
What will happen if the parties don't satisfy the terms?
What effect will the agreement have on revenue? Earnings?
Why are the parties entering into this agreement?
How does it fit with their corporate strategy?
Are there similar agreements with others?
Are more agreements in the works?

22

Grammar

WE ARE DEFINED by our words, so use them with care.

Agreement of Subject and Verb

Failure to make the verb agree in number with the subject is a common mistake, even among experienced and talented writers. Improper conjugation usually occurs when collective nouns are used.

Wrong:
> *A group of banks are meeting in Geneva.*

Right:
> *A group of banks is meeting in Geneva.*

Note that the subject of.the verb *to be* is a group, not banks. Avoid the British usage found most commonly in sports stories: *Manchester United are playing Tottenham this evening.* Correct: *Manchester United is playing Tottenham this evening.*

The lack of agreement of subject and verb is also common when *none* is the subject of a sentence. *None* can be singular or plural in construction. Use either a singular or a plural verb in a sentence such as *None of the conspirators has (or have) been brought to trial.* However, *none* can only be plural when used in sentences such as *None but his most loyal supporters believe (not believes) his story.*

An easy way to remember: Substitute *not one* for *none* to see whether the verb makes sense.

Wrong:
> *None of the Bloomberg writers make grammatical errors.*

Right:
> *None of the Bloomberg writers makes grammatical errors.*

Commas

The failure to use a comma can alter the meaning of a sentence:

I shot the cow which was fat.
I shot the cow, which was fat.

The first sentence means that the fat cow was shot. The second sentence means a cow, which happened to be fat, was shot.

Improper comma usage could be insulting to our readers, as demonstrated by the following example:

I know some investment bankers who are corrupt.
I know some investment bankers, who are corrupt.

In the first sentence, the absence of a comma before *who* creates a restrictive clause that suggests the corruption applies to the group of bankers described by the speaker. In the second sentence, the comma creates a non-restrictive clause that suggests all investment bankers are corrupt.

In general, use commas after elements that introduce the main clause (the main subject and verb) of the sentence. *In the morning, he traded stocks* is easier to read than *In the morning he traded stocks.*

Raising interest rates, the Federal Reserve tried to restrain inflation.
When the Federal Reserve raised interest rates, stocks fell.

Place a comma before a conjunction only if the second part of the sentence contains a subject and a verb:

I own stocks, and I own bonds.
I own stocks and bonds.

Hyphens

Use hyphens to avoid ambiguity or to form a single idea from two or more words. An example of avoiding ambiguity:

The president will speak to a small business organization.
The president will speak to a small-business organization.

The first sentence means that the president will speak to a business organization that doesn't have very many members. The second sentence means that the president will speak to a group of people who run small businesses.

When a compound modifier precedes a noun, use a hyphen to link all of the modifiers except the adverb *very* and all adverbs that end in *-ly*. Examples: *first-quarter profit, a full-time job, a know-it-all attitude.* In particular, use *38 million-pound charge* (singular) to refer to a charge of *38 million pounds* (plural).

This is especially important when the meaning might otherwise be unclear. One example: *Black cab driver* could mean a black driver of any cab; *black-cab driver* makes it clear we are referring to a driver of a traditional London taxi.

Some compound modifiers that are hyphenated before a noun aren't hyphenated when they occur after a noun. Examples: *The company expects to report a profit in the first quarter; she works full time.*

When a compound modifier appears after the verb *to be*, the hyphen usually must be retained. Examples: *Matt is well-known, Mike is quick-witted.* Don't use a hyphen for *French Canadian* or *Latin American.*

In headlines, always capitalize the first letter of the word following a hyphen in a compound: *State-Owned, Second-Largest.*

Only

Place *only* as close as possible to the word it modifies. Improper placement of *only*, like improper placement of commas, can change the meaning of a sentence.

I only kissed her.
I kissed only her.

The first sentence means the speaker did nothing more than kiss the woman. The second sentence means the speaker kissed one woman. *Only* is a subjective word that diminishes, and its use in our copy should be limited. What we might describe as *only* may not be *only* to a reader.

That

It's important not to overuse *that*, and just as vital to retain *that* when it enhances clarity.

That is often removed before an independent clause (a second subject and verb that could stand alone) to save space. There is no fast rule of grammar. The writer must judge whether the sentence is more or less clear without *that.*

The word often can be omitted when the independent clause follows verbs such as *say* or *think*, without obscuring the meaning:

He said that red cars are his favorite.
He said red cars are his favorite.

That usually should be retained when the independent clause follows a verb such as *assert, contend, declare, estimate, feel, make clear, point out, propose, state* or *suggest.* With some of these verbs, the absence of *that* could lead the reader to momentarily think that the words following the verb are a direct object.

Wrong:
> *Fools contend ignorance is bliss.*
> *Nigel estimates profits will fall further.*

Right:
> *Fools contend that ignorance is bliss.*
> *Nigel estimates that profits will fall further.*

That is sometimes necessary for parallel construction. If one clause is preceded by *that*, the other must be as well. Decide whether the sentence reads better with two *thats* or none.

Wrong:
> *Claudine said she went to the party and that Michel was there.*

Right:
> *Claudine said she went to the party and Michel was there.*
> *Claudine said that she went to the party and that Michel was there.*

Which

Eliminate the word from your sentence if you can do so without distorting the meaning. If you can't, be aware that some grammarians say *which* should be used only in non-restrictive clauses, while *that* should be used only in restrictive clauses. Thus, they suggest we avoid sentences like *I need a book which is by James Joyce*, because the clause describing book is restrictive. It's correct to say *The students object to reading Ulysses, which is long and dull*, because the clause describing *Ulysses* is non-restrictive.

Has and Have

These words can't be stripped out just to tighten the writing, as is commonly done. Their use is governed by grammar rules for the present perfect tense.

That tense uses forms of *to have* as an auxiliary verb to help express a time element.

Present perfect tense may be used to convey these three situations: events that began at some indefinite time in the past and are continuing in the present; actions that have been completed when the statement is made; actions that happen frequently or continuously.

These are the three errors we commonly make, and how to avoid them:

Using present perfect when we should use the simple past tense for fresh news. The present perfect dilutes the sense of immediacy. The action in news stories usually is communicated best with the simple past tense. In this lead, the present perfect isn't necessary because the measures were just proposed. The action is recent and we are reporting it promptly:

> *Chicago Mayor Richard M. Daley has proposed cutting 320 vacant jobs and raising taxes on retail sales, cigarettes and hotel rooms to help close a record $220 million budget gap.*

The verb should have been the simple past tense:

> *Chicago Mayor Richard M. Daley proposed cutting 320 vacant jobs and raising taxes on retail sales, cigarettes and hotel rooms to help close a record $220 million budget gap.*

Using the simple past tense when the time element in the sentence requires present perfect. This is the reverse of the previous example. The simple past is grammatically incorrect because it doesn't reconcile the passage of time:

> *The dollar fell 2.6 percent versus the euro since government data on Oct. 18 showed foreign purchases of U.S. financial assets at a 10-month low in August.*

Use the present perfect to indicate that the action (falling 2.6 percent) had been completed at the time of writing. The dollar could fall further in the future, but the exact 2.6 percent decline is a completed action and the verb should reflect the time period (since Oct. 18):

> *The dollar has fallen 2.6 percent versus the euro since Oct. 18, when government data showed net foreign purchases of U.S. financial assets fell in August.*

Using present perfect when a specific example would result in a stronger sentence. This sentence is correct grammatically but undesirable:

> *ECB President Jean-Claude Trichet has backed away from a forecast that growth will accelerate this year.*

Be specific. Cite a particular time when he expressed such a sentiment to give a sense of how recently the statement was made. Was it last week? A year ago? Five years ago?

> *ECB President Jean-Claude Trichet backed away from his Oct. 15 forecast that growth will accelerate this year.*

Who and Whom

These are different forms of the same pronoun. *Who* is the subject form, and *whom* is the object form. *Who* is the equivalent of *he, she* or *they. Whom* is the equivalent of *him, her* or *them.*

To determine which to use, run a substitution test. Try using *he* or *him* instead of *who* or *whom.* If *he* leads to a grammatically correct sentence, then *who* is the right form. If *him* makes the sentence correct, then *whom* is right.

Question: *Who is at bat?* or *Whom is at bat?* The test: *He is at bat?* or *Him is at bat?* Answer: *He* is correct, so the right form is w*ho.* Correct: *Who is at bat?*

Question: *Whom did you speak to?* or *Who did you speak to?* The test: *Him did you speak to?* or *He did you speak to?* Since neither reads properly, flip the sentence: *Did you speak to him?* or *Did you speak to he?* Answer: *Him* is correct, so use *whom.* Correct: *Whom did you speak to?*

The same principle applies for use of *whoever* or *whomever.*

23

Words and Terms

THIS SECTION ESTABLISHES a common language for all stories in every medium, one that is understood in all regions and by every customer. This style is the result of continuing discourse by reporters and editors since we began in 1990.

Check *The Bloomberg Way* or STYL <Go>. The latest additions and changes will be disseminated in Weekly Notes, which are found in NI LESSON or BBNS <Go>. If the point isn't addressed in *The Bloomberg Way*, try the latest *Associated Press Stylebook*. Our reference for spelling is *Webster's New World College Dictionary*, fourth edition, edited by Michael Agnes.

For spelling place names, first check *The Bloomberg Way*. Then go to the *Associated Press Stylebook* and the *Webster's New World College Dictionary*. If the place isn't listed, check the U.S. Postal Service's National 5-Digit ZIP Code and Post Office Directory and its equivalent anywhere else, or the *National Geographic Atlas of the World*.

Apply standard American spelling, usage and punctuation, and not words or phrases unique to English, Australian or Indian writers of English. When the American usage would be difficult for a reader from Japan or the U.K. to understand, use words that can be grasped anywhere.

A

abbreviations and acronyms. Use only abbreviations and acronyms that are easily recognizable by a worldwide audience. Use the full name on first reference and introduce the abbreviation or acronym on second reference as a rule, though the reverse is acceptable for lengthy names such as Organization of Petroleum Exporting Countries.

When an abbreviation has more than four letters and doesn't have to be spelled out when spoken, use lowercase after the first letter. Otherwise, use uppercase. Examples: *EU, SEC, AIDS, OPEC, REIT, AFL-CIO, Nafta, Ebitda, Unesco.*

Don't assume that an abbreviation can stand alone just because it's common practice locally. When referring to the FBI, for instance, write the U.S. agency's name—the Federal Bureau of Investigation—at some point. The same goes for the IRS, the U.S. Internal Revenue Service.

Don't use abbreviations for most company names, even in headlines, to avoid making our reports look like alphabet soup. Only these abbreviations may be used—sparingly—in headlines and on second reference, because they are recognized worldwide:

AIG	American International Group
AMD	Advanced Micro Devices
BMW	Bayerische Motoren Werke
BNY Mellon	Bank of New York Mellon
CIBC	Canadian Imperial Bank of Commerce
Con Edison	Consolidated Edison
GE	General Electric
GM	General Motors
H&M	Hennes & Mauritz
IBM	International Business Machines
J&J	Johnson & Johnson
NTT	Nippon Telegraph & Telephone
P&G	Procter & Gamble

RBC	Royal Bank of Canada
RBS	Royal Bank of Scotland
RIM	Research in Motion
SocGen	Societe Generale
UPS	United Parcel Service
Varig	Viacao Aerea Rio-Grandense
WaMu	Washington Mutual

In addition, HP may be used for Hewlett-Packard when necessary in a quotation. The full name is preferable in text. Use the initials without periods or a hyphen.

Other company names should be spelled with full words in text and story headlines. They may be abbreviated in stand-alone headlines only when the fit is rigorously tight.

Don't abbreviate titles in stories or headlines, because the abbreviation may be unfamiliar worldwide. Use full titles: *Governor Andrew Cuomo, Senator Dianne Feinstein, Representative Nancy Pelosi, General Hugh Shelton, Rear Admiral Craig Quigley.*

Standard abbreviations such as *Dept.* and *Co.* require a period. One exception: *vs* is lowercase, no period.

For non-U.S. dollars, use these abbreviations in all references: A$ for Australia, C$ for Canada, HK$ for Hong Kong, NZ$ for New Zealand, S$ for Singapore, NT$ for Taiwan.

Avoid abbreviations in story headlines.

In flash headlines only—to make space available for company tickers—some abbreviations are acceptable: Govt for government; Intl for international; Ops for operations and Cont Ops for continuing operations; Qtr for quarter and Yr for year; Mln, Bln, Tln for million, billion and trillion; 1Q for first quarter; 1H for first half; FY for fiscal year; Yr for year and similar abbreviations for other periods; Qtrly for quarterly; Rev for revenue; EPS for earnings per share; Div for dividend; CEO for chief executive; CFO for chief financial officer; COO for chief operating officer; Pnds for British pounds.

Flash headlines also may shorten million, billion and trillion to M, B and T. Put the letter immediately after the number: $300M, $2B. When it's obvious that the figures are per share, it's acceptable to drop *Share* altogether.

Include country references in headlines when necessary to prevent confusion. FTC can stand for the U.S. Federal Trade Commission and Japan's Fair Trade Commission. TSE can stand for both the Tokyo and Toronto stock exchanges.

about. Use *about* rather than approximately or around to specify that a figure isn't exact. See **rounding**.

above. Refers to location or direction, while *more than* refers to amount: *The light is above me. He received more than 51 percent of the votes.*

Abu Dhabi. Stands alone as the capital of the United Arab Emirates.

academic degrees. Use *MBA*, without periods, to abbreviate master's degree in business administration.

Other academic degrees take periods: *B.A., M.S., Ph.D.* It's always acceptable, and often smoother, to avoid abbreviations and write a phrase such as *doctorate in mathematics* or *master's degree in marine biology.*

accents. Omit accent marks. For German and Swedish umlauts, use a vowel without an umlaut followed by the letter *e*: *ae, oe, ue.*

For Nordic accents, use *aa* to represent the letter *a* with a circle above it, *ae* to represent *a* and *e* joined together, and *oe* to represent *o* with a slash through it.

In all other cases, write the vowels without accents.

accretive. Explain this jargon used to describe mergers and acquisitions that increase earnings. Specify the amount and timing of the increase.

acquisition. When one company buys another. Most transactions are acquisitions, not mergers, because one company is dominant. On second reference, to avoid a word echo, *merger* may be used.

Some acquisitions are completed when the purchase is arranged with cash or non-equity securities that may enable one company to buy another with a greater market capitalization.

When the would-be buyer plans to pay in stock, calculate the value of the offer at the previous day's closing price. Don't update the value until after the official close of trading. Until the deal is completed, update the calculation every day there's a new story because the value can change over time as the acquirer's stock fluctuates.

M&A is acceptable on second reference and in headlines for the phrase *mergers and acquisitions*. Use sparingly.

acronyms. See **abbreviations**.

activity. When attached to a noun as in *manufacturing activity, market activity* or *trading activity*, activity is redundant.

address. Avoid as a verb when we mean considering a question.

administration. Lowercase, as in *the Obama administration*.

admit. Use as a synonym for *said* only in a quotation or in a legal context such as court testimony, because *admit* indicates a subjective judgment.

ADR. Acceptable in headlines and on second reference to American depositary receipts, which represent a stake in a non-U.S. company and trade mainly in the U.S. stock market. Refer to American depositary receipts rather than American depositary shares.

advancers. Say how many stocks in a market rose instead of using this jargon.

advertisement. Not *advert*.

adviser. Not *advisor*, except in a company name.

affect. As a verb, to influence; as a noun, a feeling. Don't confuse with *effect*: as a verb, to bring about; as a noun, a consequence.

Afghan. Use to describe people born or living in Afghanistan rather than *afghani*, the term for the country's currency.

African-American. See **black.**

after-hours trading. Be specific: *after the close of trading on the New York Stock Exchange.*

after-tax. Not *aftertax* or *post-tax.* Use only when distinguishing from *pretax.*

age. Include for any newsmaker in a story. Age is a benchmark of life and is as important as any anecdote. Stories usually don't need ages for spokesmen, analysts, economists, government employees or others who are commenting or supplying information in a formal capacity. Include age when it's relevant to the situation. If a trader says, *I've always known Joe Executive to be dependable and honest,* it matters whether the trader is old enough to have known Joe for more than a few years.

agreed. Something arranged or settled by common consent is *agreed on.* Something accepted is *agreed to.* A preposition is needed, rather than writing a phrase such as *agreed a partnership, agreed a deal* or *agreed bid.*

agreed bid. Jargon derived from British takeovers. Phrases such as *agreement to buy* are preferable.

ahead of. Awkward as a synonym for *before,* which is preferable.

aims to. When writing about plans, goals or any action or event, it's better to quote someone discussing the aim than to make the assertion.

air bag. Not *airbag.*

all-time. Used as a modifier, all-time high and all-time low are better said as *record.*

alleged, allegedly. These terms don't protect us against libel or other lawsuits and are often extraneous. If we are reporting what someone says, contends or charges, it isn't necessary to insert *alleged* or *allegedly* with what was said, contended or charged. These modifiers don't provide any benefit or protection. Use the terms when we are passing along unproven facts, which is sometimes the case in press summaries.

allow to. Use *let.*

almost. Use almost to refer to amount or degree; use nearly to refer to distance: *We hiked almost four hours and covered nearly 3 miles.* Almost is imprecise as a qualifier, as in *almost entirely complete.*

al-Qaeda. Muslim terrorist organization that was led by Osama bin Laden.

although. Clauses containing *although* often confuse more than they clarify because the word connects dissimilar ideas in a single sentence and takes readers in different directions. Focus on the part of the sentence to emphasize rather than put it in opposition to another point.

aluminum. Not *aluminium*, except in a company name.

America. When appropriate, specify North America, South America or Latin America.

American depositary receipts. Not *depository.* They represent a stake in a non-U.S. company and trade mainly in the U.S. stock market. *ADR* is acceptable in headlines and on second reference. Avoid the alternative American depositary shares.

American Indian. Preferable to *native American.*

amid. Use only where there isn't any clear cause and effect to link events. Otherwise, *because of* or similar words are preferable.

Amsterdam. Stands alone as the capital of the Netherlands.

and. In all company and organization names, substitute an ampersand rather than writing *and*, even when the company uses *and* in its formal name: *Mahindra & Mahindra Ltd.*, not Mahindra and Mahindra Ltd.; *Winkler & Duennebier AG*, not Winkler + Duennebier AG. Use *and* for government agencies: *U.S. Securities and Exchange Commission.*

For compositions such as books, movies, magazines and television shows, follow the original use of & or *and* in the title: *"The History of the Decline and Fall of the Roman Empire;" Food & Wine magazine; the Globe and Mail; "Law & Order."*

anecdotal leads. Stories with anecdotal leads should return to the subject of the anecdote later in the story. People who are important enough to put in the lead might as well be protagonists and should be considered important enough to be acknowledged again by the middle of the story.

another. Refers to duplicate amounts: *Five widgets were distributed and another five were stockpiled.* Use *more* when referring to different amounts: *Five widgets were distributed and eight more were stockpiled.*

anticipate. Not a synonym for *expect.* If investors anticipate an event, they are taking steps to deal with it before it happens.

antitrust. Not *anti-trust.*

APEC. Asia-Pacific Economic Cooperation, a group that promotes economic ties and removal of trade barriers in the region. The abbreviation is acceptable on second reference. Members are Australia, Brunei, Canada, Chile, China, Hong Kong, Indonesia, Japan, Malaysia, Mexico, New Zealand, Papua New Guinea, Peru, the Philippines, Russia, Singapore, South Korea, Taiwan, Thailand, the U.S. and Vietnam.

Refer to APEC economies or APEC members, rather than APEC nations or APEC countries.

apparent. If something is apparent, it isn't necessary to say so.

application. Use the full word on first reference and in headlines. The short form, *app,* may be used on second reference for smartphone and computer applications.

approximately. Use *about.*

arbitrager. Someone who seeks to profit from price discrepancies between markets by buying a cheaper asset and by selling a more expensive asset. Not *arbitrageur.*

as. Not a synonym for *because.*

ascribe. To *ascribe* is to attribute. Don't confuse with *subscribe.*

Asia-Pacific. Hyphenate as a compound modifier: *Asia-Pacific region, Asia-Pacific markets, Asia-Pacific division.* Don't use Asia Pacific as a stand-alone name.

asset-backed. Hyphenate this modifier: *asset-backed bonds, asset-backed securities.*

Association Cambiste Internationale. Paris-based group of currency dealers. Co-sponsors two sets of benchmark money-market rates: Euribor, the euro interbank offered rate, and Eonia, the euro overnight index average, an effective overnight rate for loans between banks.

Athens. Stands alone as the capital of Greece.

Atlanta. The U.S. city stands alone.

attribution. Be precise. *Sources said*, or *according to a source*, is imprecise. Specify whether the information comes from a person, a document, a report or elsewhere.

For press releases that come from a distributor such as Business Wire or PR Newswire, include the distributor's name in the citation until someone at the company confirms publication of the release. Call a company official right away for confirmation, and make an effort to advance the story by asking the official to provide additional information.

If a source is someone hired to represent a company, rather than a company employee, mention that in the citation. Rather than *Joe Smith, a company spokesman*, write *Joe Smith, a spokesman with the company's public-relations firm, Smith & Jones Inc.*

Avoid broad attribution such as *analysts said* or *traders and analysts say* or *investors said*. Identify the speakers and why they matter.

Attribute an idea to one individual, not to one person as representative of a group. Instead of writing *analysts including John Smith of UBS Warburg said* or *regulators including Pierre Dubois, France's chief securities official, said*, credit that one person. If direct or indirect quotes from additional sources are worth including, do so within the limits of space and flow. Introduce speakers one by one.

Official statistics don't need any attribution in headlines. If the U.S. Commerce Department or the U.K. Central Statistical Office releases a report, the headlines present details from the report as facts. The same holds true for most company announcements.

Statistics from non-government organizations need attribution in headlines. So does information about companies and other organizations that doesn't come from them directly.

Examples:

U.K. March New Car Sales Rise 11% Versus Year Ago, Trade Group Says
(For figures from Britain's Society of Motor Manufacturers and Traders.)
JPMorgan Is Said to Cut 10% of European Investment-Bank Jobs
(For news that the company didn't confirm.)
Daiei May Sell Additional Lawson Stock to Pay Debt, Nikkei Says
(For a story summarized from Japan's Nikkei English News.)

Media summaries should be attributed to the specific news outlet that is the source, not to a parent company. Use BBC Radio 4 or BBC News 24 television, for example, rather than British Broadcasting Corp.

In summaries of media reports that rely on one or more people who aren't identified, always make it clear that they are anonymous: *according to unidentified people familiar with the situation.*

In quotations, always provide the attribution at the first convenient break, usually the end of the first sentence. Don't make readers jump to the end of a passage to find out who is speaking

Avoid using these verbs for attribution: *concede, note, announce, claim, explain, exclaim* and *warn*. They can add bias, suggesting a judgment by the writer.

The preferred choice is *said* because it's neutral. *Admit* may be used in legal stories, when someone is officially admitting wrongdoing.

Confirm should be used only when we have first introduced the subject. For example: *Widgets Inc. is in talks to buy Acme Corp. for as much as $880 million. Acme President Eustace Smith confirmed a New York Times report that an agreement may be announced as early as next week.*

Acknowledge and *deny* are acceptable when used appropriately.

Stories that include interviews from Bloomberg Television signature shows should contain the names of the programs in the attribution. Other stories originating from broadcast interviews should include the interviewer's name in the byline.

Auckland. The New Zealand city stands alone.

auction. Sale to the highest bidder.

Australia. Size and scope on Australian entities should recognize that it is a separate country or part of the Pacific region, not part of Asian markets.

author. Use as a noun, not as a verb.

auto parts. Not *autoparts.*

automaker. Not *auto maker.* See **-maker.**

automated teller machine. Dispenses cash, takes bank deposits and can perform other functions. Not *automatic teller machines.* Use *ATM* on second reference.

average, mean, median. *Average* is the same as *mean* for our purposes. Don't confuse with *median,* which is the middle number in a range ordered from low to high. We use the median when we survey analysts for forecasts of government economic reports or company earnings.

avian influenza. Use the full name of this infectious disease, *avian influenza,* on first or second reference. It's acceptable to use *bird flu* in the headline and lead, as long as the full name is used next. Later references also may be shortened to *avian flu.*

B

Baby Bell. Not everyone knows or remembers what it means. Baby Bell should be introduced conversationally or prefaced by *so-called.* The phrase doesn't need to be used unless something about the history is relevant to the news: *Baby Bells, the local-telephone companies spun off from AT&T Corp. in 1984* or *So-called Baby Bells, the regional local-phone companies resulting from the breakup of AT&T Corp.*

Baghdad. Stands alone as the capital of Iraq.

Baltimore. The U.S. city stands alone.

Bancorp. No period is needed on this standard abbreviation for Bancorporation.

Bangkok. Stands alone as the capital of Thailand.

Ban Ki-moon. This is the preferred spelling for the name of the United Nations secretary-general.

Bank of America. Write *Bank of America Corp.* on first reference for all arms of the company. Describe the relevant business generically—brokerage, investment banking, etc.—and without capitalizing.

BofA is acceptable in headlines that have a tight fit. Use BofA in stories only in direct quotations.

Bank of Japan. Japan's central bank. BOJ is acceptable in headlines and on second reference.

bankrupt. In the U.S., acceptable on first reference to describe companies in bankruptcy proceedings. Specify the type of proceeding and what it entails: Chapter 7, which leads to liquidation, or Chapter 11, which enables companies to reorganize. Bankruptcy laws vary by countries.

The expression *emerge from bankruptcy* is trite. Some alternatives: *Come out of bankruptcy. Complete the company's bankruptcy reorganization. Finish its bankruptcy reorganization.*

Bank Sarasin. Use Bank Sarasin on all references. Don't use AG or Cie. as part of the name, to prevent confusion with the nomenclature for closely held private banks in Switzerland.

Barclays. Barclays Bank Plc is spelled without an apostrophe. The possessive is Barclays's.

bargain hunting. Jargon. So-called bargains become bigger bargains all the time. Give the price at which people may buy.

barring major news. Never use this phrase, because it goes without saying.

based. Use this word for a company or organization that has headquarters in one place and extensive operations elsewhere. For example: *Cincinnati-based Procter & Gamble Co.*

When an entity operates almost entirely at one location, it's better to write *in Boston.*

Putting *-based* after several locations in one sentence or paragraph may be cumbersome. Put the locations inside commas after the subject.

Basel. Not *Basle.* Needs *Switzerland* on first reference.

basic earnings per share. One of two earnings figures that U.S. companies report. Based solely on common shares outstanding. Avoid using unless a company doesn't provide diluted earnings per share, which also include securities such as options, warrants and convertible bonds that may become common shares.

basis point. Define the term in stories as the equivalent of 0.01 percentage point. Use to describe yield, not price: *The bond yields 50 basis points more than the benchmark 10-year Treasury note.*

Use numerals for two-digit numbers, counting fractions as a digit, and use words for one-digit numbers: *75 basis points, 4 1/2 basis points, three basis points, one basis point.*

battle. Not for describing routine disputes and takeover contests. A battle involves more than mild resistance, and we should supply evidence of a protracted controversy or an intense struggle. Justify use of the term by writing that a takeover target hired three banks and adopted a poison pill, or a company being sued spent years in court and millions on lawyers.

beef up. Explain the action instead of using this cliche.

Beige Book. Capitalize both words, in keeping with the Federal Reserve's practice. On first reference, describe the report as the Federal Reserve's latest assessment of regional economies in the U.S.

Beijing. Stands alone as the capital of China.

believe. Not a synonym for *say.* Journalists don't know what people believe, feel, hope or think. They know only what people say and what they do.

benchmark. Benchmark refers to a standard by which others in a category can be measured. Both for financial terms and in other contexts, explain what the benchmark is measuring: benchmark bond, benchmark stock, benchmark index, benchmark for Beaujolais Nouveau, benchmark for industrial design.

Don't use *benchmark* alone.

Berlin. Stands alone as the capital of Germany.

Bernanke. Include the middle initial for the Federal Reserve chairman, *Ben S. Bernanke.*

between. Not to be used for a range that includes the number on each end. *A price between $6 and $10* means $6.01 to $9.99. To include them, use the *to* construction: *The price is $6 to $10.*

Big Three. Outdated reference to General Motors Co., Ford Motor Co. and Chrysler Group LLC.

bilateral. Superfluous when talking about negotiations between two parties.

bird flu. Use the full name of this infectious disease, *avian influenza,* on first or second reference. It's acceptable to use *bird flu* in the headline and lead, as long as the full name is used next. Later references also may be shortened to *avian flu.*

black. We say that someone is *black* rather than African-American. Ethnic descriptions used in hyphenation with "American" are best reserved for immigrants or first-generation Americans.

President Barack Obama's father was from Kenya and his mother was from Kansas, so it's precise to say Obama is African-American. Arnold Schwarzenegger is an Austrian-American because he emigrated from Austria. Henry Kissinger, born in Bavaria, is German-American.

We don't say former President George W. Bush is German-American or Irish-American, although he has German and Irish ancestors, because he is generations removed from those ancestors.

Use these descriptions only when they are relevant to the news.

blog. Acceptable on first reference for *Web log.*

Bloomberg data. When citing statistics or other information compiled by Bloomberg, use *according to data compiled by Bloomberg* on first reference. We can be more succinct in later references: *according to Bloomberg data.*

This applies whether the information was harvested from a function, phone calls, e-mail or previous stories.

When reporters or editors survey sources to tally estimates or forecasts, use a specific reference as well: *according to 14 analysts surveyed by Bloomberg News.*

Bloomberg name. First references to our editorial product should be *Bloomberg News.* Stories from all arms of our news operation fall under that umbrella. Later references may be more specific, such as *published in the January issue of Bloomberg Markets.*

Stories and press summaries about Michael Bloomberg should include a disclaimer: *Bloomberg is the founder and majority owner of Bloomberg LP, the parent of Bloomberg News.*

blue chips. Jargon that is supposed to mean the largest and most well-known companies in a stock market. Be specific: *One of the 30 stocks in the Dow Jones Industrial Average.*

BMW. Short for Bayerische Motoren Werke AG. BMW is sufficient on first reference. Use the full name once in any story referring to the German automaker.

board of directors. Use just *board* or *directors* when referring to U.S. companies, which have only one board. Some European countries have a two-tier system; a *management board* runs the business and a *supervisory board* of outside directors makes strategic decisions. When referring to one board or the other, be specific and explain its duties.

Bogota. Stands alone as the capital of Colombia.

bolsa. Acceptable as substitute for *stock exchange* in nations where the term is used.

Bombay. Former name of Mumbai, a city in India that stands alone. Mention the former name when appropriate.

Bombay Stock Exchange. Use Bombay Stock Exchange rather than Mumbai stock exchange. The larger National Stock Exchange also is in Mumbai.

bond coupons. Express bond coupon percentages as decimals rather than fractions. Write *3.5 percent bond*, not *3 1/2 percent bond*.

bondholder. Not *bond holder*.

bond ratings. Here are the rating scales of Standard & Poor's and Moody's Investors Service:

Investment grade bonds						
S&P	AAA	AA	A	BBB		
Moody's	Aaa	Aa	A	Baa		
Junk bonds						
S&P	BB	B	CCC	CC	C	D
Moody's	Ba	B	Caa	Ca	C	

S&P uses plus and minus signs to distinguish between borrowers within the AA to CCC categories. Use these signs in all references, rather than writing *plus* or *minus*. Moody's uses 1, 2 or 3 on all ratings in the Aa to B categories for the same reason.

Don't put quotation marks around ratings: *The bonds received an AA rating from Standard & Poor's.*

Don't use *upgraded* or *downgraded* when referring specifically to rating changes. Write *Moody's cut its rating on Widget's senior debt to Baa from A3* instead of *Moody's downgraded Widget's debt.*

Junk is acceptable on first reference if we explain immediately that it means *high-yield, high-risk debt.* Elaborate lower that they are *rated below BBB– by Standard & Poor's and Baa3 by Moody's,* or give the exact rating.

Use either *company* or *service,* rather than *agency,* in all references to rating providers. They are corporations, not governmental organizations. McGraw-Hill Cos. owns Standard & Poor's, and Moody's Corp. owns Moody's.

For more details on credit ratings, enter RATD <Go>. For a company's rating history, enter its ticker symbol and <Equity> CRPR. For a country's rating history, enter CSDR <Go>.

Bonn. The former German capital stands alone.

book citations. In book reviews and other stories that name a recently published book, include a citation with publication details in parentheses. Give the publisher's name, number of pages and price, in that order:

> *What led up to that moment, and all that followed, is the subject of James Green's "Death in the Haymarket" (Pantheon, 383 pages, $26.95).*

book value. Measure of a company's net worth, typically defined as shareholders' equity. It's calculated by taking the value of assets and subtracting the value of liabilities. Often stated on a per-share basis.

Boston. The U.S. city stands alone.

bought deal. Jargon. In securities underwriting, a commitment to purchase an offering from a company.

brackets. Direct quotes should be the exact words of the speaker. Paraphrase or use partial quotes when tempted to use brackets.

Brasilia. Stands alone as the capital of Brazil.

break. Jargon when used as a synonym for climb or fall or reach. Gold doesn't break $300 an ounce. It falls below $300 an ounce. One exception: A quote such as *We finally broke $300 an ounce* is acceptable, provided that it's accompanied by the appropriate context.

break even, break-even. Two words as a verb; hyphenate as an adjective. *Widgets Inc. said it will break even in the fourth quarter. Widgets Inc. forecast break-even per-share earnings.*

BRIC, BRICS. Use *BRIC* to refer jointly to Brazil, Russia, India and China. Use *BRICS* for those four countries plus South Africa.

Both terms are written in all capitals. Avoid *the BRICs*, which refers to the four BRIC countries but could be misconstrued as BRICS.

The countries should be named on first reference unless it is in a lead or quote. In those instances, name the countries soon afterward.

British Bankers' Association. Trade group that provides London interbank offered rates, or Libor, a benchmark for money-market rates in the dollar, the euro and eight other currencies.

British spelling. Acceptable only in proper names. Use *Labour Party* rather than Labor Party when referring to the U.K. political party. Use American spelling otherwise: *the labor union.*

broadly. Meaningless when used before higher or lower to describe markets. Be more specific: *Three stocks rose for every one that fell.*

Brussels. Stands alone as the capital of Belgium.

Btu. Acceptable in headlines and on second reference as an abbreviation for *British thermal units*, used to measure amounts of energy.

Bucharest. Stands alone as the capital of Romania.

Budapest. Stands alone as the capital of Hungary.

Buenos Aires. Stands alone as the capital of Argentina.

bulk up. This term is best avoided because it carries a negative connotation.

bullets Use to highlight a list of points in text. Use two hyphens (--) to indicate a bullet. Indent before the hyphens and leave a space after them. Here's a sample of a listing using bullets:

These companies have restated results because of accounting issues:
-- Rite Aid Corp., the third-largest U.S. drugstore chain, said in July 2001 it would restate for fiscal 1998 and 1999, erasing $1 billion in profits.
-- Enron Corp., the energy trader that filed the largest U.S. bankruptcy, said in November 2001 it would restate $586 million in profits since 1997 after disclosing accounting irregularities.
-- Xerox Corp., the world's largest copier maker, was ordered by the SEC in May 2001 to restate results. The SEC levied a record $10 million fine for prematurely booking $3 billion in equipment-lease revenue over a four-year period starting in 1997.

business. Use sparingly as a synonym for a company or for particular units or divisions.

Write *French companies* rather than French businesses; *finance company* rather than finance business.

For parts of a company, it's better to be specific: *the axle-making unit* instead of axle business; *the storage-systems division* instead of storage business.

business model. Explain what the corporate strategy is, rather than use this stuffy phrase.

but. Use only when the intent is to signal an about-face. Repeated use in a narrative often confuses more than it clarifies.

buy. Use only as a verb, not as a noun. *Widget Plans Acme Buy* isn't acceptable in a headline. Use *Purchase* or *Takeover* instead.

buyback, buy back. One word as a noun; two words as a verb.

buying. Not a reason for price movements, as in *stocks rose in heavy buying.* Every trade has a buyer and a seller.

buyout, buy out. One word as a noun; two words as a verb.

buy side, sell side. *Buy side* and *sell side* are jargon. When they occur in a quote that is otherwise compelling, spell them as two words. Hyphenate as modifiers: *sell-side advice, buy-side investors.*

C

Cairo. Stands alone as the capital of Egypt.

Calcutta. The former name of the Indian city of Kolkata, which stands alone. Mention the former name when appropriate.

Calgary. The Canadian city stands alone.

call options. Contracts that provide the right—but not the obligation—to buy a security, currency or commodity at a set price within a set period. Also can be used to bet on the direction of an index such as for stocks or interest rates. When using the term, define immediately after the first reference.

calls on. Specify whether someone is asking or demanding.

can. Knowing that anything can happen, use *may*, which poses a possibility, or *might*, which adds a greater degree of doubt to the possibility, when reporting on potential outcomes.

cap, capped. Explain that prices may be little changed or lower, rather than writing gains may be capped.

Cape Town. The city in South Africa stands alone.

capital controls. Government-imposed limits on how money enters or leaves the country. Be specific: *The government barred anyone from taking its currency out of the country.*

capital increase. Write instead that the company is selling additional shares.

capitalization. Market capitalization, or the total value of a company's shares. It's better to refer to a company's *market value* than its market capitalization.

Avoid the abbreviation *cap*, which often follows *large-*, *mid-*, *small-* and *micro-* in categorizing companies by total value.

capitals. A nation's capital city isn't a substitute for referring to a people or a government. Washington isn't the American people; Moscow isn't the Medvedev government. Capitals are places.

Caracas. Stands alone as the capital of Venezuela.

carmaker. Not *car maker*. See **-maker.**

carry trade. Define this term when used in our stories.

In a currency carry trade, the investor makes money by borrowing in a country with low interest rates, converting the money to a currency where interest rates are higher, and lending the money at that higher rate. The profit comes from the spread between the borrowing and lending rates; the risk is that exchange rates may change.

cash earnings. Profit figure that excludes an assortment of items, mainly charges, that a company sees as unrelated to its main business. Also known as *pro-forma earnings*. Avoid this phrase because items included or excluded from the figure vary among companies. Specify the items that aren't included: *EBay said profit excluding stock-based pay, amortization and certain other costs was $197.7 million, or 29 cents a share.*

cash flow. Define this financial measure because it has several variations, such as cash flow from operations, cash flow from investing, or free cash flow. Some use the term to mean earnings before interest, taxes, depreciation and amortization, or Ebitda, which is called operating cash flow. Be specific because cash flow and Ebitda are not necessarily the same.

cash reserves. This colloquial expression implies that a company has cash set aside for a specific purpose. The company may or may not have plans for using the money. Say exactly what the company has on hand, cash or cash and short-term investments. Exception: *Cash reserves* has a more specific meaning in the accounting for financial institutions. It's appropriate to use the term for banks and insurance companies, which are required to have certain levels of cash reserves as part of their total cash holdings.

casualty. Not a synonym for *fatality*. It refers to those killed or seriously injured. Military casualties can include those who are captured, interned, sick or missing.

Explain where we got our facts about casualties in military conflicts. Name the government, combatant group or news service that provided them.

cautious. Be more specific and describe the action or behavior.

cautiously optimistic. Cliche. People are either optimistic or pessimistic.

cease-fire. Use as a noun, not *ceasefire* or *cease fire*.

central bank. Use the Anglicized name except when the name in the local language is well-known, such as the Bundesbank, or necessary for clarity.

cents. Use when referring to the currency of countries that use cents as a monetary unit, such as the U.S. and Canada. Don't use *penny* for these countries unless referring to a coin.

Use *penny* for references to the currency of countries that officially have pennies as a monetary unit, such as the U.K.

Make sure it's clear which country's currency is involved. *Cents* is acceptable if used when the Canadian dollar or euro has already been specified. Without a dollar reference nearby, write *Canadian cents* or *euro cents* to prevent confusion with U.S. currency.

We prefer to write *cents* when used in a story headline. If we must abbreviate, use lowercase: *Acme Fourth-Quarter Profit Rises to 3 Cents a Share; Acme Forecasts Fourth-Quarter Profit of 3c a Share.*

The uppercase *C* is acceptable in stand-alone flash headlines sent by editors: *ACME FORECASTS 4TH-QTR NET INCOME OF 3C-SHARE.*

chair. Use as a noun for furniture, not as a verb. Not a substitute for *chairman* or *chairwoman.*

chairman, chairwoman. Not chairperson. In Europe, use only when referring to the head of a company's supervisory board. When referring to the head of the management board, use *chief executive officer.*

A female company chairman should be referred to as *chairman* unless she has expressed a preference to be called chairwoman.

When someone is both chairman and chief executive officer, provide both titles so readers don't assume that someone else holds one of the positions.

champagne. Lowercase when referring to the sparkling wine from the Champagne region of France.

charge. In general, *charge* means something that reduces earnings. It isn't an official accounting term and doesn't have an exact meaning. It's preferable to use a specific term, such as *cost, expense, writedown, investment loss, severance pay, loss from an asset sale.* If the company only uses the word *charge*, we can use it in initial headlines and stories while we press for details.

Chicago. The U.S. city stands alone.

chief executive. Use *chief executive officer*, rather than *chief executive*, for all first references in stories. *Chief executive* or the abbreviation *CEO* may be used on second reference.

CEO is acceptable in headlines when necessary for clarity or to fit important information.

The executive's name usually is more meaningful, so avoid falling back on the abbreviation all the time. Refer to the person as *chief,* as *chief executive,* or by name, as in *Intel's Otellini.*

In Europe, use *chief executive officer* when referring to the head of a company's management board.

chip. *Semiconductor, chip, microchip* and *integrated circuit* all mean the same thing. Be specific and explain what kind of chip: *computer chip, memory chip, mobile-phone circuit chip.*

Don't use *computer chip* unless the chip is used in computers. A memory chip used in phones isn't a computer chip. *Microprocessor* refers to certain chips that are used in PCs, mobile phones and many other devices. It isn't a synonym for semiconductor or microchip.

chipmaker. Explain what kind of chip the company makes: *Intel Corp., the world's biggest computer-chip maker,* or *Nvidia Corp., the world's biggest computer-graphics-chip maker.*

Chubb. Chubb Corp. is a U.S.-based provider of business insurance. Chubb Plc is a U.K.-based provider of security services such as locks and safes. Include enough of the company name in headlines to avoid confusion between them.

Cincinnati. The U.S. city stands alone.

cities. The following cities can stand alone in copy or headlines:

Abu Dhabi, Amsterdam, Athens, Atlanta, Auckland.

Baghdad, Baltimore, Bangkok, Beijing, Berlin, Bonn, Bogota, Boston, Brasilia, Brussels, Bucharest, Budapest, Buenos Aires.

Cairo, Calgary, Cape Town, Caracas, Chicago, Cincinnati, Cleveland, Copenhagen.

Dallas, Damascus, Denver, Detroit, Dubai, Dublin.

Edinburgh.

Frankfurt.

Geneva, Gibraltar, Guatemala City.

The Hague, Hamburg, Havana, Helsinki, Hong Kong, Honolulu, Houston.

Indianapolis, Istanbul.

Jakarta, Jerusalem, Johannesburg.

Kolkata, Kuala Lumpur, Kuwait City.

Las Vegas, Lima, Lisbon, London, Los Angeles, Luxembourg.

Madrid, Manila, Marseille, Melbourne, Mexico City, Miami, Milan, Milwaukee, Minneapolis, Monaco, Montreal, Moscow, Mumbai, Munich.

New Delhi, New Orleans, New York.

Oklahoma City, Oslo, Ottawa.

Panama City, Paris, Philadelphia, Phoenix, Pittsburgh, Prague.

Quebec City.

Rio de Janeiro, Rome, Rotterdam.

St. Louis, Salt Lake City, San Antonio, San Diego, San Francisco, San Marino, Santiago, Sao Paulo, Seattle, Seoul, Shanghai, Singapore, Stockholm, Sydney.

Taipei, Tehran, Tel Aviv, Tokyo, Toronto.

Vancouver, Vatican City, Vienna.

Warsaw, Washington.

Zurich.

city of. Lowercase when necessary to identify a location precisely: *The city of New Orleans.* Often it can be dropped.

claim. Use only in a legal context, such as an allegation: *In his suit, he claimed that the restaurant served spoiled food.* This isn't the same as an assertion that doesn't involve the law: *He said the restaurant served spoiled food.*

Class A, Class B shares. Not class A, class B.

class-action lawsuit. Use only in connection with suits that a judge certified as class actions. Before then, plaintiffs seek class-action status for their suit.

clean coal. Jargon for coal that has been treated or whose emissions are captured to reduce pollution. It's better to write *cleaner coal*, and explain what steps are being taken to make it less damaging.

cleanup. Use this as a noun and adjective, *clean up* as a verb.

Cleveland. The U.S. city stands alone.

cliches. Words whose overuse obscures any value or meaning.

---

against the backdrop	*at this point in time*
barring major news	*big business*

(*continued*)

breath of fresh air	*campaign trail*
claimed the life of	*court of public opinion*
deer in the headlights	*financial circles*
hit the ground running	*in the wake of*
in this day and age	*laid to rest*
navel gazing	*no holds barred*
no uncertain terms	*poster child*
powers that be	*pushing the envelope*
reaping the benefits	*ruffled feathers*
stretched too thin	*take the helm*
the perfect storm	*trial by fire*
unanswered questions	*wake-up call*
war-torn country	*win-win situation*
what a difference a year makes	
climbed the corporate ladder	

clinical trials. The U.S. Food and Drug Administration requires three stages of human trials for testing drugs. When referring to these trials, *human trial* is preferable to clinical trial.

Phase I trials, done on a few dozen healthy volunteers, determine a drug's safety.

Phase II trials involve several hundred patients and focus on the drug's power to combat a disorder.

Phase III tests involve several thousand patients, last for years, and are designed to assess a drug's optimum dosage and longer-term safety.

closed-end funds. Mutual funds that have a fixed number of shares outstanding. They usually trade on a stock exchange. See open-end funds and exchange-traded funds.

closely held. Company controlled by a few people. May have publicly traded shares. Preferable to privately held. Not hyphenated because closely is an adverb ending in *-ly*.

closure. Not a substitute for *closing*.

Cnooc Ltd. Use this spelling for the Chinese oil company.

code-sharing. Agreements in which airlines link their flights in reservation system computers. Explain the term and describe the agreements.

collateralized-debt obligations. Securities that bundle bonds or loans, or both, from a variety of issuers such as companies or countries. Banks create them by grouping lower-rated assets into securities that are worth more than the total value of the underlying assets. Interest payments on the underlying bonds or loans are used to pay investors.

The abbreviation CDO is acceptable on second reference and in headlines. Describe the securities in other ways as well, so stories aren't jammed with initials. One alternative is *customized securities backed by bonds, loans, real estate, commodities and a variety of material assets.* On later references, we can write *these customized securities.*

collateralized-mortgage obligations. Hyphenate.

Colombia, Columbia. Colombia is the South American country's name. Columbia is the name of a river and several cities in North America.

comfortable with. When a company executive uses this phrase to describe his or her view of analysts' earnings estimates, it's nonsense. Estimates come largely from what a company says about itself. Don't use it in stories, and ask an executive who uses it to be more specific.

committee names. Capitalize the formal names of U.S. congressional committees, such as the Appropriations Committee, Agriculture Committee or Budget Committee. When referring to more than one, lowercase committees: *the House and Senate Appropriations committees.*

common. Write *common shares* rather than *ordinary shares.*

Common Agricultural Policy. The European Union's agricultural subsidy program, under which the EU pays direct subsidies to farmers, guaranteeing them minimum prices for their products. Accounts for about 50 percent of EU spending. Use CAP on second reference.

compact disc. Not compact disk.

Compagnie. Abbreviate to *Cie.* in all company names.

Companhia, Compania. Abbreviate to *Cia.* in all company names.

company names. Generally follow the company's spelling and punctuation on first reference, and use the entire name.

Shorten to one or two words in headlines and on second reference. The first word is enough when it's unique. Cadbury refers only to the U.K.'s Cadbury Schweppes Plc. Use more than one word for common names, especially in headlines, to distinguish the company from others. Differentiate in headlines between Continental AG and Continental Air, Prudential Financial and Prudential Plc, and Chubb Corp. and Chubb Plc.

When shortening to two words, don't put a comma between them even if one appears in the full name. Skadden, Arps, Slate, Meagher & Flom LLP thus becomes *Skadden Arps* in headlines and on second reference; Gresham, Smith & Partners becomes *Gresham Smith.*

Use these spellings for company designations: AB, AG, AS, Bancorp, Bhd., BV, CA, Cia., Cie., Co., Cos., Corp., GmbH, Inc., KGaA, Ltd., LLC, LLP, LP, NV, Oy, Oyj, Pcl, Plc, Pte, Pty, SA, Saca, Sdn., SpA. Omit any comma that immediately precedes them in the full name.

Some companies, such as Elan Corp. Plc, use more than one designation. Include only the first one except when a second is necessary to distinguish between companies with similar names.

Don't use *The* at the beginning of a name even if a company does: *Limited Inc.*, not The Limited Inc.

Abbreviate words only if the company itself does so: *Warner Bros.* Write *Citigroup* and *Citibank*, not *Citi*. Write *Coca-Cola*, not *Coke*.

Give unabbreviated company names, even in headlines, so that our reports don't look like alphabet soup. Only these abbreviations may be used—sparingly—in headlines and on second reference, because they are recognized worldwide:

AIG for American International Group, AMD for Advanced Micro Devices, BMW for Bayerische Motoren Werke, BNY Mellon for Bank of New York

Mellon, CIBC for Canadian Imperial Bank of Commerce, Con Edison for Consolidated Edison, GE for General Electric, GM for General Motors, H&M for Hennes & Mauritz, IBM for International Business Machines, J&J for Johnson & Johnson, NTT for Nippon Telegraph & Telephone, P&G for Procter & Gamble, RBC for Royal Bank of Canada, RBS for Royal Bank of Scotland, RIM for Research in Motion, SocGen for Societe Generale, UPS for United Parcel Service and WaMu for Washington Mutual.

In addition, HP may be used for Hewlett-Packard when necessary in a quotation. The full name is preferable in text. Use the initials without periods or a hyphen. PricewaterhouseCoopers may be shortened in headlines to PwC only when necessary to fit essential elements. Don't abbreviate as PWC or Pricewaterhouse.

Other company names should be spelled with full words in text and story headlines. They may be abbreviated in stand-alone headlines only when the fit is rigorously tight.

When a name begins with a lowercase letter, capitalize the first letter in all references: *EBay*, not eBay; *EasyJet*, not easyJet.

If more than three letters in a row are capitalized, use lowercase for all but the first letter if the name doesn't have to be spelled out when spoken: *ABN Amro*, rather than ABN AMRO. Simplify overly capitalized, symbolized or stylized names. Write *Delia's* for dELiA*s; *DirecTV* for DIRECTV; *LCH Clearnet* for LCH.Clearnet.

Eliminate spaces between words, abbreviated words or initials as long as the name is readable: FedEx, PepsiCo, PetroChina, AstraZeneca, NCSoft.

If a company's name includes an Internet domain, such as .com or .net, retain the dot-com in headlines and on first reference: *Amazon.com, Priceline .com*. A shortened name may be used on later references: *Amazon, Priceline*. Don't toggle back and forth.

Use an ampersand rather than the word *and* (or equivalents such as *und, et, y*), even when the company uses *and* in its formal name. *Bradford & Bingley Plc*, not Bradford and Bingley Plc. Replace a plus sign with an ampersand. *Gruner & Jahr*, not Gruner + Jahr.

When a company uses an exclamation point, include it only for the first reference. *Yahoo! Inc.* on first reference; *Yahoo* on second reference and in headlines.

Generally use the full name of the parent company on first reference. When the news is about a well-known unit, such as the American Airlines business of AMR Corp., put the unit's name in the lead and the parent's lower.

For brokerages, use the parent's name when it is similar to the unit's, such as Goldman Sachs Group Inc., except when the context of the story requires drawing a distinction. When the names are dissimilar, such as BB&T Corp.'s Scott & Stringfellow, use the brokerage name first and note who owns it lower.

It's acceptable to omit the parent name of well-known financial-services units that supply information used in stories. We can cite credit ratings from Standard & Poor's without saying it's a unit of McGraw Hill Cos.

Don't write *the company* throughout a story. Drop in the name at least occasionally. When two companies in a story have similar names, make sure to distinguish them within the first four or five paragraphs.

company value. When using some amount of currency to refer to the value of a company, always provide specifics. For industrial companies, *sales* is the preferable measure. For financial companies, use *assets*.

comparable. *Comparable Treasury securities* and similar phrases aren't specific enough when comparing yields in bond stories. There are many ways to compare bonds—maturity, duration, rating, etc. *Securities of comparable maturities* is preferable.

compared to, compared with. Use *compared to* when citing similarities between items that are essentially different: *UAL is often compared to a rhinoceros.* Use *compared with* when citing differences between items that are essentially similar: *UAL had a first-quarter profit of $3 million, compared with a loss of $97 million a year earlier.*

When numbers are directly comparable, use an active verb: *UAL's shares outstanding fell to 12.3 million from 36.2 million.*

concern about, concern that. When *concern* is used to describe an emotion, follow with *that* rather than *about* and give a detailed explanation of what may happen or the apprehension. *As concern about corporate debt grows* is less precise than *As concern increases that rating companies will downgrade corporate debt in a slowing economy.* Also, be sure to identify who is concerned.

conference calls. When a company schedules a conference call to discuss a news event, provide details in a trashline at the end of the story and the byline. Explain how to obtain access:

(PG&E will hold a conference call at 11:30 a.m. San Francisco time to discuss first-quarter results. Members of the public can listen through a link on the company's website. To reach the site, enter http://www.pgecorp. com. To hear a replay, dial (800) 947-3657.)

Complete addresses are preferable to <Equity> CWP, a function that retrieves companies' Web pages, because this reference will appear on Bloomberg's website as well as the Bloomberg Professional service.

confirm. This term implies that people are aware of a previous news report, and is rarely needed. It's almost always preferable to use a verb such as *said*.

conglomerate. Name a company's main businesses instead: *United Technologies Corp., which makes aircraft engines, elevators, helicopters and air conditioners.* Don't use in combination with an industry, as in financial conglomerate.

Congo. Include a reference to the former Zaire or say *formerly known as Zaire.* In references to the similarly named country, use the full name *Republic of Congo* to differentiate.

congress. Uppercase only in proper names, such as the U.S. Congress. Lowercase when used as a generic reference to a country's legislature.

congressional terms. Use these guidelines when writing stories about the U.S. Congress:
Don't include the names of bills. In almost every case, they are pure propaganda.
Include the number of government bills so that it's easier to find relevant stories about U.S. congressional legislation.
At the end of the story write *The bill is H.R. XX.* (for the House of Representatives) or *The bill is S. XX.* (for the Senate.)

Example:

Senator Olympia Snowe, a Maine Republican who helped defeat the legislation, has called for passing a separate unemployment assistance measure. The bill defeated today was S. 76.

Use *pass* only for action by the full House or Senate: *The House passed the banking bill.*

The House and Senate *adopt* resolutions and amendments. They don't pass them.

Committees *approve* bills and resolutions. They don't pass or adopt them.

Avoid *markup, chairman's mark, whip* and any other terms that have little or no meaning outside the halls of Congress. It's better to write that a committee will *act on a bill* rather than mark up a bill. Describe a chairman's mark as a draft of a bill.

Words such as *reconciliation* may be unavoidable even though they aren't familiar to many people worldwide. When using them, provide explanations.

Clear has a very specific meaning in Congress. Use it only when Congress completes action on a bill and sends it to the president.

congressional titles. *Representative* and *senator*, along with their plurals, shouldn't be abbreviated in references to members of the U.S. Congress. Capitalize titles in front of names: *Senator Richard Lugar.* Also write party affiliations and state names without abbreviating.

Always include the affiliation and state somewhere in the story. Try to weave them into the narrative when possible: *Arizona's Republican senator, John McCain.* Otherwise, put them after the name: *Representative Duncan Hunter, a Republican from California.*

Don't capitalize titles when they are used without a specific name: *McCain said no other senator would vote for the bill. Hunter said no other representatives would oppose the bill.*

consensus. Not a synonym for *average* or *mean* in earnings estimates.

consortium. Use *group*.

consultancy. Use *consulting firm* or *consultants*.

Continent. *The Continent* and *Continental* aren't synonyms for *Europe* and *European.* Use a more precise description.

continue. What continues isn't news. Better to use an historical comparison if nothing has changed. *The economy grew for the sixth straight quarter* is preferable to *The economy continued to grow.*

contractions. Use contractions in place of two-word phrases when the second word is *not*—*wouldn't, wasn't, isn't, can't, don't, won't, hasn't.*
It's is acceptable when used occasionally, not repeatedly.
Other contractions with forms of *to be* or *to have* may be used when they sound natural: *it's, you've.* Spelling both words in full often reads better. Don't use *it'll,* or *they'd* or *mayn't,* for example.

contract manufacturer. Company that makes products, especially computers and electronics, for other companies to sell under their own brand names. Describe in stories.

convexity. An adjustment to duration, which is an estimate of how much the price of a bond will change when interest rates rise or fall. Typically applied to callable bonds, whose prices tend to drop more for an increase in yield than rise for a decrease—a trait known as negative convexity. Positive convexity means a bond's price rises more for a drop in yield than it declines for the same increase in yield. Explain in stories. See **duration**.

convince, persuade. Convincing involves a person's beliefs, while persuading involves a person's actions. Someone is *convinced of, convinced that* or *persuaded to.*

Copenhagen. Stands alone as the capital of Denmark.

core. Companies often describe something they consider essential to their strategy as a core business or core asset. Describe the business or assets, instead.

corporate America. Lowercase *c*: corporate America.

correction. Jargon in market stories. Prices aren't mistakes, so markets can't have corrections.

could. Anything could happen. Use *may*, which poses a possibility, or *might*, which adds a greater degree of doubt to the possibility, when reporting on potential outcomes.

couldn't be reached. Imprecise. Explain the efforts that were made to reach a person. *Acme Chief Executive Officer John Smith didn't return phone calls made to his office. Acme's public-relations department didn't return calls seeking comment. Calls to Smith's office and home were connected to recorded messages. Smith's assistant Jane Jones said he wasn't available to comment.*

Council of Europe. Forty-seven-nation forum designed to promote human rights and democracy. Based in Strasbourg, France. Oversees the European Court of Human Rights. Isn't part of the European Union.

cram-down. Hyphenate as a noun or adjective. Two words as a verb.

credit. Saying that central banks eased or tightened policy isn't accurate. They ease or tighten credit through policy changes. It's preferable to say that a central bank raised or lowered interest rates.

credit crunch. Provide a definition, such as saying people and businesses are having trouble paying their bills or banks are refusing to lend, and why.

credit-default swaps. Credit-default swaps are contracts based on bonds and loans that are used to speculate on a borrower's ability to repay debt or to hedge against losses on the debt. The buyer of a swap pays a premium and gets the face value of the debt in exchange for the underlying securities or the cash equivalent if the borrower fails to adhere to its debt agreements. The price of a credit-default swap typically declines when the perception of a borrower's creditworthiness improves, and vice versa. Give prices of credit-default swaps in basis points rather than a currency. Stories should include a definition.

credit derivatives. A broad group of securities that let buyers guard against a borrower's missed debt payments. Credit derivatives include credit-default swaps, which are the most common, and collateralized-debt obligations. Explain in stories.

credit lines. We usually mean *bank financing* or *loan agreements*, which are better terms to use.

credit ratings. See **bond ratings**.

creditworthy. Not *credit-worthy*.

currencies. Use the currency of denomination in all references, including earnings and takeover values. After the first reference to non-U.S. dollar amounts except for share prices, provide a dollar conversion in parentheses immediately afterward: *Sales increased 20 percent to 400 million euros ($487 million)*. Round off conversions to the nearest million when the original amount is less than 1 billion, and to one decimal place for amounts of 1 billion or more. Examples: *Profit rose to 674 million euros ($821 million) during the third quarter. Sales climbed to 3.8 billion euros ($4.7 billion).*

Use only the $ sign in all references to U.S. dollars. For non-U.S. dollars, use these abbreviations: A$ for Australia, C$ for Canada, HK$ for Hong Kong, NZ$ for New Zealand, S$ for Singapore, NT$ for Taiwan. For values less than $1, skip the dollar sign: *22 Canadian cents*, not C$0.22.

It's acceptable on second reference to use a nickname for dollar currencies—Canada's loonie, New Zealand's kiwi, Australia's Aussie and the U.S. greenback—to provide variety and reduce word echoes. Avoid overusing.

These European currencies may be abbreviated in stand-alone headlines and in speed fills when referring to amounts: EU for euro, SF for Swiss franc, DK for Danish krone, NK for Norwegian krone, SK for Swedish krona. Place the abbreviation before the figure, no space. Not acceptable in story headlines. Examples: *NK500 Million, SF3.5 Billion.*

Write other currencies as full words after the figure in all uses. Don't use symbols for currencies such as the yen, the euro and the British pound. Example: *500 Million Pounds.*

For amounts of less than one unit, identify the country before the measure when necessary to distinguish between currencies: *10 Canadian cents, 25 Mexican centavos*. Round all the amounts to whole numbers: 5 cents, not 4.8 cents.

When referring to emerging-market currencies' record highs or lows, include dates to reflect devaluations and changes in the currency.

To convert currencies, use FE11 <Go>.

currency band. Range within which a government allows a currency to fluctuate. If it trades outside the range, the government buys or sells the currency to bring it back into the zone. Explain in stories.

currency board. Maintains a government-set, fixed exchange rate for the country's currency by taking control of monetary policy from a central bank. The board backs the country's notes and coins with reserves of another currency, such as the dollar or the euro. Provide the description rather than use this term.

currency peg. Link to another currency or fixed exchange rate, typically resulting from government fiat or decree. Hong Kong pegs its dollar at the rate of 7.8 per U.S. dollar; supply and demand in foreign-exchange markets then establishes a market rate. Other links can take the form of a crawling peg, in which a government targets its currency's depreciation against the U.S. dollar or some other currency.

currency swap. An agreement between two parties to exchange their periodic interest-rate payments based on a set amount of money, though in different currencies, for a set amount of time. Typically involves the exchange of principal so that each party has an asset that can generate interest payments. Explain in stories.

D

Dallas. The U.S. city stands alone.

Damascus. Stands alone as the capital of Syria.

damp, dampen. *Damp* refers to cooling or restraining: *damp a furnace, damp the economy, damp earnings. Dampen* refers to moistening: *dampen the mop.*

data. When citing statistics or other information compiled by Bloomberg, use *according to data compiled by Bloomberg* on first reference. Be more succinct in later references: *according to Bloomberg data.*

This applies whether the information was harvested from a function, phone calls, e-mail or previous stories.

When reporters or editors survey sources to tally estimates or forecasts, use a specific reference as well: *according to 14 analysts surveyed by Bloomberg News.*

database. Not *data base* or *data-base.*

datelines. The date in a dateline should be the current day in the city where the main news occurred. When writing an anecdotal lead, use the date that is today for the location of that anecdote. Don't let a story published one day cross into the next. In other words, we don't update after midnight local time where the story takes place. Start a fresh story, which is an opportunity for us to take another look at the news and advance it.

dates. Put the date after the month, and abbreviate long months: *May 27, Sept. 2, Jan. 13, 1994.* When combined with a date, abbreviate as Jan., Feb., Aug., Sept., Oct., Nov., Dec. Never abbreviate March, April, May, June, July.

Months shouldn't be abbreviated in stand-alone references such as *September*, or in month-year references such as *January 2002.* Don't abbreviate when using months to define a range: *January-March, October-December.* Avoid using this format to define periods: *fourth quarter* is preferable to *October-December quarter.*

days of the week. Name days of the week only when necessary in a quotation: *"Monday is the final deadline," the prime minister said.*

Choose one of these alternatives for time references: Use *yesterday, today* or *tomorrow.* Name the exact date (Sept. 29). Or convey a time frame: *two weeks from now; four days ago; in about three months; earlier this month.* Use the reference that sounds smoothest and meets the required degree of specificity. For opinion polls, always use exact dates.

Most of our stories should say when the main news happened, which is almost always *today.* The day should appear on the first screen and often will fit well in the second paragraph. The day doesn't need to be in the lead unless it is germane to the news. We don't need later references to today unless the time frame has been changed and must be brought back to the present for clarity.

Use *earlier today* when needed to indicate that the news is a reaction to something that happened hours ago. Make the progression of time clear.

One exception is market stories. Readers know that reports about the trading in stocks, bonds, currencies, commodities, etc. are that day's news, so we don't need to say *today*.

In shares-up and shares-down stories, it is clear that the stock trading is today's news because we give a time of day for the price. Specify the day of the news that triggered the move. Stocks may react to news from today, yesterday or even two or three days ago.

In press summaries, say when the news happened. We don't need to add the date of publication or broadcast unless it is relevant. If the source material doesn't make the time element clear, then omit it from our summary.

The day in a story should reflect the time where the news happened, not where the reporter or editor is located.

deal. Too vague for use on first reference. Describe the transaction or agreement: *contract, merger, acquisition.* Acceptable on later references to avoid word echoes.

dealers. *Traders* is preferable.

debt. In referring to the cost of a takeover, use this word by itself only when an acquirer plans to exchange bonds for shares. Write *assumed debt* when the target company owes the money already and the buyer will take on the debt.

debt holder. Not *debtholder.*

decimals. Use CV <Go> to convert to fractions if needed. For details on rounding, see **rounding**.

decimate. In modern use, this word means to destroy or severely damage.
The original meaning of killing every 10th person, a punishment sometimes inflicted by Roman commanders, is obsolete.

declined comment. *Declined to comment* is the proper phrase.

decliners. Say how many stocks in a market fell instead of using this jargon.

deflation. Deflation is the opposite of inflation. It means a general drop in prices, often as part of a severe economic slowdown. Don't confuse with *disinflation*, a slowing of inflation. Explain in stories.

demerger. Jargon word for a company's decision to split into two or more companies, or to reorganize part of its business into a separate company. Don't use.

Denver. The U.S. city stands alone.

derivatives. Either of these definitions for derivatives may be used, depending on how full an explanation is needed in the context:

Derivatives are contracts whose value is derived from stocks, bonds, loans, currencies and commodities, or linked to specific events such as changes in interest rates or the weather.

Derivatives are financial instruments used to hedge risks or for speculation. They're derived from stocks, bonds, loans, currencies and commodities, or linked to specific events like changes in the weather or interest rates. Options and futures are the most common types of derivatives.

despite. Clauses containing *although, but, despite* and *however* often confuse more than they clarify because the words connect dissimilar ideas in a single sentence and take readers into two different directions. Focus on the part of the sentence to emphasize rather than put it in opposition to another point. Sometimes *and* is what we mean.

detail. Not to be used as a verb meaning *provide details.* Acceptable as a verb for meticulously cleaning, such as a car.

Detroit. The U.S. city stands alone.

deutsche mark. Not *deutschemark.*

devaluation. Decline in currency's value that results from a change in government fiat or decree. Differs from *depreciation*, which results solely from changes in supply and/or demand in currency markets.

Diet. Acceptable in references to Japan's legislature, or parliament.

diluted earnings per share. One of two earnings figures that U.S. companies report. *Diluted* reflects all securities that may become common shares, such as options, warrants and convertible bonds. Use these numbers when possible instead of basic earnings per share, which are based solely on common shares outstanding.

dip. A brief drop followed by a rise. It shouldn't be used when there has been a slide and no recovery. Not a synonym for *decline.*

discount. Price below face value. Used most often when referring to the share price of a company targeted for takeover, and to bond prices. Be specific when referring to this difference: *The stock closed at $10 a share, 4 percent less than the offer's value,* not *The stock closed at $10, a 4 percent discount to the offer's value.*

disinflation. Disinflation means a slowing of inflation, often during a recession. See deflation.

distance. Use the measuring system—metric or U.S.—of the country that is the main subject of the story. Provide a conversion in parentheses on first reference. To do conversions, enter UCNV <Go>.

dividends. Some companies pay an interim dividend at midyear and a final dividend after the year ends. Avoid referring to the payment as an *interim* or *final* dividend. Refer to *first-half* or *second-half dividend.* When the dividend is quarterly, specify which period.

dot-com. Use this as a noun or adjective: *dot-coms, dot-com companies.* When referring to companies that have .com in their names, include the .com on first reference: *Amazon.com,* not Amazon. Use a shortened version, such as *Amazon, Priceline* or *Overstock,* on later references. Don't toggle back and forth.

double-digit. A double-digit percentage change could range from 10 percent to 99 percent. Be specific: *Earnings rose 13 percent.* If someone says *double-digit,* press for a more exact figure. Avoid *single-digit a*s well.

Downing Street. On first reference, information from 10 Downing Street should be attributed to the British prime minister's advisers or to the person who supplied it. On second reference, attribution to Downing Street is acceptable.

downside. Jargon when referring to the decline of a security or market.

downstream. Refers to refining and marketing businesses in the oil industry. Provide the description instead.

downturn. Not a synonym for *decline* or *drop*.

downward. Bad on its own, because *-ward* is unnecessary. Worse in front of *pressure* to describe something headed lower. Don't use.

Dragon bonds. Debt securities denominated in U.S. dollars and sold in Asian countries outside Japan.

Dubai. This city in the United Arab Emirates stands alone. Dubai also is the name of one of the seven emirates making up the UAE.

Dublin. Stands alone as the capital of Ireland.

DuPont Co. Acceptable in all references to E.I. duPont de Nemours & Co. Write DuPont as one word, not two.

duration. An estimate of how much the price of a bond will change when interest rates rise or fall. Bonds with longer maturities, such as 10 or 30 years, typically have greater duration than shorter-term debt of two or five years, for instance. That means a drop of 1 basis point in the yield of a 10-year note will push the price up more than a similar move in yield on a two-year note. Explain in stories. See convexity.

Dusseldorf. Not *Duesseldorf.* Needs *Germany* on first reference.

Dutch auction. Offer in which investors can specify the price, within a set range, at which they are willing to buy or sell. Explain in stories.

E

E. coli. Not e.coli, e-coli or E-coli. Short for the bacterium Escherichia coli.

earnings. The more general *results* shouldn't be used unless the company has yet to release its financial statements for a given period and either analysts or the company itself expect a loss.

earnouts. Payments made by the buyer of a business to the seller if profits exceed a set limit. Explain rather than use this jargon.

earthquakes. The Richter and Mercalli scales for measuring earthquakes aren't used much anymore. Seismologists measure moment magnitude, or the amount of energy that the quake released based on the physical area of the moving fault. All three scales produce relatively close numbers; a quake that ranks 2 on one scale won't rank 7 on another.

Refer to *preliminary magnitude* in early reports. Large quakes are often reassessed later, leading to a more precise figure that can just be called *magnitude*. Intensity is a measure of the shaking and damage that a quake causes, not the strength.

easing. Saying that central banks ease policy isn't accurate. They ease credit through policy changes. It's preferable to say that a central bank *pushed interest rates lower*.

Eastern Europe. The term *Eastern Europe*, with both words capitalized, refers to the former East bloc political alliance. For a geographic reference, use eastern Europe.

eastern Germany. Use only as a geographic reference for the eastern part of the current Germany. East Germany ceased to exist Oct. 3, 1990.

Ebitda. Earnings before interest, taxes, depreciation and amortization. Measures profitability of companies, especially those dependent on debt financing or operating under bankruptcy protection. This is not the same as most types of cash flow. Ebitda is acceptable in headlines. Write the full term on first reference in text and then explain.

Ecofin. Council of European Union finance ministers, which normally meets once a month in Brussels. Avoid this term and refer to *meetings of EU finance ministers*.

e-commerce. Electronic commerce, or the selling of goods and services over the Internet. Acceptable in headlines and on second reference. Provide a more specific reference in the story first.

Edinburgh. Stands alone as the capital of Scotland.

edging higher, edging lower. Prices don't edge higher or lower; they move up or down. Use a neutral word, such as *rose* or *fell*, when moves are relatively small.

effect. As a verb, to bring about; as a noun, a consequence. Don't confuse with *affect*: as a verb, to influence; as a noun, a feeling.

ellipsis. A series of periods (. . .) used to indicate an omission, especially of letters or words. Don't use ellipses in quotations. Direct quotes must be the exact words of the speaker. Use partial quotes or paraphrase if necessary.

e-mail. Acceptable in all references to electronic mail. Not *Email* or *email*.

Emirates. Emirates is the one-word name of this airline owned by the Dubai government. When identifying its business, use *airline* in lowercase: *Dubai's Emirates airline is in talks with Boeing Co.*

end. Not to be used in market stories to mean *close*. *Stocks closed higher*, not *stocks ended higher*.

English. Our style is to use standard American English.
Slang such as *gonna* doesn't belong in our stories, even in quotes. We write stories in accepted spelling and should use *going to*, no matter how the speaker pronounced it.

Eonia. Euro overnight index average, an effective rate for overnight loans denominated in euros. Calculated from money-market trading between banks in countries that have adopted the European currency. Published by the European Banking Federation, based in Brussels.

Ericsson AB. Acceptable in all references to Telefonaktiebolaget L.M. Ericsson.

estimate. For company earnings and sales, write that analysts give estimates while companies supply *forecasts*. The figure from analysts is an *estimate*, a rough calculation, because they don't have as much information as the company.

The company's number is a forecast because it is a projection based on more complete knowledge.

Euribor. Euro interbank offered rate, a benchmark for money-market rates in euros. Calculated from bank rates in countries that have adopted the European currency. Published by the European Banking Federation, based in Brussels. Euribor is acceptable in headlines and on second reference.

euro. A single currency used by 17 countries in the European Union. Eleven countries introduced the euro on Jan. 1, 1999.

One euro consists of 100 cents. Write *20 cents* rather than 0.2 euro, *15.70 euros* rather than 15.7 euros, *36 euros* rather than 36.00 euros. Never use the symbol for the euro.

Estonia began using the euro in January 2011, joining Austria, Belgium, Cyprus, Finland, France, Germany, Greece, Ireland, Italy, Luxembourg, Malta, the Netherlands, Portugal, Slovakia, Slovenia and Spain.

Eurobonds, euro bonds. A Eurobond is corporate or sovereign debt issued in a different currency than the one in the market where the borrower is based. The term predates the 1999 establishment of the euro.

A euro bond is debt issued in euros by borrowers within the currency bloc.

Joint euro bonds or common euro bonds refers to debt instruments that may be issued jointly by the nations in the euro region.

Eurodollars. Dollars held in banks outside the U.S. and typically used to settle international transactions. The Euro- prefix also applies to other currencies. Japanese yen deposited outside Japan are called Euroyen.

euro group. Informal group of finance ministers from countries that have adopted the European currency. Normally convenes before monthly meetings of the council of European Union finance ministers.

euroland. See **euro zone**.

European Banking Federation. Brussels-based trade group that publishes two sets of benchmark money-market rates: Euribor, the euro interbank offered rate, and Eonia, the euro overnight index average, an effective rate for overnight loans between banks. Its full name is the Banking Federation of the European Union.

European Central Bank. Sets monetary policy for countries that have adopted the euro. The Governing Council, consisting of a six-member Executive Board and the governors of the countries' central banks, makes policy decisions. Succeeded the European Monetary Institute on July 1, 1998. Based in Frankfurt.

European Commission. Brussels-based executive body of the European Union. Use *commission* on second reference. Never abbreviate to EC, which stands for the European Community, the EU's predecessor. Refer to commissioners by their titles: the *EU's digital agenda commissioner, Neelie Kroes.*

European Court of Justice. Final arbiter of disputes arising from European Union treaties or legislation. Based in Luxembourg.

European Investment Bank. Lending arm of the European Union. Based in Luxembourg.

European monetary union. Process that led to the creation of the euro. Don't use the abbreviation EMU.

European Parliament. Elected assembly of the European Union. Based in Strasbourg, France. Plays a role in shaping legislation and managing the EU budget.

European Union. Twenty-seven European countries with economic and political links. Succeeded the European Economic Community. EU is acceptable on second reference.

Member states are: Austria, Belgium, Bulgaria, Cyprus, Czech Republic, Denmark, Estonia, Finland, France, Germany, Greece, Hungary, Ireland, Italy, Latvia, Lithuania, Malta, Luxembourg, the Netherlands, Poland, Portugal, Romania, Slovakia, Slovenia, Spain, Sweden and the U.K.

Three countries are working toward admittance, Croatia, Iceland and Turkey.

Eurostat. Statistics agency of the European Union. Based in Luxembourg.

euro zone. Acceptable reference to the European Union countries that have adopted the euro as their currency, though phrases such as *countries that share the euro, euro region, euro area* are preferable. Hyphenate as an adjective: *euro-zone economy.* Don't use the term *euroland.*

ever. *Ever* is redundant when describing something as the biggest, largest, fastest, highest, etc. It tells the reader more when we can be specific: *the biggest gain since the company went public five years ago* rather than the biggest gain ever.

ex-. This prefix should be placed before the entire subject, not inserted in the middle. Write *ex-Tyco director*, not Tyco ex-director.

exceptional item. In the U.K., this phrase describes an after-tax gain or charge. In parts of Asia, the definition is more flexible. Use *gain* or *charge* if a more specific description isn't available, and say whether the amount is before taxes. See extraordinary item.

exchange rate. Value of one currency in terms of another. The rate can be fixed or floating. Fixed rates are tied to a specific value of another currency, such as the dollar or the euro, or a commodity such as gold. Floating rates reflect the supply and demand in foreign-exchange markets.

exchange-rate mechanism. Established as part of the European monetary system to limit the extent of movement, or price fluctuation, in exchange rates between the participating countries. Succeeded on Jan. 1, 1999, by exchange-rate mechanism-2. Avoid the abbreviations ERM and ERM-2.

exchange-traded funds. Mutual funds that combine features of closed-end and open-end funds. Their shares trade on stock exchanges, and they don't have a fixed number of shares outstanding. Avoid the abbreviation ETF. See **closed-end funds** and **open-end funds**.

expected. News is a surprise, and something that is expected doesn't qualify. Using *plans, may* or *will* is preferable. When the alternatives don't work, make it clear who is doing the expecting on first reference: *Economists expect the report to show*, rather than *The report is expected to show.*

expert. The word lacks transparency. Use terms that are clear and precise: *doctor, medical researcher, professor, tax lawyer, economist, money manager, educator, mechanical engineer.*

expiry. Use *expire* and *expiration* when referring to futures and options contracts, not expiry.

extend. Too mild a term when referring to debt payments that a government or company can't make on time. As an alternative, write that it wants to *postpone* payments.

extraordinary item. In the U.K., this phrase describes a pretax gain or charge. In parts of Asia, the definition is more flexible. Don't use this, even when a company does. Use *gain* or *charge* and specify whether the amount is before taxes. See exceptional item.

eye. Use this only as a noun, not as a verb, including in headlines.

F

401(k). Tax-deferred retirement savings plan provided by U.S. companies. Employees can contribute as much as 15 percent of pretax salary to the plan, and many companies match at least part of their contributions.

facilities. Be specific: *the plant, the office building, the headquarters.*

factors. Often used as a synonym for *reasons*, which is preferable except when writing about retailing or mathematics.

In the retail industry, factors buy unpaid bills, or receivables, from companies such as garment makers and assume the risk of collection.

fall. Not to be used as a noun to describe a change in value. *Traders Encouraged by Bonds' Fall* isn't a grammatical headline.

false titles. Putting a job description in front of a name turns it into a false title. *Richard Bove, an analyst at Rochdale Securities,* is preferable to *analyst Richard Bove at Rochdale Securities.* See **titles**.

Fannie Mae. Use the full name of Fannie Mae on all references.

farther, further. *Farther* refers to distance: *He ran farther down the street. Further* refers to extent: *They moved further toward the goal of independence* or *Her projections look further into the future.*

FBI. Acceptable in headlines and on first reference to the Federal Bureau of Investigation. Use the full name in a later reference high in the story.

fear. It's a presumptuous judgment to describe people as fearful unless they are on the record saying "I'm afraid." That attributed evidence should be supplied in the story.

federal. Lowercase when used as an adjective to distinguish from state, county or other jurisdictions. Capitalize for corporate or governmental bodies that use the word as part of their formal names.

federal funds. Money that U.S. banks have on deposit at Federal Reserve banks. In the federal funds market, banks borrow and lend deposits that exceed the Fed's reserve requirements. *Fed funds* is acceptable in headlines and on second reference.

The Fed sets a target for the rate on overnight loans. On first reference, write *the Fed's interest-rate target for overnight loans between banks*, unless the story has already defined *fed funds*. On second reference, *the fed funds target* is enough. Avoid referring to *the Fed's target interest rate*. The Fed doesn't have a target interest rate per se.

Federal Open Market Committee. Determines U.S. monetary policy. Includes the Federal Reserve Board's seven members and the president of the New York Federal Reserve Bank, one of 12 regional banks. Four other Fed bank presidents are entitled to vote on a rotating basis; the rest only participate in the panel's discussions. Sets target for the overnight federal funds rate, at which U.S. banks lend money to each other, and approves Fed statements assessing conditions in the economy and financial markets. FOMC is acceptable in headlines and on second reference.

Federal Reserve. U.S. central bank. Run by the Federal Reserve Board, consisting of a chairman, vice chairman and five governors who oversee the Federal Reserve System's 12 regional banks. All board members and some bank presidents are voting members of the Federal Open Market Committee, which determines monetary policy.

Federal Reserve is sufficient on first reference in most cases. Fed is acceptable in headlines and on second reference.

Write *governor* as a full word rather than abbreviating in all references: *Federal Reserve Governor Daniel Tarullo* or *Daniel Tarullo, a governor at the Federal Reserve.*

feel. Not a synonym for *say.* Journalists don't know what people feel, believe, hope or think. They know only what people say and what they do.

fewer. Use for things that can be counted: *fewer bowls of cereal, fewer hours of work, fewer feet of space.* Use *less* for things that can't be counted: *less work, less space.*

final dividend. Description for the second payout at many non-U.S. companies that pay dividends semiannually. Refer to the *second-half dividend* instead.

finalize. Don't use this synonym for *complete.*

finished. Not to be used to describe the end of a trading day. Trading will resume the next business day. It isn't over for good.

Finra. The Financial Industry Regulatory Authority, or Finra, oversees U.S. securities firms. It was created in July 2007 after the merger of the NASD and a regulatory unit of the New York Stock Exchange.

fire. Use *fired* or *dismissed* rather than euphemisms such as *laid off* or *made redundant* when workers lose their jobs without the probability of being rehired. We can also say that the positions were *eliminated* or *cut.* Reserve *laid off* for workers who may be called back from employers such as airlines or auto plants.

firm. Use when referring to accounting, law or brokerage firms. Typically applies to entities that are, or originally were, partnerships. Don't use as a synonym for *company.*

first. Writing *first month in three* or *first day in four* is awkward. Write *first time in three months* or *first time in four days.*

fiscal periods. Only specify the last day of a fiscal reporting period when it doesn't correspond with the calendar. Otherwise it's redundant. *The first quarter ended March 15* is fine. *The first quarter ended March 31* isn't, as quarters typically end on March 31, June 30, Sept. 30 or Dec. 31.

For companies that report semiannually, the standard ending dates are June 30 and Dec. 31 except in Japan, where periods end Sept. 30 and March 31.

Include the last day of a non-standard fiscal period on first or second reference. When doing the latter, use *fiscal* on first reference to tip off the audience unless the word bogs down the lead. Put the word before the number of the period: *fiscal third quarter,* not *third fiscal quarter.*

Avoid using *at* before a specific date, such as *total assets at March 31.* Use *as of* or *on* instead. Use *ended* if the fiscal period is over, *ending* if it isn't:

> *Earnings in the fiscal first quarter rose 28 percent.*
> *Revenue in the quarter ended July 31 fell 2 percent.*
> *The company forecast net income of 3 cents a share for the quarter ending Nov. 30.*

flagship. Overused. A fleet has only one flagship, which carries the admiral.

flat. People don't say that a market is curved or round, so don't write that it's flat. *Unchanged* or *little changed* is preferable.

flotation. Boats float. Stocks don't. Use *sale* when writing about share sales.

-fold. Suffix that serves as a multiplier. An increase of 100 percent is the same as doubled or two times. An increase of 200 percent is tripled, or three times, or threefold. Hyphenate when the number is 10 or more: *sevenfold, 10-fold, 100-fold.* The verbs after *quadruple* (*quintuple, sextuple,* etc.) are awkward and should be avoided.

footprint. Jargon to describe a company's geographic reach, such as where a service will be available. Describe rather than using this term.

forecast. For company earnings and sales, write that companies supply *forecasts* while analysts give *estimates*. The figure from analysts is an estimate, a rough calculation, because they don't have as much information as the company. The company's number is a forecast because it is a projection based on more complete knowledge.

forego, forgo. *Forego* means to go before, to precede. *Forgo* means to do without, to abstain.

foreign. What is foreign to one person isn't always foreign to another. Use only in well-established terms such as *foreign currency* or *foreign exchange*. Determine what the word is trying to convey and be specific: *overseas sales, European accounting laws, South American customs, international laws.*

foreign reserves. Write *foreign currencies* when referring to central banks' holdings of currencies other than their own. *Foreign reserves* could refer to a German company's coal mine in Russia, for instance.

foreign words. Use only foreign words and abbreviations that have become widely accepted in American English. *Bon voyage* is universally understood, while *hoi polloi*, Greek for the common people, isn't. If use of an unfamiliar foreign term is necessary, place it in quotation marks and attribute to its source.

forwards. Agreements to buy or sell assets such as currencies or metals at a set price and date. Forwards differ from futures in that they aren't traded on exchanges and can be tailored to a buyer's or seller's needs. See futures.

fractions. Use words for fractions whose denominator is two through nine: *a half, a fourth, two-thirds.*

Use numerals when the denominator is 10 or more, and when the value is more than 1: *a 10th, a 16th, 2 1/2 years, 1 1/4 points.* The fraction counts as a digit in the last two examples, and two-digit numbers are written that way.

Avoid unnecessary use of fractions, which can be hard to read. Some numbers need to be that precise. In other situations, it's easier for people to comprehend if the number is rounded. Instead of saying *the highest price in 2 1/2 months*, write *the highest price in more than two months.*

Use CV <Go> to convert to decimals if necessary.

Frankfurt. The German city stands alone.

Freddie Mac. Use the full name of Freddie Mac on all references.

FTC. Abbreviation for both the U.S. Federal Trade Commission and Japan's Fair Trade Commission. When the abbreviation appears in headlines, add the country name as necessary for clarity.

fundamentals. Fine when used in a quotation with attribution. Avoid as a catch-all for economic variables that may affect the price of securities. Be specific and refer to *economic growth, inflation* and so forth.

fundraiser, fundraising. Use *fundraiser* as a noun, and *fundraising* as a noun and adjective.

funds from operations. Used to measure performance of U.S. real estate investment trusts, or REITs, and to determine dividends. Defined as net income plus depreciation and amortization, excluding gains or losses from joint ventures or property sales. Explain in stories.

futures. Agreements to buy or sell assets at a set price and date. Futures differ from forwards in that they trade on exchanges and are standardized. Futures often are bought as a bet on price fluctuations and sold before the delivery date. See **forwards.**

futures orders. Clothing- and shoe-industry term for orders that retailers place ahead of time, typically as much as six months in advance. Explain in stories.

G

G-7, G-8, G-10, G-20. Acceptable in headlines and on second reference for the Group of Seven, Group of Eight, Group of 10 and Group of 20, respectively. For membership, see individual entries under **Group of.**

GAAP. In the U.S., refers to generally accepted accounting principles. The abbreviation is acceptable on second reference.

gaining ground, losing ground. See **cliches**.

gasoline. Use the full word *gasoline* rather than the shortened *gas*, to prevent confusion with *natural gas*. The short form is acceptable in idioms such as *gas station* or *gas-guzzling cars.*

Geneva. The Swiss city stands alone.

Gibraltar. The British territory stands alone.

glitch. Specifically refers to a minor malfunction or false electronic signal caused by a brief power surge. *Breakdown* is usually a better choice.

global. Overused. Rather than referring to *global sales at Coca-Cola*, use *sales* and mention the number of countries where Coca-Cola does business.

global bonds. Debt securities sold simultaneously in several markets. Global bonds are generally more available to individual U.S. investors than eurobonds.

global depositary receipts. Not *depository.* These securities represent a stake in a non-U.S. company and usually trade outside the U.S. GDR is acceptable in headlines and on second reference. Avoid the alternative global depositary shares.

global depositary shares. Use global depositary receipts.

going forward. Awkward transitional phrase that usually can be omitted. If a transition is essential, better choices include *soon, later, eventually.*

GM, GMO. Write *genetically modified* or *genetically modified organisms*, rather than GM or GMO, in headlines and copy.

Goldman Sachs. Parent company is Goldman Sachs Group Inc. Brokerage unit is Goldman, Sachs & Co. on first reference, Goldman Sachs in later references. Use the unit's name in all references except those related specifically to the parent's operations, such as earnings.

goodwill. The amount exceeding fair value of the net assets paid for in an acquisition at the time of purchase. Fair value is the market price of the related assets and liabilities at the time of acquisition.

The goodwill that is recorded on an acquirer's books at the time of a purchase is evaluated at least annually under U.S. accounting rules. If the value of the acquired assets permanently declines, the company writes down goodwill to the amount of the residual amount.

GOP. Not an acceptable synonym for the Republican Party in the U.S.

Gotterdammerung This opera by Richard Wagner may be spelled without the extra *E*s that we usually insert as a substitute for umlauts.

This is an exception to our policy on German and Swedish words spelled with umlauts. The other exception is *Dusseldorf.*

For details, see **Accents**.

government spokesman. This isn't specific enough in countries that have a division of power. In those cases, the attribution should say whether the spokesman is speaking for the president, prime minister or another official. Don't use a broad attribution such as *the Kremlin said.*

governor. Capitalize before the name of a U.S. Federal Reserve Board member or a U.S. state's top official: *Federal Reserve Governor Daniel Tarullo*, Arizona Governor Jan Brewer. Don't abbreviate as *Gov.*

grand jury. When writing about investigations, be precise in order to avoid confusion. U.S., state and federal grand juries examine evidence presented by prosecutors in suspected crimes to determine whether there is probable cause to show that someone broke the law.

Once an investigation begins, a company or an event can be the subject of a probe. If a grand jury begins to focus on a suspect, it will send a letter stating that the subject is now a target. If the jury finds probable cause, it issues a *bill of indictment* or a *bill of information*. An indictment is similar to a criminal charge. A bill of information is usually a prelude to a guilty plea.

Grand juries *return* or *issue* an indictment. They don't *hand up* or *hand down* an indictment. Those terms are used colloquially but we shouldn't use them in stories.

greater. Use a word such as *more, bigger* or *larger.*

green. *Green* and *environmentally friendly* are vague. Give specific examples of what a company, government or institution is doing or has done.

greenback. Acceptable on second reference for the U.S. dollar, to provide variety and reduce word echoes. Avoid overusing.

gross margin. Shows how much a company earned after paying production expenses, including the cost of raw materials, production workers' salaries and plants' utility bills. Expressed as percentage of sales. Can also be stated as cents per dollar of sales, or the equivalent in local currency. Define in stories.

group. Not to be used as a synonym for *company* except as part of a name.

Group of Eight. Consists of Russia and the Group of Seven countries: Canada, France, Germany, Italy, Japan, the U.K. and the U.S. Created by the G-7 in 1998. G-8 is acceptable in headlines and on second reference.

Group of Seven. Consists of Canada, France, Germany, Italy, Japan, the U.K. and the U.S. G-7 is acceptable in headlines and on second reference.

Group of 10. Consists of the Group of Seven countries—Canada, France, Germany, Italy, Japan, the U.K. and the U.S.—along with Belgium, the Netherlands and Sweden. G-10 is acceptable in headlines and on second reference.

Group of 20. Consists of the European Union and 19 countries with the biggest industrialized and emerging economies. Finance ministers expanded beyond the G-10 after the Asian financial crisis in 1997, and member finance chiefs began consulting at regular meetings in November 2008.
   Members are Argentina, Australia, Brazil, Canada, China, France, Germany, India, Indonesia, Italy, Japan, South Korea, Mexico, Russia, Saudi Arabia, South Africa, Turkey, the U.S., the U.K. and the EU. The membership should be listed in stories other than briefs.
   G-20 is acceptable in headlines and on second reference.

grow. Use as a transitive verb only for living things: *grow flowers, grow a mustache, grow antlers*. Avoid using grow with a direct object when we mean expand or increase. Don't say *grow the business, grow revenue, grow enrollment*.

Grow is acceptable as an intransitive verb meaning expand or increase. A surplus, profit or membership may grow.

Guatemala City. Stands alone as the capital of Guatemala.

guidance. Specify the earnings forecasts that analysts and investors obtain from companies, rather than using this jargon.

Gulf. It's acceptable on second reference to write *the Gulf* for specific locations, such as the Persian Gulf and the Gulf of Mexico.

H

Hague, The. The Dutch city stands alone.

haircut. Jargon as a financial term. Use *haircut* only in unavoidable situations such as a direct quote from an official.

halve. Lacks grace as a verb for decline. *Fell 50 percent* has more impact than *halved*.

Hamburg. The German city stands alone.

Hanover. Not *Hannover*. Needs *Germany* on first reference.

hard goods. This term and *hardline goods* are jargon used in retailing to describe items such as electronics and furniture. Be specific.

Havana. Stands alone as the capital of Cuba.

headquarters. Use only as a noun. Don't use *headquarter* as a verb, and don't use *headquartered* as a synonym for *based*.
Every company that plays a role in the news should be identified by where it is based. We don't need to give the headquarters for a company mentioned only in passing.

health care. Not *healthcare* as a noun. Hyphenate as an adjective: *health-care stocks, health-care industry, health-care reform*.

heavy. Jargon for describing the amount of buying or selling in a market. There is a buyer for every seller and vice versa. Instead, provide a figure for the day's total trading and compare it with a daily average of at least three months.

hedge funds. Hedge funds are mostly private pools of capital whose managers participate substantially in the profits from their speculation on whether the price of assets will rise or fall. Write *hedge fund* rather than hedge-fund firm.

hedging. Using financial instruments to guard against adverse swings in interest rates, currencies or other securities. For example, a European investor buying U.S. stocks might reduce currency risk by locking in an exchange rate for the dollar for the period of the investment.

Helsinki. Stands alone as the capital of Finland.

Hezbollah. Use this spelling. The name means Party of God. Stories should include background on what the group is and where it comes from.

High Street. U.K. phrase referring to the center of town and the shops typically found there, similar to *Main Street* in the U.S. Avoid both terms.

high technology. This phrase, and the alternative *high tech*, can mean everything from computers, software and the Internet to drugs and synthetics. Explain what the technology is and does.

high-yield bonds. *Junk bonds* is acceptable on first reference, followed by an explanation that they are *high-yield, high-risk debt*. Elaborate lower that they are *rated below BBB– by Standard & Poor's and Baa3 by Moody's*.

hike. Often used after *price* or *rate*. More precise words, such as *increase*, are preferable.

historical cost. One of two ways in which U.K. oil companies' financial statements handle inventories. Based on first-in, first-out, or FIFO, which links the cost of goods sold to the cost of the oldest purchases. The other is *replacement cost*, based on last-in, first-out, known as LIFO. This method links the cost of goods sold to the cost of the most recent purchases. Use *replacement cost*, and make clear in the story that the earnings were calculated on that basis. Explain in stories.

hit. Use when writing about people engaged in target practice, military conflict, baseball, boxing or some other form of sport or aggressive behavior. In other contexts, be precise and affirmative: *Stocks climbed to a record high*, rather than *Stocks hit a record high*.

hive off. Use the appropriate term in American English when referring to a company's disposal of a business: *spin off*, *divest* or *sell*.

holders. Noteholders, stockholders, bondholders, debt holders, debenture holders.

holy. Inappropriate as a label describing a place that may be sacred to followers of one or more religions.

Hong Kong. The Chinese city stands alone.

Honolulu. The U.S. city stands alone.

hope. Not a synonym for *say*. Journalists don't know what people hope, believe, feel or think. They know only what people say and what they do.

Houston. The U.S. city stands alone.

however. Clauses containing *although, but, despite* and *however* often confuse more than they clarify because the words connect dissimilar ideas in a single sentence and take readers into two different directions. Focus on the part of the sentence to emphasize rather than put it in opposition to another point.

hurricane. Capitalize in front of an officially named hurricane. Capitalize the plural in front of two storm names.

The same style applies to tropical storms and typhoons. Tropical cyclones are named in some parts of the world and not in others. Examples: *Hurricane*

Camille, Hurricanes Katrina and Rita, Tropical Storm Tammy, Typhoon Longwang, Cyclone Pyarr.

hyphens. When a compound modifier precedes a noun, use hyphens to link each word except when the modifier begins with *very* or an adverb that ends in *-ly*. Examples: *first-quarter profit; full-time job; larger-than-estimated loss; closely held company.* Use *38 million-pound charge* (singular) to refer to a charge of 38 million pounds (plural). Don't place a hyphen between the number and its adjective: *38-million-pound charge.*

Hyphens are essential when the meaning might otherwise be unclear. *Black cab driver* could mean a black driver of any cab; *black-cab driver* makes it clear we're referring to a driver of a traditional London taxi.

Many compound modifiers that are hyphenated before a noun aren't hyphenated after a noun: *analysts estimate that the company will report a larger profit for the first quarter; she works full time.*

When a compound modifier appears after the verb *to be*, the hyphen usually must be retained: *George is well-known.* Don't use a hyphen for French Canadian or Latin American.

In headlines, always capitalize the first letter of the word following a hyphen in a compound: *State-Owned, E-Mail, Second-Largest.*

I

if. *If* means in the event that, while *whether* suggests alternatives. *I can't go if you drive; whether I go depends on who is driving.*

If shouldn't be used to suggest a hypothetical in a story unless it is attributed to a source. Substituting the word *should* doesn't countermand this practice and often leads to stilted, awkward language. When the hypothetical comes from a source, use *if* and attribution. Otherwise, the passage should be rewritten with neither word.

Capitalize *If* in headlines.

impact. Acceptable as a noun. Don't use as a verb to mean *affect.*

impeachment trial. An impeachment is an indictment, and the trial is a separate event.

impending. Be specific about when events will take place rather than using this term.

implied volatility. A measure of a security's expected volatility reflected by the market price of the options traded on the security. It's used to value options.

including. Attribute an idea to one individual, not to one person as representative of a group.

Instead of writing *analysts including John Smith of UBS Warburg said* or *regulators including Pierre Dubois, France's chief securities official, said*, credit that one person.

If direct or indirect quotes from additional sources are worth including, do so within the limits of space and flow. Introduce speakers one by one.

Avoid attribution such as *analysts said* or *traders and analysts say* or *investors said*. Identify the speakers and why they matter.

income. Operating profit, operating income and operating loss are used differently in different industries and by different companies. Define them each time: *Operating profit, or sales minus the cost of goods sold and administrative expenses, rose 66 percent to 32.6 billion yen.*

indexes. Not *indices.*

Indianapolis. The U.S. city stands alone.

industry rivals. Redundant. If companies are rivals, they have to be in the same industry.

inflation. Rising prices. Inflation may accelerate, or the inflation rate may rise. Writing *rising inflation* or *higher inflation* is redundant.

inflationary pressure. Refer to *signs of accelerating inflation.*

infrastructure. Acceptable as long as we define to say it refers to roads, bridges, power plants and other essentials.

ING Groep NV. Use the Dutch spelling of *Group* in all references to the financial-services company.

initial public offering. The first time that a company sells stock to the public. IPO is acceptable in headlines and on second reference. Write *initial public offering* rather than initial public offer.

innovative. Few programs, policies or people are truly original. Save the word for such rare occasions.

insiders. Officers, directors and major shareholders of a company. Always provide the definition.

interbank rates. Rates at which banks will lend money to each other for a specified period. Use *offered rates*, not offer rates. Capitalize only the first letter of all abbreviations, such as Libor for the London interbank offered rate, Euribor for the euro rate, Tibor for Tokyo and Sibor for Singapore.

interest-rate swap. This exchange of cash flows is one of the most common types of derivatives. It's an agreement between two parties to exchange their periodic interest-rate payments for a set amount of time. Typically, one party will swap its variable-rate payments on a set amount of money for another's fixed-rate payments.

   Borrowers use swaps to match the type of interest rates on their debt with the rates on their income, which can help reduce borrowing costs. Lenders and speculators use swaps to profit from changes in the direction of interest rates. A bet on higher rates, for example, means paying fixed rates and receiving variable.

interim dividend. Description for the first payout at many non-U.S. companies that pay dividends semiannually. Don't use the phrase. Call it *first-half dividend.*

intermediate term. Be specific: *three to five years.*

international bonds. Any bond sold outside the country of the seller's domicile. These include eurobonds, Yankee bonds and Samurai bonds.

intervention. We may use *intervene* or *intervention* to describe government actions in the currency markets as long as we provide a specific explanation of the term. Central banks intervene when they buy or sell currencies to influence exchange rates.

interview. When using comments and news from our print, radio or television interviews, use the phrase *said in an interview*. It's not necessary to specify which medium.

inventory. Not *inventories*. When companies attribute an earnings shortfall to excess inventory, focus on the events that led to the excess, such as lower-than-expected demand or a glut of competing products.

Investor AB. A holding company owned by Sweden's Wallenberg family. Include the AB identifier in all headlines to avoid confusion.

IPO. Acceptable in headlines and on second reference to an *initial public offering*, the first time that a company sells stock to the public. Stories about a company's IPO should note the security's ticker: *The shares will trade on the New York Stock Exchange under the symbol "XYZ."*

iPad, iPod, iTunes. Follow the company style for capitalization in text: *iPad, iPod, iTunes*. In headlines, capitalize because the words are nouns: *IPad, IPod, ITunes*.

Iraq War. Capitalize Iraq War. It's also acceptable to write *the war in Iraq* or *the Iraq conflict*.

ironic. Unnecessary. The audience will determine whether an anecdote or situation is ironic, and doesn't need to be told.

issuance. Bond-market word for *sale*, a better choice.

issue. Not a synonym for *topic* or *subject* when no argument is involved. Reserve it for a point, matter or question that is disputed or to be decided.

issuer. In connection with securities sales, name the seller, such as a company or government.

Istanbul. The Turkish city stands alone.

it's. Contraction for *it is*. *The company is releasing earnings next week* might become *It's releasing earnings next week*. Don't use *it, it's* and *its* so much that a sentence becomes difficult to follow.

its. Possessive form of *it*. *The company's earnings were released last week* might become *Its earnings were released last week*. Don't use *it, it's* and *its* so much that a sentence becomes difficult to follow.

-ize. Verbs created with this suffix are overused. Acceptable ones are those in long use and for which there may be no graceful alternative, such as realize, canonize, authorize. Find better language for more recent coinages such as privatize, finalize, prioritize, containerize.

J

Jakarta. Stands alone as the capital of Indonesia.

jargon. Fields such as business, finance, economics, science and technology are rife with jargon: *choppy trade, intervene, guidance, to the upside, price target*. Translate jargon into language that everyone can understand. If a term is unavoidable, include a short definition.

Jeddah. Needs *Saudi Arabia* on first reference.

Jerusalem. Stands alone as the capital of Israel.

jet. A type of engine. Use *jetliner* or *jet plane* when referring to aircraft powered by jet engines.

jitters. We don't know whether the latest event has people shaking in their seats, as the word implies. Use *concern*.

Johannesburg. The South African city stands alone.

JPMorgan Chase & Co. Not J.P. with periods.

junk bonds. Acceptable on first reference if we explain immediately that they are *high-yield, high-risk debt*. Elaborate lower that the bonds are rated below BBB– by Standard & Poor's and Baa3 by Moody's.

K

key. Acceptable as a noun. When an adjective is needed, look for a more precise word such as *crucial* or *pivotal*.

Kohlberg Kravis Roberts & Co. No commas in the name. KKR is acceptable in headlines and on second reference.

Kolkata. The Indian city stands alone. Mention that it was formerly known as Calcutta when appropriate.

Koninklijke. Dutch word for *Royal*. Appears in some company names. Use *Royal* in all references: *Royal Philips Electronics NV*.

Koran. The holy book of Islam. Don't use Quran.

kroner. Plural of Norway's krone and Denmark's krone.

kronor. Plural of Sweden's krona.

Kuala Lumpur. Stands alone as the capital of Malaysia.

Kuwait City. Stands alone as the capital of Kuwait.

L

large-cap. Abbreviation for large-capitalization, used to describe a stock market's largest companies by market value. Provide a range of values, such as *more than $10 billion*, instead. Descriptions of large-cap stocks vary, so always ask for a definition.

Las Vegas. The U.S. city stands alone.

latest. Writing that someone or something is the latest doesn't help distinguish what's new. Be specific and use facts: *Widgets is the ninth company to go public this week* says more than *Widgets is the latest company to go public*.

launch. Reserved for ships, spacecraft and missiles. Governments, agencies and companies *sell* securities. Companies *start* services or *introduce* products.

layoff. *Layoff* as a noun, *lay off* as a verb. Don't use either as a synonym for firing or dismissal, as companies often do when they are cutting a large number of positions. When people are laid off, they may be recalled to work. When they are fired, they won't.

leading. Not to be used as a synonym for *biggest* or *best.* Say what we are measuring and how: *the world's biggest airline, based on revenue passenger miles; the largest U.S. household-goods maker* (noting later that the yardstick is sales).

Avoid vague references such as *leading maker of liquid-crystal displays* or *leading maker of passenger planes.* Be specific.

lead manager. Write *a group of investment banks led by (company name).*

lead underwriter. Write *a group of investment banks led by (company name).*

legal action If someone will be sued, say so.

legal citations. The legal citation should be listed in the last paragraph of any story that discusses specific court cases: *The case is: Widget Inc. v. Acme Corp., 104CV023646, Santa Clara County Superior Court.* If the case documents are available on the Bloomberg system, attach them to the story or provide a clickable link.

legislature. Capitalize this word when referring to a specific state:

The Georgia Legislature voted against the bill.
In Nevada, the Legislature approved the bill.
The Legislature was under pressure, Delaware Governor Smith said.

Don't capitalize in generic or plural uses:

Three state legislatures delayed voting.
The Kentucky and Ohio legislatures failed to act.
No legislature has considered taking action.

Refer to the *Associated Press Stylebook* entries on general assembly, assembly, governmental bodies, house of representatives and senate as well as legislature.

less. Use for things that can't be counted: *less steam, less work, less space.* Use *fewer* for things that can be counted: *fewer bowls of cereal, fewer hours of work, fewer feet of space.*

level. Ask whether *level* is extraneous or whether another word might be a better choice than this overused and often misused term.

Statistics that are presented as a percentage, rather than an absolute number, are a rate rather than a level: *French unemployment climbed to the highest rate in 22 months in July.*

Level works when a word such as *lowest* used alone would be hard to read: *Sales of previously owned homes in the U.S. fell in April to the lowest level in almost four years.*

Level isn't needed when it's clear what the superlative is referring back to: *A measure of the supply of homes for sale rose to the highest since August 1992.*

A foreign-exchange rate is not a level: *The single currency traded at $1.3440 versus the dollar, close to the rate before the figures were released.*

Price is a more precise term when money is involved: *Dell jumped 1.8 percent to $27.37, its highest price since November 2006.*

Libor. London interbank offered rate. The rate at which banks in London are willing to lend money to each other for a specified time period. Benchmark for money-market rates. Libor is acceptable in headlines and on second reference.

lift. Not to be used as a substitute for *raise* or *increase.*

light. Not to be used for characterizing the amount of trading in a market. Provide the current day's total and compare it with a daily average of at least three months.

like. Synonymous with *similar to.* Not a substitute for *such as.*

likely. Not an adverb substituting for *probably: She likely will vote for the bill.* Acceptable as an adjective: *The bill is likely to pass* or *Jones is a likely candidate.*

Lima. Stands alone as the capital of Peru.

Lisbon. Stands alone as the capital of Portugal.

listed company. Company whose shares are listed on one or more stock markets. Write *public company* except in stories about a market where shares trade.

listing. Membership in the ranks of companies whose shares can trade in a specific market. Better to write that a company *plans to go public* or *plans to sell shares to the public* than to write that it will list shares.

little changed. Acceptable, but look for a more interesting way to tell the story. Rather than writing *European stocks were little changed*, focus on stocks and/or industry groups that rose or fell substantially.

London. Stands alone as the capital of the U.K.

London Club. Forum for countries seeking relief from debt owed to commercial banks. Each debtor country has a separate "club," formed at its request and dissolved when an agreement is signed.

long dated. Be specific: *more than 10 years, three to five years.*

long term. Be specific: *more than 10 years, three to five years.*

looks to. Imprecise. Write about what the person or organization wants or expects. Instead of *Brown is looking to the election to gain a mandate*, write *Brown expects to gain a majority of at least 165 seats in the election.*

loonie. Acceptable on second reference for the Canadian dollar, to provide variety and reduce word echoes. Avoid overusing.

Los Angeles. The U.S. city stands alone.

loss. Losses widen and narrow; they don't rise or fall: *The company's first-quarter net loss widened to $39 million, or 10 cents a share, from $27 million, or 7 cents, a year earlier.*

loss-making. Awkward. Use *unprofitable* or *money-losing.*

Luxembourg. Stands alone as the capital of Luxembourg.

-ly. Adverbs ending in *-ly* don't take hyphens: *closely held company, most actively traded shares.*

M

Macau. This city needs *China* on first reference. Not Macao.

Macedonia. Use *Republic of Macedonia* on first reference. Later references can say *Macedonia.*

A size and scope lower in stories should mention that the country formerly was part of Yugoslavia, to prevent confusion with the Macedonia regions of Greece and Bulgaria.

mad cow disease. Acceptable on first reference. Be sure to include the scientific name high in a story: *bovine spongiform encephalopathy.*

Madrid. Stands alone as the capital of Spain.

main board. Used in some countries, such as Malaysia and Indonesia, to refer to the main section of the stock exchange where the largest companies often trade. Referred to as *first section* in some exchanges. Avoid this jargon. Be more specific or explain how big a company must be to trade in the different parts of an exchange.

Main Street. U.S. phrase referring to the center of town, and the shops typically found there, similar to High Street in the U.K. Avoid both terms.

-maker. One-syllable words can take *-maker* as a suffix if they refer to established trades or industries: *drugmaker, steelmaker, glassmaker, toymaker. Automaker* also is acceptable. Keep *maker* as a separate word otherwise: *aircraft maker, computer-chip maker, policy maker.* Don't use if the combination of letters makes it awkward. *Deal maker*, for example, should be two words.

Maker usually is preferable to longer synonyms, such as producer or manufacturer.

management board. One of two tiers of company directors in some European countries. Runs the business, while a *supervisory board* of outside directors makes strategic decisions.

Manila. Stands alone as the capital of the Philippines.

margin. Measure of profitability. Expressed as a percentage of sales or revenue in earnings analysis, and as a dollar amount in oil markets. Margins widen or narrow; they don't rise or fall. Use plural *margins* only when referring to more than one part of a company or more than one type of margin. Analysts track several margins, so be specific in any reference. See gross margin, operating margin and profit margin.

market expectations. Markets don't have voices or opinions; people do.

Marseille. The French city stands alone.

MBA. Use MBA, without periods, to abbreviate *master's degree in business administration.*

Other academic degrees take periods: *B.A., M.S., Ph.D.* It's always acceptable, and often smoother, to avoid abbreviations and write a phrase such as *doctorate in mathematics* or *master's degree in marine biology.*

mean, median, average. *Average* is the same as *mean* for our purposes. Don't confuse with *median*, which is the middle number in a range ordered from low to high. We use the median when we survey analysts for forecasts of government economic reports or company earnings.

measurements. Use the system of units—metric or U.S.—in the country that is the main subject of the story. Provide a conversion to the other in parentheses on first reference. Stories from the U.S. might refer to *2,500 miles (4,000 kilometers)*, assuming the distance in miles was approximate. If the measurement is precise, *2,500 miles (4,022 kilometers)* is preferable. Stories from countries that use the metric system should put the distance in kilometers first. To calculate equivalents, enter UCNV <Go>.

median, average, mean. The *median* is the middle number in a range ordered from low to high. We use the median when we survey analysts for forecasts of government economic reports or company earnings. *Average* is the same as *mean* for our purposes.

medium. References to size or time should be specific: *$250 million to $1 billion* or *the next two to three years*, rather than *medium-size* or *medium-term*.

Melbourne. The Australian city stands alone.

members. Stock markets consist of companies, not members. Write *companies in the S&P 500 Index*, rather than *members of the S&P 500 Index*.

merger. Acceptable on second or subsequent reference for *acquisition*. *Merger* is appropriate only when the companies are essentially equal partners. If one will have a dominant role in the merged company, use alternatives such as *acquisition, purchase* or *takeover*.

To determine which company will be dominant, consider the composition of the resulting board, the ownership of the combined company's shares, the choice of the chief executive and the location of the future headquarters.

When the would-be buyer plans to pay in stock, calculate the value of the offer at the previous day's closing price: *Molson Inc. and Adolph Coors Co. agreed to merge in a $3.4 billion share swap*. Don't update the value until after the official close of trading. Calculate the new value with each successive day until the transaction is complete.

M&A is acceptable on second reference and in headlines for the phrase *mergers and acquisitions*. Use sparingly.

metric. Acceptable as an adjective for the system of measurement that uses meters and grams. Don't use as a noun to describe an indicator of a company's performance: *the company's metrics are improving*.

metric ton. Equivalent to 2,204.62 pounds. When citing metric tons, identify them as metric on first reference. *Tons* is enough for later references as long as there aren't any figures in short tons. Don't use the synonym *tonne*.

Mexico City. Stands alone as the capital of Mexico.

Miami. The U.S. city stands alone.

mid-cap. Abbreviation for *mid-capitalization*, used to describe companies with too little market value to be among the stock market's largest and too much value to be considered small. Provide a range of values such as *$1 billion to $10 billion*. Descriptions of a mid-cap stock vary, so always ask for a definition.

mid-size. Be more specific, such as *$250 million to $1 billion*.

Milan. The Italian city stands alone.

million. Always use figures before the word: *2 million; 100 million*.

Milwaukee. The U.S. city stands alone.

ministry. Capitalize only when naming a specific ministry: *The Foreign Ministry declined to comment; The ministry declined to comment*.

Ministry of Finance. Japanese government agency. MOF acceptable in headlines and on second reference.

Minneapolis. The U.S. city stands alone.

minus sign. Don't use the minus sign in copy or headlines. Spell the word because the symbol could be overlooked: *The temperature was minus 10 degrees Fahrenheit* or *Confidence among manufacturers fell to minus 1.3 points in the three months ended Dec 31*.

Exception: Use the minus sign in bond ratings: *BBB– is Standard & Poor's lowest investment-grade rating*.

miracle. Save for miraculous events. Miracle escape, for instance, is a cliche.

Mitsubishi. Use at least two words of the name in headlines on Mitsubishi Corp., a Japanese trading company, or affiliates whose names begin with Mitsubishi: *Mitsubishi Heavy, Mitsubishi UFJ*.

Mitsui. Use at least two words of the name in headlines on Mitsui & Co., a Japanese trading company, or affiliates whose names begin with Mitsui: *Mitsui Chemicals, Mitsui Engineering*.

mixed. Use the word to describe markets only when benchmark measures differ substantially: for instance, when the Dow Jones Industrial Average is up 100 points and the Nasdaq Composite is down 50 points. Otherwise, use *little changed*. Market stories ought to focus on the most newsworthy moves; leads that say prices *were mixed* aren't compelling.

mobile phone. *Mobile phone* is the preferred term in all references except direct quotes. While many people continue to use the term *cell phone*, the technology is no longer cellular.

modest. A vague and opinionated modifier. Give a percentage: *earnings rose 2.5 percent*, rather than *a modest earnings increase*.

modifiers. Modifiers except those derived from specific details are unnecessary. A headline that says industrial production rose *a more-than-expected 0.2 percent* serves by providing a comparison with the expected percentage change. A headline that says industrial production rose *a modest 0.2 percent* makes a judgment that may be debatable. The first headline is precise; the second is imprecise.

Hyphenate compound modifiers: *first-quarter earnings, health-care stocks, lower-than-average returns*.

When a compound modifier begins with a numeral, hyphenate between the numeral and the unit of measure: *10-year period, 12-day rally, 25-basis-point increase*. Exceptions are currency amounts and percentages: *$14 trillion industry, 28 percent gain*.

Avoid language in front of a name or as an appositive that may be judgmental. When a person is accused of a crime or other misbehavior, that information should not be used as a label, which might prejudice the reader. Instead, use a parenthetical description, in headlines and text.

Monaco. Stands alone as the capital of the principality of Monaco.

money manager. Preferable to *portfolio manager* because the manager is paid to handle other people's money.

Montreal. The Canadian city stands alone.

Moody's Investors Service. Unit of Moody's Corp. that provides credit ratings, research and financial information.

Moscow. Stands alone as the capital of Russia.

most. Whether *most* people in any category are doing something is rarely known. Use *many* or *few* when referring to anecdotal evidence gathered through several interviews.

most favored nation. Trade status under which the U.S. applies the lowest possible tariffs to imports from a specific country. Available to most other countries on a reciprocal basis.

Muammar Qaddafi. Longtime leader of Libya.

mull. *Consider* is preferable.

multibillion. Hyphenate in a compound: *multibillion-dollar agreement.*

multimedia. More than one medium, such as newspapers, magazines, radio, television and the Web.

multimillion. Hyphenate in a compound: *multimillion-dollar agreement.*

Mumbai. The Indian city stands alone. Mention that it was formerly known as Bombay when appropriate.

Munich. The German city stands alone.

Muslim. Not *Moslem.*

Myanmar. Indicate that the country was formerly known as Burma.

N

named. The ambiguous use of *named* when people or organizations appear in a lawsuit or official statement implies judgment we don't wish to make.

The word is imprecise because it might mean that the party has been sued or that it has merely been mentioned.

names. Provide full names of companies, organizations and people on first reference.

For people's names, consider personal preferences. William Jefferson Clinton encourages Bill Clinton as standard usage. Rupert Murdoch goes by his middle name rather than his first name, Keith. Refer to people's Bloomberg Profile entries, available under <Help>, as a reference for their names.

If a person has a middle initial on his business card and it is used in news releases from his company, government or organization, we should use it as well.

For people under age 18, use first name rather than last name for second reference. The exception is when a child is accused of a crime. Use the last name for a child involved in this adult situation.

Family names come first, rather than last, in Asian countries such as China and Korea. Many Indonesians use only one name. See the Asian Names section for details about these countries and others in the region.

In Dutch surnames, use lowercase for inserts such as van, de, den, der, van der, van den, in 't, op 't and ter: *Cees de Jager, Cees van der Hoeve.* When referring only to the surname, use uppercase for one-word inserts and for the first word of two-word inserts: *De Jager, Van der Hoeve.*

In company names, the first word often will suffice in headlines and on second reference. LVMH is fine for LVMH Moet Hennessy Louis Vuitton SA of France because it's unique to the company.

When the first word is a common name, use as many additional words as necessary to distinguish a story's subject from others with similar names. Use Continental AG in headlines about the German tire-maker and Continental Air in headlines about the U.S. airline.

Always substitute *&* in place of *and, et, und, y* and similar words in company names. For more details, see company names.

Capitalize all brand names of prescription and over-the-counter drugs: *Contac, Tagamet, Valium.* Don't capitalize generic or chemical names: *aspirin, penicillin.*

narrow. Losses, deficits and margins do this when they get smaller. Preferable to confusing words such as *decline* or *fall.*

narrowly. Meaningless when used as *narrowly higher, narrowly lower* or *narrowly mixed* in describing markets. Be specific.

native American. Use *American Indian.*

NATO. Acceptable in headlines and on first reference to the North Atlantic Treaty Organization. Provide the full name on second reference.

near. Not precise enough for establishing context. *Less than 1 percent from a two-year high* is preferable to *near a two-year high.*

near future. People use this pompous term when they mean *soon.* Use *soon* if you must. Be more specific when you can. See **term.**

nearly. Use nearly to refer to distance; use almost to refer to amount or degree: *We had covered nearly 3 miles after hiking amost four hours.* Don't use nearly as a qualifier; *nearly unique,* for example, isn't acceptable.

negative equity. When liabilities exceed assets.

negative territory. There is no such place on Earth. Specify what has declined.

net income, net loss. The bottom line in earnings stories, even for countries where pretax income is the more common benchmark for profit and for companies that focus on some other measure. Avoid phrases such as *net earnings* or *net profit.*

net interest income. Interest that banks receive on loans and on investments such as bonds, minus the interest paid for deposits.

net interest margin. Difference between what a bank pays on deposits and receives on loans and investments. Expressed as a percentage of assets.

New Delhi. Stands alone as the capital of India.

new economy. Used to describe companies whose business is associated with the Internet. The term isn't precise.

New Orleans. The U.S. city stands alone.

news reports. Specify sources on first reference.

newspaper names. Put *the* in lowercase at the beginning of a name even if the newspaper doesn't: *the New York Times,* not *The New York Times.*

Newspaper shouldn't be truncated to *paper,* such as when attributing information. Write *the newspaper said* rather than *the paper said.*

New York. The U.S. city stands alone.

In headlines, abbreviate New York City as *NYC* and New York state as *N.Y.*

Also use *N.Y.* in the shortened form of newspaper names in headlines: *N.Y. Post, N.Y. Daily News, N.Y. Times.* For the Times, *NYT* also is acceptable.

next generation. *New* is a better, and shorter, way to describe new products. Explain how they improve upon previous ones, too.

non-. Most words prefixed with *non-* don't carry a hyphen: *nonprofit, nonoperating.* Follow *Webster's New World College Dictionary.*

non-core Companies often use this phrase before *business* or *assets* to define whatever they no longer consider essential to their strategy. Describe the business or assets instead.

non-interest income. Banks' income from sources such as fees on checking accounts and credit cards, service charges, and sales of securities or mutual funds.

notch. Use *level* or *grade* for raising or cutting a credit rating.

numbers. Write one through nine as words unless the number precedes a unit of measure or refers to someone's age: *two-year note, four-time winner, seven sheep, 1 million, 8 euros, 9-year-old boy.*

Points aren't a unit of measure, so use words rather than numerals for one-digit numbers: *four percentage points, a two-percentage-point increase, 3 1/4 basis points, 19 basis points.*

Use numerals for 10 or more unless the numbers refer to a quantity of products known by numbers instead of names: *10-year note, 27 sheep, thirty 777s*.

Write first through ninth as words and use numerals for 10th or higher in all references, including trashlines. Exceptions: Use numerals for Paris's municipal districts and for names that are part of a sequence: *4th arondissement, 3rd Congressional District, 6th Fleet, 7th Ward*.

Don't have a number on one line in a story and the unit of measure on the next line. Use a paragraph mark to put them side by side on the same line.

Before:

> *The company said net income set a quarterly record of $4.5 million.*

After:

> *The company said net income set a quarterly record of $4.5 million.*

Use numerals when referring to ratios: *a 3-for-2 stock split*. Use hyphens in all cases: *a 5-to-1 ratio; a ratio of 5-to-1; split the stock 5-for-1*.

Odds are expressed as a ratio: *Bookies put the odds of a Conservative Party victory at 7–3*. Percentages shouldn't be used with the word *odds*. Instead: *Smith said the bill has an 80 percent likelihood of passing*.

Use a comma in all numbers of 1,000 or more, including indexes: *The FTSE 100 Index fell 0.9 percent to 4,338.4. Sage Group rose 2.3 percent to 254.3 pence in London*.

When a numeral begins a compound modifier, hyphenate between the numeral and the unit of measure except with currency amounts and percentages: *10-year period, 12-day rally, 25-basis-point increase, $14 trillion industry, 23 billion-pound purchase, 28 percent gain*.

For ranges, repeat the unit of measurement in text: *$10 million to $15 million*. In headlines, repeat the unit or find another way of expressing the amount, such as *More Than $10 Million* or *Up to $15 Million*. Don't write *$10–15 Mln* to save space.

With *-fold*, use a word and no hyphen through *ninefold*, numerals and a hyphen starting with *10-fold*. Make it *sevenfold, 15-fold, 37-fold*.

When a fraction follows a whole number, use numerals rather than words. *Half a year; 3 1/2 years. Two-thirds of a cup; 1 2/3 cups.* Percentages often are easier to grasp and more precise than fractions: *increased by 31 percent*, rather than *increased by almost a third*.

For ages, use numerals with people. With objects, use words through nine, numbers for 10 and up. *The 5-year-old boy. He was 32 years old. The four-year-old program. The 10-year-old building.*

Headlines, subheads and sentences should begin with words rather than numerals. Don't start with years, numbers preceded by a dollar sign, or other numerals. The only exception is a name, such as 3M Co.

When noting an historic level—a stock price fell to *a three-year low* or an economic statistic was *the highest in 18 months*—don't use a number that is rounded up. These thresholds are treated like birthdays. You aren't 30 until you reach that exact date. Being 29 years and 10 months doesn't count.

We can use *almost* in certain cases, especially for larger numbers, but do so sparingly. It's acceptable to say *General Motors' shares are at the lowest in almost 14 years* when it has been 13 years and 11 months. Don't round to say they hit a 14-year low until it is accurate to the day.

For smaller numbers, use discretion with *almost*. It may not make sense to say a number was the highest *in almost 14 months* when it has been 13 months and 17 days. It's better to round down to 13 months or write *in more than 13 months*.

For additional style guidelines related to numbers, see **fractions; percentages; rounding;** and **records**.

Nuremberg.   Not *Nuernberg* or *Nurnberg*. Needs *Germany* on first reference.

O

obscenities.   Acceptable in quotations only when the comment was made in a newsworthy context and is compelling. An executive editor must sign off on the decision.

Newsworthy context is when the words were uttered in a public forum, at a newsworthy event or in the execution of public duty. That excludes private interviews with reporters.

The words also must help drive a story. Don't use obscenities gratuitously or for color.

Write with hyphens substituting for letters after the first letter of the obscene term: *"Have you ever tried to get cow s--- out of a Prada purse?" she said. "It's not so f---ing simple."*

observers. Lacks precision, as in *observers said.* Identify people in detail.

offered rate. Not *offer rate.*

offer, offering. Offer and offering may be used when writing about the sale of securities: *Spirit previously planned to offer 20 million shares at $14 to $16.*

offset. Try to identify a theme that stands out and introduce others later. Don't tie together all of a story's forces or themes by using this word in leads.

oil patch. Not *oilpatch.*

oilfield. Use this as an adjective, *oil field* as a noun.

OK. Acceptable only in quotes. Unacceptable as a synonym for *approve.* Don't spell as *okay.*

Oklahoma City. The U.S. city stands alone.

old economy. Used to describe companies whose business isn't associated with the Internet. The term isn't precise.

one-off. Write *one-time.*

one-time. As in *one-time charges, one-time gains.* Use this rather than words such as *extraordinary, nonrecurring* or *exceptional,* and only when appropriate. Don't assume that a charge or gain is one-time just because a company presents the item that way.

ongoing. Acceptable only in quotes. If an investigation is under way, for instance, it's ongoing by definition.

online. Use *online*, one word, both as adjective and adverb.

When referring to the Internet, use *Internet* or *Web* on first reference because there are other ways of going online.

on offer. Write *for sale*.

on the year. This phrase could mean year to date, from a year earlier, the past year or the fiscal year. Be specific.

on track. Vague when used as *the stock index is on track for its biggest weekly decline in a decade*. We usually can find a better way of conveying what we're trying to say: *the stock index is headed for its biggest weekly decline in a decade*.

OPEC. Acceptable in headlines and on first reference to the Organization of Petroleum Exporting Countries. Use the full name on second reference.

Stories also should identify OPEC's 12 member nations: Algeria, Angola, Ecuador, Iran, Iraq, Kuwait, Libya, Nigeria, Qatar, Saudi Arabia, United Arab Emirates and Venezuela.

open-end funds. Mutual funds that sell new shares continuously and buy back shares. Holders can only trade directly with the fund. See closed-end funds and exchange-traded funds.

open-market operations. Jargon. Write that central banks buy and sell government securities.

operating margin. Shows how much a company earned after paying expenses for production, sales and marketing, research and development, and administration, and after taking accounting charges to reduce the value of its assets. Expressed as percentage of sales.

operating profit, operating income, operating loss. These terms are used differently in different industries and by different companies. Define them each time: *Operating profit, or sales minus the cost of goods sold and administrative expenses, rose 66 percent to 32.6 billion yen.*

operation. Not a synonym for *business*. Hewlett-Packard Co. has a *printer unit*, not a *printer operation*.

options. Contracts granting their buyers the right—but not the obligation—to buy or sell a security, a commodity or an index's cash value at a set price. There are two basic types: *Call options*, conveying the right to buy, and *put options*, representing the right to sell. *American-style options* can be exercised at any time before they expire; *European-style options* can be exercised only at the time of expiration. Explain in stories.

The contracts are said to be *in the money* when the underlying asset has a price above the strike price of a call option and below that of a put option. The contracts are called *out of the money* when the underlying asset price is below the call's strike and above that of a put option.

ordinary share. Use *common share*.

organized labor. This phrase lacks precision. Better to refer to specific unions, such as the International Association of Machinists and Aerospace Workers.

Osama bin Laden. Not *Usama*. Capitalize *bin* when *Bin Laden* appears by itself in headlines or at the start of sentences.

Oslo. Stands alone as the capital of Norway.

others. Meaningless by itself, especially in headlines, because it is vague. *Philip Morris, Others Seek Reduction in Taxes on Cigarettes* is imprecise because *others* could refer to tobacco companies, retailers, health groups or other organizations. Better: *Philip Morris and R.J. Reynolds Seek Cigarette-Tax Cut* or *Philip Morris, Other Cigarette Makers Seek Tax Cut*. If we need to indicate additional items on a list, either name them or provide a more specific reference: *Burger King, McDonald's and other restaurant chains*.

Ottawa. Stands alone as the capital of Canada.

out of. Pompous when used in phrases such as *news out of the Middle East*. Use *from*.

outage. Use *failure* instead in references to power failures.

outlook. A company can increase or reduce its earnings forecast. That means its outlook improved or worsened. The company didn't increase or reduce its outlook.

output. Simplify this favorite among economists. Instead of *gross domestic product, the total output of goods and services produced*, for instance, use the equally clear *gross domestic product, the total of goods and services produced*.

outside of. Not to be used as a synonym for *excluding*, which is preferable.

outside spokesman. Name the person and identify his or her firm, in addition to the company being represented.

outsized. Meaningless. Specify.

outsourcing. Practice of shifting work to contractors, often in other countries, from employees. Define in stories.

outweigh. Try to identify a theme that stands out and introduce others later. Don't tie together all of a story's forces or themes by using this word in leads.

over. Not to be used as a synonym for *during* or *more than*.

overall. Use *total* when that is the intended meaning. *Overall* often is extraneous and can be deleted.

overbought. Favorite jargon of analysts. Better to write that a security or market is *poised to fall* and to explain the indicators used in reaching that conclusion.

oversold. Favorite jargon of analysts. Better to write that a security or market is *poised to rise* and to explain the indicators used in reaching that conclusion.

oversubscribed. Describes a stock or bond sale in which investors offer to buy more securities than the total amount available. Explain and provide specific amounts.

oversupply. Write instead that *at current prices, people aren't willing to buy as much as producers want to sell*.

overweight. Describes a market segment, such as an industry group or a country, that accounts for a larger percentage of a portfolio than it does of a benchmark index. Instead of using the word, provide specifics.

P

Palestine. Palestine signifies different territory in different contexts.

The land historically belonged to the kingdoms of Israel and Judah. Palestine represented the area west of the Jordan River that was a British mandate from the 1920s until the creation of modern Israel in 1948.

Today, Palestine includes parts of Israel and Jordan. Use *Palestine* in the context of geography, not as a substitute for the Palestinian Authority, Palestine Liberation Organization or any other political body.

Panama City. Stands alone as the capital of Panama.

pandemic. Not to be confused with a global outbreak. The H5N1 strain of avian flu in humans is not a bird-flu pandemic.

The lethal virus spreading among poultry doesn't easily infect people because it doesn't have many of the characteristics of human flu.

If avian flu mutates to become highly contagious among people, it will no longer be an avian flu strain, rather a *pandemic influenza virus*. Scientists call the global outbreak of avian flu in animals a *panzootic*.

paper. Not to be used as a synonym for *securities* or for *newspaper*.

paper says. In headlines on media summaries, identify the publication.

parentheses. Direct quotes should be the exact words of the speaker. Paraphrase or use partial quotes instead of parentheses.

Paris. Stands alone as the capital of France.

Paris Club. Forum for countries seeking relief from debts owed to other countries. There are 19 members, whose representatives meet informally in Paris to provide coordinated assistance. Provide the explanation and use the name only when necessary to set up a quote.

partner. Use as a verb only for ballet. For other alliances, say *teamed, joined,* or *formed a partnership.*

passthrough. Type of mortgage-backed security entitling its owner to receive principal and interest payments on home mortgages. The homeowners' money passes through a government agency or investment bank before reaching investors. Define in stories.

pause. In market reporting, markets don't pause when prices are little changed. Investors don't pause when they consider what is happening.

pence. Don't use *p* as an abbreviation for pence. Spell pence in all references, including stock prices.

penny. Use when referring to the currency of a country that officially has pennies as a monetary unit, such as the U.K. Use *cents* when referring to the currency of a country using cents as a monetary unit, including the U.S. and Canada. Penny is acceptable for referring to 1-cent coins. See cents.

Pentagon. On first reference, information from the Pentagon should be attributed to the U.S. Defense Department or the person who supplied it. Attribution to the Pentagon is acceptable on second reference.

per. Use *a* instead of *per* when referring to amounts: *50 cents a share, 50 planes a year, $50 a barrel.* Exceptions are *earnings per share* or *per-share earnings*, when an exact figure isn't included, and *miles per hour.*

perceived. Identify the source of the perception or just state it as fact: *The Federal Reserve raised the target rate for overnight bank loans*, not the perceived target.

percent. Spell the word *percent* in stories. Use the % symbol in story headlines, Top headlines and tables.

percentages. *Percent* isn't the same as *percentage point.* The Federal Reserve, for instance, may raise or lower its target rate for overnight bank loans by 0.25 percentage point, not 0.25 percent.

Express percentages as numerals. For numbers less than 1, include the 0 before the decimal point: *0.9 percent*, not *.9 percent*. The 0 isn't needed after the decimal for a whole number: *5 percent*, not 5.0 percent.

Round off percentages of less than 10 to one decimal place unless the rounded figure is a whole number: *9.7 percent*, not 9.68 percent. For percentages of 10 or more, round off to whole numbers: *15 percent*, not 15.3 percent.

Take amounts to more decimal places when the added precision is required. It's better to write *Fund A rose 18.4 percent, while Fund B rose 17.6 percent* than to write that both funds gained 18 percent.

For percentages of about 100 or more, making a general comparison is usually better than providing specific figures: *first-quarter earnings more than doubled*, rather than *first-quarter earnings rose 109 percent*.

Don't hyphenate percentages in compound modifiers: *14 percent gain*, not 14-percent.

When calculating percentages, use the most complete figures available, not rounded figures.

Points aren't a unit of measure, so use words rather than numerals for one-digit numbers: *four percentage points*, a *two-percentage-point increase*.

Percentages shouldn't be used with the word *odds*. Instead: *Smith said the bill has an 80 percent likelihood of passing*. Odds are expressed as a ratio: *Bookies put the odds of a Conservative Party victory at 7–3*.

period. *Period* may be used on second reference for a time span in earnings or sales stories. The first reference must specify quarter, half, week or month.

Persian Gulf. The Persian Gulf is surrounded by Saudi Arabia, the United Arab Emirates, Qatar, Kuwait, Iraq and Iran. If a quotation refers to it as the Arabian Gulf, add a line of explanation that some countries use that name for the body of water.

persuade, convince. Convincing involves a person's beliefs, while persuading involves a person's actions. Someone is *convinced of, convinced that* or *persuaded to*.

Philadelphia. The U.S. city stands alone.

Phoenix. The U.S. city stands alone.

phonetic spelling. Our style is to use standard American English.

Slang such as *gonna* doesn't belong in our stories, even in quotes. We write stories in accepted spelling and should use *going to*, no matter how the speaker pronounced it.

physical. In commodity markets, an actual commodity as opposed to a contract to buy or sell. *Delivery* will suffice instead of *physical delivery*.

pipeline. Jargon that sometimes refers to all products and services that a company, especially a drugmaker, is developing. Explain the term and don't overuse.

Pittsburgh. The U.S. city stands alone.

players. Investors, traders, executives and politicians aren't players. They are professionals. *Players* is a conceit of journalism. Use *participants* if necessary, and a more descriptive word or phrase if possible: *traders and investors.*

pleaded. Not *pled*. Past tense of *plead*.

plug. Confusing when used in conjunction with a budget deficit. Write that borrowing will be used to *finance* or *fund* a deficit.

poison pill. Type of takeover defense that typically gives shareholders the right to buy new stock at a discount. Introduce conversationally or preface with *so-called* on first reference.

policy maker. Not *policymaker* or *policy-maker*.

policy making. Not *policymaking*. Hyphenate when used as a compound modifier: *policy-making panel.*

political labels. Judgments such as *liberal, conservative, moderate, left* and *right* should be avoided unless we provide specific examples of their meaning.

poll. Use in describing results of scientific sampling with a quantifiable margin of error. Otherwise, *survey* is preferable. We survey analysts and economists.

portfolio. We prefer to leave portfolios to artists. Don't succumb to press agents extolling business portfolios. Just identify the investments: *stocks and bonds.*

portfolio manager. *Money manager* is preferable, because the manager is paid to handle other people's money.

positive territory. There is no such place on Earth. Specify what has risen.

possessives.

    Singular nouns. Add *'s,* even when the word ends in a letter that sounds like *s* or *sh*: *Xilinix's earnings, Onex's IPO.*

    Singular nouns that end in *s*. Add *'s: the witness's response, the boss's decision.*

    Singular names that end in *s*. Add *'s,* whether the final *s* is pronounced or not: *Sears's sales, American Express's customers, Arkansas's budget.* Exceptions where only the apostrophe is used: Classical names such as *Sophocles' Antigone* or *Artemis' bow.* Names with more than one syllable when the last syllable starts and ends with *s* or an *s* sound and the final syllable is unaccented: *Moses' staff, Massachusetts' governor.*

    Nouns that take the same form whether singular or plural. Add *'s: one moose's tracks, three moose's tracks.*

    Plural nouns that don't end in *s*. Add *'s: the women's achievements, the men's decisions.*

    Plural nouns that end in *s*. Add only an apostrophe, including when the plural noun represents a singular entity: *the accountants' review, the CEOs' compensation.*

    Nouns plural in form but singular in meaning, including names. Add an apostrophe: *the measles' effects, General Motors' earnings.*

    Compound phrases. Add the punctuation after the word nearest to the object that is possessed: *attorneys general's research, inspector general's request.* Add the punctuation only after the last word if the possession is joint: *Bush* *and Blair's agreement.* Add punctuation after both words in the phrase if the objects are individually owned: *Germany's and France's budgets.* Do not add an apostrophe after a word that ends in *s* that functions primarily as a descriptive element: *a reporters manual, the dockworkers lockout.*

Common expressions that are possessive in form. Add only an apostrophe when the expression ends with *s* or an *s* sound and is followed by a word that begins with *s: for goodness' sake, for appearance' sake.* Otherwise, use *'s.*

Double possessives. A double possessive occurs when a possessive follows *of.* Use *'s* for the possessive when the word following *of* is an animate object and the word preceding *of* involves only part of the animate object's possession: *A friend of Jim's,* not *a friend of Jim.* (Animate object and only one friend is involved.) *A friend of the college,* not *a friend of the college's.* (Inanimate object.) *The friends of George Washington,* not *the friends of George Washington's.* (All of the friends are involved.)

possible. Use a more precise word. Anything is possible.

post-. Words with this prefix generally don't require a hyphen unless the first letter that follows it is capitalized: *postwar, post–World War II.*

posted. Make sure this word goes with an appropriate noun. Companies can post earnings, but a factory can't post orders. *Reported* or *had* is often preferable because the terms are less jargonistic.

pounds. Never use the pound symbol when referring to the U.K. currency. Write the word *pound.*

power outage. Use *power failure* for this utility-industry phrase.

Prague. Stands alone as the capital of the Czech Republic.

pre-market trading. Be specific: *In trading before exchanges opened.*

preferred. Write *preferred shares* rather than *preference shares* or *preferential shares.*

In earnings stories, use dollar amounts before payment of dividends on preferred stock. Use per-share amounts after the dividends, and make clear that they reflect the dividend payments.

premium. Price above face value. Used most often when referring to the share price of a company targeted for takeover, and to bond prices. Be specific when referring to this difference.

prepositions. In headlines, capitalize prepositions of four or more letters: *About, Above, After, Among, Behind, Between, From, Into, Over, Through, Toward, Under, Until, Upon, With, Without.*

Shorter prepositions usually are lowercase: *at, but, by, for, in, of, off, to, up.* Capitalize the short ones when they are part of an expression: *Fed Up, Hang On, Check Off.*

Use prepositions such as *below, under, above* and *over* to denote a physical relationship. Don't use them as substitutes for *less than* or *more than.*

presence. Companies say they are expanding their presence, or trying to increase it. These phrases are meaningless, so don't use them. Give specifics about what the company is attempting.

pretax. Not *pre-tax.* Use amounts before taxes in earnings stories only when after-tax figures aren't available, and always label them.

price. Express the price of a commodity as a singular rather than plural.

price-earnings ratio. Share price divided by earnings per share. The amount that an investor has to pay for every currency unit, such as a dollar or a euro, of earnings. Define this in all cases. Avoid the phrase *price-to-earnings* when referring to the ratio.

price quotes. Provide the time when quoting prices for stocks, bonds, futures and currencies, or indicate that the price was at the close. Include the location that correlates with the time. Electronic trading makes it imprecise to specify a stock exchange.

Silvercorp fell 16 percent to C$6.52 at 11:47 a.m. in Toronto, the biggest decline since Nov. 19, 2008.

Commonwealth Bank of Australia, the nation's largest lender by market value, sank 4.1 percent to $145.45 in Sydney, its lowest closing price in more than two years.

The FTSE 100 fell 1.6 percent to 5,129.62 at the close in London as all but eight companies retreated.

The Bovespa declined 0.5 percent to 55,412.37 at 12:15 p.m. in Sao Paulo. Forty-one stocks dropped on the index, while 23 rose.

Wheat futures for December delivery fell 0.3 percent to settle at $7.2725 a bushel on the Chicago Board of Trade.

The S&P GSCI Index retreated 2.5 percent at 12:42 p.m. in New York. Arabica coffee for December delivery fell 2.6 percent to $2.767 a pound on ICE Futures U.S.

The U.K. currency strengthened 0.4 percent to $1.6049 at 4:43 p.m. in London, after earlier falling to $1.5913, the weakest level since July 13. The pound appreciated 1.2 percent to 87.12 pence per euro, after slipping 0.4 percent yesterday.

U.K. 10-year bond yields gained two basis points, or 0.02 percentage point, to 2.36 percent at 9 a.m. in London, according to Bloomberg Bond Trader prices. The 3.75 percent bond, due September 2020, rose 0.61, or 6.10 pounds per 1,000-pound ($1,597) face amount, to 111.90.

price target. Jargon that analysts use to describe the price they expect a stock to reach by a certain date or within a certain period. Give the price, along with the date or period.

primary offering. Give specifics on what the company is doing rather than writing *primary offering* or *secondary offering*.

prime bank notes. Bogus securities. Sellers have claimed that the notes come from one of the world's top 100, or prime, banks and offer returns of as much as 300 percent with virtually no risk.

prior to Use *before*.

private equity. When using the terms *buyout firm, private-equity firm* or *LBO firm*, explain exactly what the company does. If it specializes in leveraged buyouts, for example, specify that.

private placement. Securities sale to a relatively small number of investors, typically institutions. In the U.S., companies that use private placements don't have to register the securities with the Securities and Exchange Commission before selling.

privately held. In many countries, privately held means that the company is owned by investors rather than by the state. When referring to companies whose shares aren't traded, write *closely held*, whether the shares are held by one person or a few.

privatization. Use *the sale of state-owned businesses* or an equivalent phrase.

problem. Specify. Phrases such as *the country's economic problems* aren't precise. People become interested when problems become specific: *the country's inability to tame inflation.*

producer. Use *producer* and *produce* only to avoid word echoes. *Maker* and *make*, respectively, are shorter and usually will suffice.

profit. The plural *profits* should be used only when referring to earnings of more than one company or more than one period.

profit margin. Percentage of sales that a company earns after subtracting some or all of its costs and expenses. *Gross margin* reflects production costs. *Operating margin* also subtracts expenses for sales and marketing, administration and research, as well as charges taken to reduce the value of assets. *Pretax margin* subtracts financing costs as well. *Net margin* is based on net income. Be specific in identifying which kind of margin.

profit-taking. Could be loss-taking, depending on the purchase price. It's usually impossible to know. Explain the reasons why people are more inclined to sell, rather than writing phrases such as *profit-taking, cashing in* or *locking in profits.*

profit warning. This phrase refers to a company's failure to meet earnings forecasts, and suggests that it's detached from the failure. Better to be descriptive: *The company lowered its forecast for third-quarter earnings,* not *The company gave a third-quarter profit warning.*

pro forma. Once used only to identify earnings that were restated as if a recent takeover had taken place earlier. Now refers to earnings before an assortment of items that a company sees as unrelated to its main business. Also known as *cash earnings.* Don't use. Just explain.

program trading. Trading related to stock-index arbitrage and other strategies that require use of computers. Use a more specific term, such as *computer-guided trading* or *computer-driven trading.*

Prudential. Prudential Financial Inc. is a U.S.-based insurance company. Prudential Plc is a U.K.-based insurer whose shares trade in U.S. markets. Include enough of the company name in headlines to avoid confusion.

put options. Contracts that provide the right—but not the obligation—to sell a security, currency or commodity at a set price within a set period. Also can be used to bet on the direction of an index, such as for stocks or interest rates. When using the term, define immediately after the first reference.

Q

Qaddafi, Muammar. Longtime leader of Libya.

Quebec City. The Canadian city stands alone.

quiet. Don't use when referring to trading. If we're referring to the volume of trading, be specific: *The smallest daily trading volume so far this month.*

quiet period. Companies seeking to sell securities to U.S. investors sometimes cite a *quiet period* imposed by the Securities and Exchange Commission as their reason for declining to comment on a news event. The SEC's restrictions on what can be discussed are less restrictive than what many companies and their lawyers cite.

quotation marks. Financial terms such as collateralized-mortgage obligation or junk bond don't require quotes. Don't put ticker symbols or bond ratings in quote marks.

The official name of an operation, program or product doesn't require quote marks. These names generally are capitalized, while a descriptive term isn't.

Compassion Forum
Operation Desert Storm
Martin Luther King Jr. Scholars Program
Hokey Pokey Elmo
Windows Vista
Canadian mining operations
nurse training program
hydroelectric power project

When our goal is to alert readers to a term that may be unfamiliar, use conversational wording rather than quote marks: *also known as Naxalites; nicknamed Big Bertha; called hoagies by local residents.*

In rare instances, quote marks are needed to convey that the speaker used a term ironically, meaning the opposite of the word's definition: *The offer was "too generous" to accept, she said.*

Never use *so-called* and quote marks together on one term. *So-called* indicates that a term is popularly used but unofficial, sometimes almost slang. It should be used sparingly.

quotations. A direct quotation must convey exactly what the person said. We don't tinker with the words within quotation marks. Don't change a speaker's grammar or incorrect words. If language mistakes make the person appear ignorant or foolish, the only alternative to a direct quote is an accurate paraphrase.

All quotations need named attribution. When a person declines to allow his or her name to be used, find someone else to quote.

It's acceptable to skip parts of the quote and start with the insightful part, as long as we don't distort the speaker's meaning. Use a partial quote, omitting throat-clearing introductions such as *I think, Of course, As you know, In effect* or *Indeed*. Prune hang-on expressions at the end of a quotation that don't add substance.

Put quotations at the beginning of paragraphs. Don't bury them in the middle. Make sure the quotation moves a story forward and doesn't just reiterate earlier text, such as the lead.

Place commas and periods before closing quotation marks, rather than afterward. Colons and semicolons are the only forms of punctuation that sometimes go after closing marks.

If using a quote that wasn't obtained today, indicate when it was said. Provide context about the circumstances of older comments. What was the speaker discussing? Who was the audience? Where?

Only include quotations that are complete as presented. Don't use an ellipsis (. . .) to connect one part of a sentence to another, or to link complete sentences. Use partial quotes or paraphrase.

Always introduce the speaker at the first convenient break, usually the end of the first sentence. Don't make people jump to the end of a passage to find out who is speaking: "*The feeling is that interest rates will continue to drift lower,*" *said Charles Henderson, chief investment officer at Chicago Trust Co., which oversees $7 billion.* "*That's a very positive backdrop for stocks.*"

Don't use parenthetical explanations within quotes, as in "*It (the central bank) should raise interest rates.*" Put the explanation before or after the quote instead, as in *The central bank "should raise interest rates."* If it's impossible to divorce them from the statement, paraphrase rather than use a quote.

Quotes at the top of a story should support the theme set out in the lead and should come from a person of authority. Spokesmen rarely should be the source of a lead quote.

R

raise. Use it to refer to lifting or collecting items, rather than increasing: *The company increased the amount it plans to raise through bond sales by 25 percent to $1 billion.*

rally. A short, steep rise in a market or security price after a period of downward or sideways movement. A rally can *end* but it can't *stall.*

ramp up, ramp down. Companies often use these jargonistic phrases when they mean *increasing* or *decreasing*, which are preferable.

range-bound. Write about what the range is and how long it has lasted before stooping to such market jargon.

rankings. Use an abbreviation and number when referring to a ranking, rather than full words: *No. 1*, not Number One.

Rankings of No. 1, No. 2 and No. 3 are helpful size and scope because they alert the reader that the subject is important in its field. Lower rankings don't have to be mentioned until later in a story, if at all. When naming one of the top three, we usually should name the other two as well.

The *No.* nomenclature should be used only when the ranking is indisputable. Include what measure is used to make the ranking: sales, market capitalization, market share, number of stores, earnings, number of subscribers, assets, etc. When a ranking is in the lead, the yardstick can be dropped within the next few paragraphs to avoid cluttering the lead.

Rankings such as third-highest are hyphenated when used as a compound modifier in front of a noun: *second-largest U.S. discount retailer, fourth-wettest day on record.* Also use a hyphen when the modifier stands alone after a form of the verb *to be*: *The cable maker is the world's second-biggest.*

rate. On first reference, specify what type of rate: *interest rate, swap rate, exchange rate, absorption rate, inflation rate, occupancy rate.* Don't assume the reader knows which rate we mean by the context.

ratepayer. Use *customer*.

realized. Describes gains or losses on investment sales, a preferable way to refer to them. Differs from *unrealized* gains or losses, which are based on changes in the value of investments.

rebound. Signals a springing back from a bad situation, such as returning to profit after having a loss. Be specific about the time element: rebounded from when? It could be the fourth time in a row that the company has gone to a profit from a year-ago loss, and we could startle those who know that it's been profitable in recent quarters.

recession. Define this term precisely. While many people consider two consecutive quarters of falling gross domestic product as a recession, that definition doesn't count among academic or business economists when it comes to the U.S. economy. They defer to the National Bureau of Economic Research, a nonprofit group in Cambridge, Massachusetts, that makes its own judgment.

record. *New record* and *all-time record* are redundant.

records. When noting an historic level, such as a stock price falling to a three-year low, don't round up the number. These thresholds are like birthdays. You don't reach them until you get all the way there.

Almost may be used in certain cases, especially for larger numbers. It's acceptable to say that General Motors shares are at the lowest in almost 14 years when it has been 13 years and 11 months. Don't round to say a 14-year low until it is accurate to the day.

For smaller numbers, use discretion with *almost.* It may not make sense to say *in almost 14 months* when it has been 13 months and 17 days. It's better to round down to 13 months or write *more than 13 months.*

reengineering. Jargon. Process of reassessing what a company does and finding new and improved ways to do it.

reform. One person's idea of reform is another person's idea of a step backward. We have no way of knowing who will turn out to be right, and shouldn't make a judgment.

refute. Not a synonym for *dispute, deny* or *rebut.* To refute is to disprove. To dispute, deny or rebut is to make an effort to disprove, and that effort may fail.

regions. Capitalize only regions that are well-known worldwide: *San Francisco Bay area, central Boliva, Southeast Asia, Southern California, U.S. Northeast.*

reinvent. Use a simple word such as *change.*

relief. When describing taxes or utility rates, *tax break* and *rate increase* are preferable, for instance, to *tax relief* or *rate relief.*

remain. What remains isn't news, so avoid this. Markets are always moving, for instance. They don't remain anywhere. Just say whether prices, yields or values are higher or lower than they were at the previous day's close.

reopen. *Reopen* is acceptable only after an exceptional closing. Give a time frame: *will reopen after a four-day trading halt; reopened eight months after Hurricane Katrina flooded the building; will be reopened next year under a new name.*
    Stick with *open* for a daily or other regular schedule of opening and closing.

reorganization. Obscures more than clarifies and sounds pompous. Be precise about what the company, government or other organization is doing and why: *said it will shut two of its six divisions and merge three others.*

replacement cost. One of two ways in which U.K. oil companies' financial statements handle inventories. Based on last-in, first-out, known as LIFO, which links the cost of goods sold to the cost of the most recent purchases. The other is historical cost, which calculates the value of unsold oil based on first-in, first-out, or FIFO. This method links the cost of goods sold to the cost of the oldest purchases. Use *replacement cost*, and make clear that the earnings were calculated on that basis.

reportedly. If someone reports something, say who.

representative. Capitalize before the name of a member of the U.S. House: *Representative Nancy Pelosi.* Don't abbreviate as *Rep.*

resignation. Use only in references to someone planning to leave a position. People resign when they give notice, not when they actually depart.

resistance. Analysts use this jargon to identify a price or value that a security, commodity or index probably will struggle to exceed, based on past performance. Describe the performance instead. See **support**.

restructuring. Hackneyed. It can mean almost anything related to a change in a company's affairs. When a company merges, acquires, divests or fires, be specific: *said it will fire 2,000 mechanics, or 5 percent of its employees, close all of its plants and become a distributor.*

results. Imprecise when referring to a company's financial performance. *Earnings* or *loss* is more specific.

retail. When writing about brokerages or banking, we mean *individuals* or *consumers*.

retained earnings. The profits retained by a company after payment of dividends.

rethink. A misused and overused transitive verb that means *reconsider*, *review* or *examine*. Choose an alternative whose meaning is specific.

revenue. Preferable to sales only when writing about companies and industries whose business goes beyond selling goods and/or services. Not *revenues* or *turnover*.

reverse. Use *compared with* when comparing a profit in the latest period and a loss in the year-earlier period, or vice versa.

revitalize. Explain instead that a company has a plan to return to profitability.

rights issue. When a company distributes securities that give stockholders the right to buy additional shares, it's a *rights offer*.

rights offer. Not *rights issue*. Be sure to define this as a sale of stock to current shareholders.

Rio de Janeiro. The Brazilian city stands alone.

rise. Acceptable as a noun only when it doesn't mean *increase*, such as *the rise and fall of the company*. Employees receive a pay increase, not a pay rise. Central banks may consider an interest-rate increase, not an interest-rate rise.

rival. Often extraneous. Don't use if the context makes clear that two companies or people are competitors.

river names. Give the full, English-language name of rivers on first reference: the Amazon River, the Mississippi River, the Ganges River, the River Thames.

Exception: the Rio Grande, because *rio* is Spanish for river and Rio Grande River would be redundant.

Shortened names such as the Euphrates and the Mekong are acceptable on second reference.

roadshow. Series of meetings that companies and investment bankers hold with investors to promote securities sales. One word, not two. Use only in quotations. Otherwise, write *promotional tour* or a similar phrase.

roll out. Companies often use this when bringing out a new product or service. *Introduction* or *introduce* is preferable.

Rome. Stands alone as the capital of Italy.

Rotterdam. The Dutch city stands alone.

rounding. Round to two decimal places for numbers that are either less than 10 million, or between 1 billion and 10 billion (*9.23 million, 6.14 billion*). Round numbers to one place if they are between 10 million and 1 billion, or more than 10 billion (*324.8 million, 33.7 billion*).

Round percentages of less than 10 to one decimal place: *9.7 percent*, not 9.68 percent. For percentages of more than 10, use whole numbers: *15 percent*, not 15.3 percent.

Economic statistics of less than 10 percent should be carried out two decimal places when available. Other amounts can be rounded to more decimal places when added precision is required. It's better to write *Fund A rose 18.4 percent, while Fund B rose 17.6 percent* than to write that both funds gained 18 percent.

Round merger valuations, currency translations and other estimated numbers below 1 billion to the nearest million (*325 million*) and amounts of 1 billion or more to one decimal place (*1.7 billion*).

The converted number shouldn't be more exact than the original, except when precision is necessary to show an important contrast. Usually, 30 centimeters should be rounded to 12 inches, not 11.8; 6 meters is 20 feet, not 19.7.

When the context makes clear that the number is approximate, such as *about 60 miles*, the conversion should be equally round, 100 kilometers rather than 96.5 or even 97.

Round values stated in cents or similar currency units to whole numbers, including earnings per share: *5 cents*, not 4.8 cents.

Round stock-trading statistics to reflect the minimum size for a typical trade in the local market. For instance, if daily trading averaged 45,623 shares during the past three months and the minimum is 100 shares, use 45,600.

Don't round a number differently in the headline than in the text. Numbers need to match exactly.

round trip. Not *roundtrip*.

rumor. While we don't report rumor or hearsay, we do report on speculation, which is when traders or investors buy or sell something based on rumor or other unverifiable information. See **speculation**.

S

7 Up. Soft-drink brand owned by Dr Pepper Snapple Group Inc. in the U.S. and PepsiCo Inc. internationally.

safe harbor, safe haven. Redundant. *Haven* and *refuge* are better choices.

said. Substitutes for *said*, such as *noted, announced, claimed, explained, exclaimed, warned, conceded* and *admitted*, can imply bias.

Some verbs convey attribution and make the use of *said* unnecessary, including *agreed* and *named*.

Put *said* before a person's name only when a title or description follows that takes more than a couple of words: *It's too soon, John Smith said. It's too soon, said John Smith, a lawyer representing most of the victims.*

Always identify news sources as precisely as possible. This often will mean specifying that a person communicated through a statement, speech or testimony, as opposed to an interview with a reporter.

Use the phrase *said in a statement* only when attributing remarks to an individual that come from a press release.

said it. This phrase usually isn't necessary in leads. *Smith Corp. said it may buy Widget Inc.* can become *Smith Corp. may buy Widget Inc.* as long as the story mentions what Smith said soon enough.

St. Louis. The U.S. city stands alone.

salaryman. Acceptable as a reference to Japanese white-collar workers or office workers as long as it's defined in the story.

sales. Preferable to revenue when referring to companies and industries whose business is based on selling goods and/or services.

sales force. Not *salesforce*.

Salt Lake City. The U.S. city stands alone.

same-store sales. Sales at stores open for at least a year. A performance benchmark for retailers, supermarkets, restaurants and hotels because the figure excludes actions such as openings, closings and expansions that can affect total sales. Health-maintenance organizations report same-store membership and hospitals report same-store admissions, based on plans and facilities owned for more than one year, respectively. Define in stories.

Samurai bonds. Debt securities sold in Japan by foreign governments and companies.

San Antonio. The U.S. city stands alone.

San Diego. The U.S. city stands alone.

San Francisco. The U.S. city stands alone. When referring to *the San Francisco Bay area*, keep *area* in lowercase.

San Marino. Stands alone as the capital of San Marino. We don't need to name the country, which is also called San Marino.

Santiago. Stands alone as the capital of Chile.

Sao Paulo. The Brazilian city stands alone.

SARS. Abbreviation for severe acute respiratory syndrome. The abbreviation SARS is acceptable on first reference if followed soon by the full name for the disease. Use the abbreviation sparingly.

Saudi. *Saudi* is acceptable as an adjective meaning Saudi Arabian and as a noun for residents of Saudi Arabia. Don't use it as a shortened form of the country name.

Saudi Binladin Group. Use this spelling for Saudi Binladin Group, a construction company based in Jeddah, Saudi Arabia.

scheme. Synonym for plan or proposal in the U.K. that implies illegal or unethical activity in the U.S.

school names. Refer to colleges and other schools by the full name, not a nickname, on first reference: *Virginia Polytechnic Institute and State University.* The shortened *Virginia Tech* may be used on later references.

scramble. Please leave the scrambling to the eggs.

seasons. *Winter, spring, summer, fall* and *autumn* should be avoided in time references because seasons come at different times in the northern and southern hemispheres: *The transaction will be completed by December* or *by the fourth quarter*, rather than *completed in the fall.* When this isn't possible, include a reference to the location: *the U.S. summer driving season.*

Seattle. The U.S. city stands alone.

secondary offering. Specify what the company is doing, such as selling shares for the third time in four years.

second board. Used in some countries to refer to the section of the stock exchange where relatively smaller companies trade. In some markets, this is called the *second section.* Avoid this jargon. Be more specific or explain how big a company must be to trade in the different parts of an exchange.

sector. Not a synonym for *industry* or *group. Sector* may refer to many distinct subsets of industry, an economy, markets or a society that share similar characteristics.

secure. In lending, to *secure* means the borrower has guaranteed payment by putting up assets or other collateral. *Turkey Secures $8.5 Billion Loan Agreement*

With U.S. could suggest that Turkey is backing the loan with a promise to pay. More precise: *Turkey Gets $8.5 Billion U.S. Loan for War Costs.*

seem. Report what is said and done, not what seems, which can be subjective. What seems to one person may not seem to another.

Self-Defense Forces. Use this name for Japan's military only on second reference or later. Provide a description on first reference. Don't use the abbreviation SDF.

selloff. Acceptable in the appropriate context. *Selloff* works best when a trigger event such as a surprise negative economic report sparks selling. Spell without a hyphen.

semicolons. Use this punctuation in a headline only when it includes more than one subject. When one subject takes two verbs, use a comma.

> *Widgets Names Johnson Chairman; Stock Falls*
> (In first part of the headline, Widgets is the subject. In the second part, the stock is the new subject.)

> *Widgets Names Johnson Chairman, Plans $100 Mln Charge*
> (The company is taking both actions.)

senator. Capitalize before a name: *Senator John McCain.* Don't abbreviate as *Sen.*

senior. As a modifier, doesn't mean or add anything unless it is in a direct quote or part of someone's title.

senior citizen. The two-word term *senior citizen* is preferable to *senior,* in both text and headlines. The word *senior* brings to mind students in the final year of high school or college.

Seoul. Stands alone as the capital of South Korea.

Sept. 11. The date usually can be used without the year when a story mentions the terrorist attacks on the U.S. Specify 2001 if the context doesn't make it clear. Preferable to 9/11.

In a direct quote, if a person says *nine-eleven*, write it as *9/11*. If the person says *September 11*, write it as *Sept. 11*.

settle. When using in stories about legal matters, be specific about the terms on which the sides came to agreement. Include any financial terms and any admission or finding of wrongdoing.

severe acute respiratory syndrome. Use lowercase when writing the full term. The abbreviation SARS is acceptable on first reference if followed soon by the full name. Use the abbreviation sparingly.

Shanghai. The Chinese city stands alone.

shareholder. Not *share-holder*.

shareholder value. Largely meaningless phrase that companies often use in justifying their actions. Better to write that the company wants to boost its share price or increase returns to shareholders.

share movements. Sentences giving a stock price shouldn't have a cryptic structure that starts with *Shares rose* or *Shares fell*. For a smoother read, use a modifier or an article to indicate whose shares. Instead of *Shares fell 1.9 percent*, write *Toshiba fell 1.9 percent* or *The shares fell 1.9 percent* or *Its shares fell 1.9 percent*.

sharp. Not to be used for describing behavior. It often is judgmental or superfluous.

sharply. Meaningless when used before *higher* or *lower* to describe markets. Use a strong verb instead: *The market surged*, not *The market rose sharply*. Then cite the performance of an index or security that shows why the verb is appropriate: *The increase was the largest in 14 years*.

shed. Cats and dogs shed. Stocks, bonds, currencies and commodities don't. Avoid using *shed* as a verb, as in *Crude oil shed 37 cents to $48.55 a barrel*. Better: *Crude oil fell, dropped, declined, tumbled*, etc.

shipbuilder. Not *ship-builder*.

short dated. Be specific: *less than two years; in the next six months.*

short sale. Sale of stock borrowed from shareholders. People who sell short hope to profit by repurchasing the securities later at a lower price and returning them to the holder. Define this in all cases.

short seller. Use two words and no hyphen for *short seller* and *short selling.* As an adjective, hyphenate: *short-selling strategy.*

short squeeze. Situation in which a number of short sellers buy back the shares they borrowed and sold because the price has risen, rather than fallen. Define this in all cases.

short term. Be specific: *less than two years; in the next six months.*

should. Use *may* or *might* when reporting on probable or likely outcomes.

shrugging off. Describe how security prices didn't react strongly to a piece of news rather than using this term.

sidelines. Use the term *on the sidelines* only for events that have sidelines to a playing area, such as a soccer match. Don't use the term colloquially to refer to interviews conducted outside the main action of a conference or meeting.

signed. In leads, the fact that agreement was reached usually is more newsworthy than the signing of the agreement.

since. Use only in time references: *Widget sales have fallen since the start of the year.* Use *because* when describing cause and effect: *Widget sales have fallen because of the recall.*

Singapore. The Asian city-state stands alone.

single-digit. Be specific: *Sales fell 5 percent.* A single-digit change could range from 1 percent to 9 percent. If someone says *single-digit,* ask for a more exact figure.

sit. Indexes, stocks, bonds, currencies and commodities don't sit. Don't write sentences like this one: *The Dow industrials now sit about 7 percent below their record close.*

size and scope. The size and scope should define the subject of the story—whether a company, a person, an organization or a country—and help explain what's at stake and why it matters.

Define the universe used in the size and scope. Is it the biggest in the world? The largest in a particular country or region? Or an industry? Omitting the definition forces people to make assumptions or guesses: *Intel Corp., the world's largest semiconductor maker; Nokia Oyj, the world's biggest maker of mobile phones.* Use the geographic area when needed: *Deutsche Lufthansa AG, Europe's second-largest airline; Bertelsmann AG, Europe's largest media company.* When a company isn't the largest in its industry, identify larger competitors in the story.

The basis for the ranking is often worth identifying. Sales are the usual benchmark for industrial and service companies, and assets are a benchmark for financial companies. Identify rankings based on other measures, such as market value, when they appear. The explanation can come later in the story rather than bog down the lead.

Size and scope also can say something interesting or newsworthy about the subject: *Veritas Software Corp., whose name is Latin for "truth," said Kenneth Lonchar resigned as chief financial officer after admitting he lied about having a master's degree in business administration from Stanford University.*

Make sure any reference fits the story. Referring to Johnson & Johnson as the maker of Band-Aids and baby powder in the lead may not make sense in a story about the company's drug business or medical devices.

Size and scope is usually best situated immediately after the subject: *Acme Co., the second-largest widget maker, agreed to buy XYZ Inc.* Separating the subject and its description can cause confusion: *Acme Co. agreed to buy XYZ Inc., sending shares of the second-largest widget maker higher.* Whose stock is moving—Acme's, XYZ's, or that of a third, unnamed company that makes widgets?

slash. Not a synonym for *reduce. Slash* means to cut with sweeping force. It should be used when the cuts are immediate and deep. It's often better to be precise about the size of a reduction: *Acme is reducing its workforce by 20 percent. Widgetco will trim its budget by 15 percent.*

slightly. Be specific: *rose 0.1 percent*, rather than rose slightly.

Slim. Carlos Slim uses only one surname. Don't use *Carlos Slim Helu* on first reference. For second references, *Slim.*

His son uses two family names. He is *Carlos Slim Domit* on first reference and *Slim Domit* on later references.

sluggish. Vague. If sales are sluggish, are they rising or falling? Is a sluggish economy expanding or shrinking? How much? Be specific.

small-cap. Abbreviation for *small capitalization*, used to describe companies with relatively little stock-market value. Provide a range of values, such as *$250 million to $1 billion.* Descriptions of a small-cap stock vary, so always ask for a definition.

smartphone. The term for advanced mobile phones is spelled as one word, *smartphone.*

so-called. Terms that are formal names or widely understood usually don't need to be put inside quotation marks nor be preceded by *so-called.*

So-called indicates that a term is popularly used but unofficial, sometimes almost slang. It should be used sparingly.

So-called doesn't take the place of explaining jargon or an unfamiliar term. It often signals the need for such explanation. Other times, *so-called* is extraneous and should be eliminated.

Don't use *so-called* together with quotation marks around the term.

soft goods. Jargon used in retailing to describe items such as clothes and linens. Don't use in stories.

soft landing. Jargon that economists use to describe what happens when a central bank raises interest rates enough to curb inflation without causing a recession.

soft patch. See **cliches.**

sources. Be specific: *according to police officials; according to people familiar.* See **attribution.**

Soviet Union. There are 15 former Soviet republics: Armenia, Azerbaijan, Belarus, Estonia, Georgia, Kazakhstan, Kyrgyzstan, Latvia, Lithuania, Moldova, Russia, Tajikistan, Turkmenistan, Ukraine and Uzbekistan.

space. Not a synonym for *industry, group, niche, market, business* or *potential.* Choose a more precise word or omit. When *space* is used improperly in a quotation, choose another quote, ask the speaker to rephrase, or paraphrase. *Online music industry,* not online music space.

speaker. Capitalize this congressional title only when it appears as a formal title before a person's name: *Speaker John Boehner.* Otherwise, use lowercase.

speculation. While we don't report rumor or hearsay, we do report on speculation, which is when traders or investors buy or sell based on rumor or other unverifiable information.

Don't use *speculation* when we mean *prediction, expectation* or *report.*

spike. Use a verb such as *rose* or give specifics: *The index surged 8.2 percent in three minutes.*

spinoff. Use *spinoff* as a noun, *spin off* as a verb. Use only when a public company plans to give stock in a unit to shareholders. If the company plans to sell the stock, use *sale.*

spokesman, spokeswoman. Use *spokesmen* for groups that include men and women. Use *spokeswomen* only when referring to all females. Don't use *spokesperson* or *spokespeople.*

sports metaphors. A worldwide audience isn't likely to understand sporting terms used to describe events. References to *scoring a touchdown* would make sense only to people familiar with American football. Similarly, few people in the U.S. would know the meaning of phrases such as *knocked for six,* which comes from cricket.

spread. When referring to debt, spread is the extra yield that investors demand to own a bond rather than Treasuries. Avoid using *spread* on first reference, as in *The spread between U.S. Treasury notes and European government bonds widened.* Better: *The difference in yield between U.S. Treasury notes and European government bonds widened.*

If the gap in the yield is widening, investors perceive more risk. If the spread is narrowing, holders consider the bond to be less risky relative to a Treasury and will accept less extra yield as compensation.

staffer. This informal term is best saved for quotes. Better to write *staff member* or specify the person's job.

stagnant. Not a synonym for *little changed* in earnings reports, market comments or other stories.

stake. A shareholding should reflect shares that are owned outright. If an investor owns only options that haven't been exercised, use conditional language such as: *The options, if exercised, would represent a 7 percent stake in the chipmaker.*

stall. Not appropriate to describe securities or markets, because the word implies that another move is imminent. *Little changed* is preferable.

stand. People stand. Stocks, bonds and indexes don't. So don't write sentences like this one: *The S&P 500 stands about 6.1 percent below its all-time closing high.*

Standard & Poor's. Unit of McGraw-Hill Cos. that provides credit ratings, research and financial information.

standstill agreement. Agreement in which a potential acquirer refrains from increasing its stake in a target company for a specified period. Define this when it's used.

startup. Use *startup* as a noun or adjective, *start up* as a verb.

state names. For the benefit of our worldwide audience, write full names of U.S. states in all references: *California*, not Calif. or CA. The abbreviations

N.Y. and *N.J.* may be used for New York and New Jersey only in headlines with a rigorous fit. Don't use the postal codes NY and NJ.

For the District of Columbia, *D.C.* is acceptable only when necessary to distinguish Washington from the state of Washington.

state of. Lowercase when necessary to identify a location precisely: *The state of Washington.* It can often be dropped.

state-owned. Reserved for companies owned entirely by a government. If a state company has publicly traded shares, use *state-controlled.*

steady. People don't say that a market or economic indicator is unsteady, so don't write that it's steady, which has a positive connotation. *Unchanged* or *little changed* is preferable.

steelmaker. Not *steel maker.*

stockbroker. Not *stock broker.*

stockholder. Not *stock holder.*

Stockholm. Stands alone as the capital of Sweden.

stock splits. When describing splits, begin with the number of shares an investor will have after the split. Use numerals rather than words to describe the ratios, and always tie the figures together by using hyphens: *Widgets proposed a 3-for-2 stock split. Widgets said it will split its stock 3-for-2.*

straights. Jargon used by some non-U.S. investors to describe fixed-rate bonds.

strategic alternatives. Companies often use the phrase in connection with the hiring of investment bankers. Rather than using the phrase, mention the alternatives. If a company doesn't explain the alternatives, ask if it's looking for a buyer.

streaming. Used in front of *audio* and *video* to describe broadcasting done on the Internet, rather than on radio and television.

strike price. The price at which an option can be exercised.

string of. Lacks precision. If there is more than one, mention how many there are. Instead of *Widgets has made a string of acquisitions,* write *Widgets has bought 25 companies this year.*

strong. Be precise. Modifiers such as *strong* and *weak* should be used to describe a currency, commodity, economy or government only when specifically used by an official or organization.

It's acceptable to use *strengthen* as a verb for a currency, commodity or economy.

subcommittee names. In stories about the U.S. Congress, avoid using *committee* and *subcommittee* in the same phrase. As an example, for the House Energy and Commerce Committee's Subcommittee on Health, write *a House Energy and Commerce subcommittee* on first reference and *the Subcommittee on Health* on second reference.

If a subcommittee has a long and disjointed name, such as the House Energy and Commerce Subcommittee on Commerce, Trade and Consumer Protection, use the relevant portion. It's acceptable in a story on consumer matters, for instance, to refer to the Subcommittee on Consumer Protection.

subscribe. To sign up; not to be confused with *ascribe.*

subsequently Use *later* for *subsequently* and *after* for *subsequent to.*

subsidiary. Separately incorporated business within a parent company. Acceptable alternative to *unit,* which is preferable.

sulfur. Not *sulphur.*

Sumitomo. Use at least two words of the name in headlines on Sumitomo Corp., a Japanese trading company, or affiliates whose names begin with Sumitomo: *Sumitomo Chemical, Sumitomo Heavy.*

supercommittee. Not *super-committee.*

supercomputer. Not *super-computer.*

superconductor. Not *super-conductor.*

Superfund. Capitalize in all references.

superhighway. Not *super-highway.*

superstore. Not *super-store.*

supervisory board. One of two tiers of company directors in some European countries. Consists of outside directors and makes strategic decisions.

support. Analysts use this to identify a price or value that a security, commodity or index probably will struggle to fall below, based on past performance. Describe the performance. See **resistance.**

supporting the view. Be specific; show the support.

survey. Preferable to *poll* when the results being described don't come from scientific sampling.

suspect. Often meaningless because of the absence of specific named individuals or organizations being charged, jailed, wanted or investigated in connection with a specific act.

suspend. Not appropriate when referring to debt payments. Companies or countries suspend payments when they can't pay, or won't pay.

swap rate. What borrowers pay to exchange their fixed-rate interest payments for floating ones. The gap between that and a benchmark bond yield is the swap spread. Explain in stories. See **swap spread.**

swap spread. The difference between a benchmark bond yield and the swap rate. When the swap spread widens, it becomes more expensive for borrowers to pay a fixed rate of interest and get a floating rate in return. Investors and banks monitor the spread because it is used as a guideline to price corporate debt. Explain in stories. See **swap rate.**

swaps. Stories should specify whether a swap is credit-default, currency or some other type. Weave a definition of the swap into the narrative.

swing. Use this term only when a company has a profit for the first time in a year (after four quarterly losses or two half-year losses, depending on how it reports). Or use for the first loss after a year of profits.

Don't use *swing* when the company has bounced between profits and losses during the past year. Don't use it for comparison only with the immediately preceding period.

Sydney. The Australian city stands alone.

syndicate manager. Say *a group of investment banks led by*, and name the firm.

T

tables. Countries and companies belong in alphabetical order in tables unless there is a specific reason to arrange them differently, such as a ranking in order of sales, market value or other figure. To begin a list of European Union members with a country other than Austria, for instance, the reporter and/or editor would have to decide which member is most important, or biggest, or most relevant.

Add *T on the line immediately above and below the table so that it displays properly on the Bloomberg.com site.

Taipei. Stands alone as the capital of Taiwan.

takeover. Use this as a noun, *take over* as a verb.

Taliban. Muslim fundamentalist group that took control of Afghanistan in 1996 and sheltered Osama bin Laden. In Arabic, it means students or scholars. Singular form is *talib*.

tap. Acceptable, provided it isn't overused, as a synonym for *borrow*, as in *tap into its bank financing*. Don't use tap for hiring or personnel moves, as in *Widgets tapped John Smith as its chief executive officer*.

target price. Jargon for the price that an analyst expects a stock to reach within a specified period. Be specific: *She expects the shares to reach $100 within 12 months*.

tax-loss carryforward. Tax benefit allowing companies to apply losses and credits incurred in one fiscal period against income reported for later periods. Describe as a tax benefit.

Tea Party. Capitalize Tea Party for the political movement, and Tea Partyer for its followers.

tech, biotech. Seek the editor-in-chief's permission before using these shortened forms of *technology* and *biotechnology* in headlines or text.

technical analysis. Market analysis that relies on identifying historical price patterns. Better to write, for instance: *Some traders who rely on chart patterns expect the rally to end at about 11,000 on the Dow Jones Industrial Average.*

technology. This can mean everything from computers, software and the Internet to drugs and synthetics. Be specific.

teenager. No hyphen.

Tehran. Stands alone as the capital of Iran.

Tel Aviv. The Israeli city stands alone.

telecom. Abbreviation for *telecommunications.* Acceptable only in quotes and headlines. *Telecoms*, plural, isn't acceptable.

television ratings. Two measures apply to U.S. television programs and networks: *rating*, the percentage of all homes having a television set that were tuned in; and *share*, the percentage of all TV sets in operation that were tuned in. A program at 15/40 has a 15 rating and a 40 share.

temblor. Not *trembler* when referring to earthquakes.

temperatures. Use the scale—Celsius or Fahrenheit—of the country where the main action of the story occurs. Provide a conversion in parentheses on first reference: *72 degrees Fahrenheit (22 degrees Celsius).* To calculate equivalents, enter UCNV <Go>.

tender, tender offer. *Tender* is the action taken by a company's shareholders in response to a tender offer. *Tender offer* is made by a would-be purchaser in connection with an acquisition.

term. Frequently follows *near, short, intermediate* or *long* in describing time periods. Be more specific: *Three to six months* rather than *short-term*, for instance.

territory. There is no such place as *negative territory* or *positive territory*. Prices or values are lower or higher.

terrorism, terrorist. Use *terrorism* to describe violent actions that are intended to intimidate or demoralize, especially for political reasons, and *terrorist* to describe someone associated with carrying out the actions. When evidence isn't readily available and an authority asserts that an event was caused by terrorists or that bombs were dropped on terrorist camps, qualify the assertion with *alleged* or *suspected*. When terrorists' religion is given as a reason or motivation, name it in the story.

Reserve the word *terror* for the emotion of intense fear.

test. A popular term among analysts, who might say: *The market will test support.* Don't use. Just say where they expect prices to go.

the. Omit at the beginning of company names: *Limited Inc.*, not *The Limited Inc.* For newspaper names, put in lowercase: *the New York Times*, not *The New York Times*.

think. Not a synonym for *say.* Journalists don't know what people think, believe, feel or hope. They only know what people say and what they do.

think tank. Describe what the group does: *The Brookings Institution, which does research and analysis on U.S. public policy.*

though. Preferable to *but* and *however.* Use with care because the qualifier often isn't necessary.

throughput. Jargon used in industries such as chemicals as a synonym for *capacity*, which is preferable.

Tibor. Tokyo interbank offered rate. The rate at which banks in Tokyo are willing to lend money to each other for a specified period. Benchmark for money-market rates. *Tibor* is acceptable in headlines and on second reference.

tick. Price change in a security. Don't use.

tight. Underwriters say *the deal was tightly priced* when securities were too expensive to attract investors. Economists say *the labor market is tight* when it's relatively hard for companies to find workers. Better to explain the situation.

tightening. Saying that central banks tighten policy isn't accurate. They tighten credit through policy changes. It's preferable to say that a central bank *pushed interest rates higher.*

time element. See dates and days of the week.

time of day. Separate the hour and minute with a colon, not a period, and use *a.m./p.m.,* not 24-hour time: *4:30 p.m.,* not *4.30 p.m.,* not *16:30.*
  Omit 00 when making exact references to an hour: *4 p.m.,* not *4:00 p.m.*
  Most of our stories should say on the first screen when the main news happened, which is almost always *today.* A single reference is usually enough. We don't need later references to today unless the time frame has been changed and must be brought back to the present for clarity.
  Readers know that reports about the trading in stocks, bonds, currencies, commodities, etc. are that day's news, so we don't need to say *today* in most market stories.
  Avoid confusing people with *this morning, this afternoon, this evening. Overnight,* used to describe foreign-exchange trading in another time zone, is most confusing of all. Remember that it's always some other time somewhere else.

Times. *London* isn't part of the name of the newspaper there called *The Times.* To differentiate between that *Times* and similarly named publications, write *the London-based Times.*

time zones. Terms such as *Eastern Daylight Time,* or abbreviations such as *EDT,* aren't familiar to a worldwide audience. Better to use a major city or region: *5 p.m. London time, midnight U.S. West Coast time. Local time* is also acceptable.

tipped. This term for events that either will or may happen isn't familiar to many people in the U.S. and lacks precision. If someone is likely to be named to a position, say so and provide attribution.

titles. Courtesy titles such as *Mr., Mrs., Miss* and *Ms.* are unnecessary. True titles belong to elected officials and to corporate and military officers. They take capital letters when they precede a name and are lowercase in any other position, such as when used as a description: *Executive Vice President John Smith. John Smith, executive vice president.* Do the same when referring to titles of former officers: *former Chairman Mary Jones.*

Titles shouldn't be shortened because the abbreviation may be unfamiliar to people around the world. Some examples: *Governor Andrew Cuomo, Senator Dianne Feinstein, Representative Nancy Pelosi, Rear Admiral Craig Quigley.*

Place false titles, which describe the person's job instead of his or her actual position, after a name. Refer to *Jane Smith, a bank analyst at Dresdner Kleinwort,* instead of Dresdner Kleinwort bank analyst Jane Smith. Job descriptions are always lowercase, whether they come before or after the name.

Always place long titles after the name to avoid awkward strings of capitalized words.

Titles of nobility or honorifics, such as *Lord, Lady, U* or *Tan,* aren't used on first reference. Use the name in standard form: *Margaret Thatcher* or *Paul McCartney.* If the person prefers to be known by the title or is widely known by it, use it in a later reference with an explanation of where the title comes from or what it means.

For example, on first reference: *Margaret Thatcher* or *former Prime Minister Margaret Thatcher.* On second reference: *Thatcher, who has been known as Lady Thatcher since she was elevated to the House of Lords in 1992.* Or, *since 1992, when she became a baroness.*

John Browne, a partner and managing director of Riverstone Holdings LLC. On second reference: *Browne, known as Lord Browne since being appointed a member of Parliament's upper chamber in 1997.*

Frederick Curzon, known as Earl Howe since becoming the 13th holder of the hereditary title in 1999.

When someone is so widely known by a titled name that most people wouldn't recognize the common name, try to fit both names in the headline.

For example, many people aren't aware that the Duke of Westminster's common name is Gerald Grosvenor. The best solution is to trim as many details as possible from the headline so that both names can be used. If there is no way to make them fit, use only the titled name.

Royal titles are acceptable, such as *Queen Elizabeth II, Emperor Akihito of Japan, Sheikh Ahmad al-Abdullah al-Sabah of Kuwait, King Bhumibol Adulyadej of Thailand.*

Tokyo. Stands alone as the capital of Japan.

toll-free numbers. Include toll-free telephone numbers in stories when they will help people obtain additional information about product recalls, class-action legal settlements and the like. Follow this style for U.S. numbers: (800) 666-6666. *The company said it would eliminate its toll-free number in an effort to cut costs.* Or: *The company established a toll-free number, (800) 555-5555, to handle calls from customers.*

Before putting the number in a story, call to make sure it is working. Specify if it works only in a certain country.

ton. Refers to U.S. short tons, or 2,000 pounds, as opposed to metric or long tons, or 2,204.62 pounds. When citing metric tons, identify them as metric on first reference. In later references, *tons* is enough as long as there aren't any figures in short tons.

tonne. Use *metric ton* for this unit of measure, equivalent to 2,204.62 pounds.

Toronto. The Canadian city stands alone.

Tory. *Tory* and *Tories* are acceptable when referring to the Conservative Party in the U.K.

Toys "R" Us Inc. In headlines, use single quote marks.

track. Provide more context about the relationship between one market and another instead of using jargon such as *Canada Bonds Track U.S. Bonds.*

tracking stock. Class of shares whose value reflects the performance and prospects of a unit, rather than the entire company.

traded hands. We mean *were traded* or *changed hands.*

trading, trade. When reporting about the buying and selling on stock, bond and commodity exchanges, we refer to *trading*, not trade. Eliminate expressions such as *in morning trade* and *the start of trade. Trading* shouldn't be used as a synonym for *sales*, nor *trading statement* for *sales report.*

tranche. Part of a stock or bond sale or bank loan. Use *portion* and provide a description on first reference.

trans-Atlantic. Not *transatlantic.*

trans-Pacific. Not *transpacific.*

Treasuries. Not *Treasurys* when referring to U.S. government securities.

treasury. Capitalize when referring to a national treasury; that includes Treasury bills, notes, etc.

trend. Bad as a noun, horrid as a verb. Don't write that *the trend is* or *markets are trending.* Be specific about moves.

troubled. Defections or executive changes aren't enough to justify describing a company as troubled. Supply evidence that a company is running out of money and having trouble paying its bills on time.

TSE. Abbreviation for both the Tokyo and Toronto stock exchanges. When used in headlines, add the country name as needed for clarity.

turbulence. Rather than referring to a country's *financial market turbulence*, write something like *the bonds are in default and the currency was devalued by x percent.* Show, don't tell.

turmoil. Rather than referring to a country's *financial market turmoil*, write something like *the bonds are in default and the currency was devalued by x percent.* Show, don't tell.

turnaround. Use this as a noun, *turn around* as a verb.

turnover. Not a substitute for *sales* or *revenue*. Avoid when referring to the pace at which a company sells what it makes (inventory turnover) or collects money from its customers (receivables turnover).

TV attribution. Stories that include interviews from Bloomberg Television signature shows should contain the names of the programs in the attribution. Other stories originating from broadcast interviews should include the interviewer's name in the byline.

tweet. Use *tweet* only in a compelling quotation about Twitter. *Wrote* and *posted* are better verbs to indicate Twitter use.

U

U.A.E. *United Arab Emirates* should be spelled in full on first reference. Later references may use the abbreviation U.A.E.

U.K. Use in all references to the United Kingdom except quotations.

U.S. Use in all references to the United States except quotations.

Ulan Bator. Spell the capital of Mongolia as *Ulan Bator*.

uncertain. Describe the situation instead.

under. Not a substitute for *less than*. Implies a physical relationship.

under investigation. Better to say a person or an organization is being investigated.

under pressure. Write that the stock or index is *falling, dropping* or *plunging* rather than using this market jargon.

under way. This is almost always used as two words: *The parade is under way*. One word only as a nautical adjective: *the underway flotilla*.

undersubscribed. Give specific amounts for a stock or bond sale in which investors offer to purchase fewer securities than the total amount available, rather than using this jargon.

underweight. Describes a market segment, such as an industry group or country, that accounts for a smaller percentage of a portfolio than it does of a benchmark index. Instead of using the word, provide specifics.

undetermined. By definition, this offers no news. Avoid.

Unilever. Owned jointly by Unilever NV, based in the Netherlands, and Unilever Plc, based in the U.K. The two companies operate as a single entity, though their shares trade separately.

United Nations. Write the full name, United Nations, on first reference. UN, without periods, on second reference.

unnamed. Not a synonym for *unidentified* when writing about news reports that rely on one or more anonymous sources. Everyone has a name.

unprofitable. Preferable to *money-losing, loss-making*, etc.

unrealized. Describes changes in the value of investments, a preferable way to refer to them. Differs from *realized* gains or losses, which are based on the sale of investments.

up. Not a verb, as in *ups the ante*. When using as a suffix, include the hyphen if the resulting word isn't found in *Webster's New World*.

up to. Acceptable as a substitute for *as much as* only in headlines: *Sony Will Fire Up to 3,000 Workers*. In stories, use the most precise term for what is being measured: *as much as, as many as, as deep as, as far as, as high as, as fast as, as few as*, etc.

upcoming. To quote Barney Kilgore, who transformed the *Wall Street Journal* into a newspaper with 1 million circulation from one with 33,000: "The next time I see someone use upcoming, I will be downcoming and he will be outgoing." Don't use. Be specific about when events will take place.

upside. Jargon for the increase in a security or market.

upstream. Jargon used in the oil and gas industry for exploration and production, and in telecommunications for a signal that travels from a customer's equipment to a network. Provide the description.

upswing. Advertising and promotional lingo. Don't use.

upturn. Use a term such as *advance*.

upward. Bad on its own, because *-ward* is unnecessary. Worse, when used as *upward pressure* to describe a market headed higher.

Uridashi bonds. Debt securities denominated in currencies other than yen that are sold to individual investors in Japan.

V

valuation. Security's price in relation to measures such as earnings, sales or net worth. Instead of using the word, describe the measures.

value. Not a synonym for *worth*. Worth can be subjective, whatever someone is willing to pay. When an asset or transaction is being evaluated, it's better to say *valued at*. An expression such as *$10 million worth of engines* can be shortened to *$10 million of engines*.

Vancouver. The Canadian city stands alone.

Vatican City. The independent papal state stands alone.

versus. Write the word *versus* in text and story headlines: *It's the bears versus the bulls; Widgets 2nd-Qtr Net 7c-Share Versus Loss 10c.*
Abbreviate as *v.* when citing lawsuits: *Roe v. Wade.*
Use *VS* only in stand-alone flash headlines: *WIDGETS 2Q NET 7C-SHARE VS LOSS 10C-SHARE.

vice chairman. Two words.

vice president. Two words.

video cassette, video-cassette recorder. Two words as a noun, hyphenated as an adjective.

videoconference. One word.

video game, video-game maker. Two words as a noun, hyphenated as an adjective.

video tape, video-tape recorder. Two words as a noun, hyphenated as an adjective.

Vienna. Stands alone as the capital of Austria.

visibility. Market jargon often used in connection with people's ability to predict a company's earnings or sales. When visibility is low, they aren't sure what the figures will look like.

volatility. A measure, usually expressed in annual percentage terms, of how much a price, index or interest rate varied from its average for a given period. For example: *10-day volatility* or *30-day volatility*.

volume. Be precise: *The stock rose 10 percent in trading of 2.3 million shares*, not *volume of 2.3 million*. Also, *trading volume* is redundant.

W

Wal-Mart. Use a hyphen in all references to Wal-Mart Stores Inc. and stores carrying the Wal-Mart name.

Wall Street. When *Wall Street* is used to describe the U.S. financial industry, specify on second reference which parts: *securities firms, commercial banks, insurance companies, hedge funds, mutual funds, leveraged-buyout companies.*

Geographically, Wall Street refers to the street where the New York Stock Exchange is based. It is where the biggest banks were originally located and where John Pierpont Morgan went to work.

warning. Often appears after *profit* when referring to companies' forecasts of their results. Don't write about a company's failure as if it's detached from the failure. Better to be descriptive: *The company reduced its forecasts for third-quarter sales and earnings.*

Warsaw. Stands alone as the capital of Poland.

Washington. Stands alone as the capital of the U.S. Use Washington, D.C., only when it isn't clear whether the reference is to the U.S. capital or the state of Washington.

weak. Be precise. Modifiers such as *weak* and *strong* should be used to describe a currency, commodity, economy or government only when specifically used by an official or organization.

It's acceptable to use *weaken* as a verb for a currency, commodity or economy.

-wear. One-syllable words can take *-wear* as a suffix: *menswear, sportswear.* Keep *wear* as a separate word otherwise: *ladies' wear, children's wear.*

Web
    Spelling and capitalization for Web terms:
    World Wide Web
    the Web
    website
    Web page
    webcam
    webcast
    webmaster
    Web log (blog is acceptable on first reference)

weights. Use the system of units—metric or U.S.—in the country where the main action is taking place. Provide a conversion to the other in parentheses on first reference: *200 pounds (90 kilograms).* To calculate equivalents, enter UCNV <Go>.

West. *The West* is a dated term for the U.S. and its noncommunist allies in Europe and the Western Hemisphere, best avoided today. Use *western Europe* to indicate the western side of the continent.

western Germany. Use only as a geographic reference for the western part of the current Germany. West Germany ceased to exist as a country Oct. 3, 1990.

whether or not. Redundant. Just use *whether*.

whistle-blower. Not *whistleblower*. When writing stories that develop from a whistle-blower's allegations, ask whether the person demanded any money from his or her employer and include the response. This will arm people with all the facts and help them judge the person's credibility.

white goods. Write *large household appliances* or describe the goods.

White House. On first reference, information from the White House should be attributed to the president's administration or to the person who supplied it. On second reference, attribution to the White House is acceptable.

wholly owned. Unnecessary. Describe a company's ownership of a unit only when the stake is less than 100 percent.

wide-ranging. See **cliches.**

widen. Losses, deficits and margins do this when they get larger. Preferable to confusing words such as *increase* or *rise*.

Wi-Fi. Not *Wifi* or *WiFi*.

workforce. Not *work force*.

World Trade Center. Don't abbreviate as WTC.

worry, worried, worries. These are subjective. Use only if we can quote someone saying, "I'm worried."

worth. Not a synonym for *value*. Worth can be subjective, whatever someone is willing to pay. When an asset or transaction is being evaluated, it's better to say *valued at*. An expression such as *$10 million worth of engines* can be shortened to *$10 million of engines*.

wrapping up. Better to write *completing* when referring to the end of a period, as in *completing the first week since the changeover*.

writedown. Use this as a noun, *write down* as a verb.

Explain what the company is writing down, and why.

Many writedowns occur when a company permanently reduces the value of an asset. Be transparent when a writedown stems from mark-to-market pricing of financial assets. Their value may be increased in a later report.

write-off. Use this as a noun, *write off* as a verb.

Y

Yahoo. Include the exclamation point in Yahoo! Inc.'s name only on first reference. Omit the punctuation in headlines and on second reference.

Yangon. Myanmar's capital. Indicate that the city was formerly known as Rangoon.

Yankee bonds. Debt securities sold in the U.S. by foreign governments and companies.

year earlier. The best way to refer to earnings in the previous year's quarter is usually the concise phrase *a year earlier.*

Sometimes it is appropriate to write more descriptively: *in last year's third quarter.*

Don't use *in the year-earlier quarter, a year ago, in the year-ago quarter* or *in the same quarter a year earlier.*

A year ago is inaccurate for earnings because it means a year prior to the present time, while the earnings comparison is with a period that ended more than a year ago. *A year ago* may be used in nonearnings stories when it is accurate.

year-on-year. *From a year earlier* is preferable.

Z

zero-coupon bonds. Securities that mature in more than one year and don't pay interest.

Zurich. The Swiss city stands alone.

Names

This section is a guide to understanding how to use people names.

Asian Names

Is it Li Ka-shing or Li Ka Shing? On second reference, should we refer to the billionaire as Li, Ka Shing or Shing? Mishandling an Asian name is insulting and it reflects poorly on our organization.

Unfortunately, there are few hard-and-fast rules regarding names in Asia, even within one country. The following guide is aimed at standardizing spelling, rendering and usage of Asian names. Countries are listed in alphabetical order.

Only one rule applies in all cases: Use the spelling or second reference preferred by the person.

In general, Asians can be divided into three groups: those who ought to be called by their first name, last name or whole name on second reference. Beware: Exceptions abound.

Generally, use the last name (not necessarily the family name) on second reference if the person is from Bangladesh, India, Indonesia, Japan, Pakistan, the Philippines or Vietnam.

Generally, use the first name (though not necessarily the given name) on second reference if the person is from China, Hong Kong, Korea, Laos, Malaysia, Singapore, Taiwan or Thailand.

Use the whole name on second reference if the person is from Myanmar or Cambodia.

Bangladesh

Most people have adopted a surname. Usually, use the given name first, family name last.

Use family name on second reference. *Khaleda Zia* becomes *Zia* on second reference.

Nicknames are an exception. *Hussain Mohammad Ershad*. Hussain is his given name. Mohammad is his father's name. Ershad is a nickname given by his family. Under normal rules, he would be Mohammad on second reference, but he prefers *Ershad*. That name, therefore, should be used on second reference.

Cambodia

Among Khmers, family name usually precedes given name. Use full name on second reference. *Hun Sen* is *Hun Sen* on second reference. Given name is used only by family and close friends.

For Vietnamese Cambodians, see **Vietnam** section. For Muslim Cambodians, see the **Malaysia** section.

China

The family name always precedes the given name for mainland Chinese. In the pinyin transliteration of names, there are no hyphens between syllables. Premier *Wen Jiabao* is *Wen* on second reference. Former Premier *Li Peng* is *Li* on second reference.

Some Chinese, to avoid confusion in Western countries, flip their names on business cards. Usually, the surname is capitalized and the given name is in small letters. To avoid confusion, use the surname first.

In cases where mainland Chinese adopt Western first names, use them in Western order. *Jack Liu* is *Liu* on second reference.

See entries for names in **Hong Kong** and **Taiwan**.

Hong Kong

Most Cantonese names are rendered with the Wade-Giles system of transliteration, with the given name hyphenated and the second element in lowercase. Surname precedes given name. *Li Ka-shing* is *Li* on second reference.

Some people prefer the Southeast Asian (Singapore, Malaysia, Indonesia) style of three names, without the hyphen. Family name still precedes both given names.

Spelling follows the British style of romanizing the Cantonese dialect.

Most Hong Kong Chinese have both a Chinese and Western name, such as *Li Ka-shing's* son, who prefers *Richard Li* to *Li Tzar Kai* or *Li Tzar-kai*. In any case, *Li* is still used on second reference. Many Chinese living in the West have reversed their names to agree with the Western style of naming. *I.M. Pei* is *Pei* on second reference, because Pei is the family name.

India

In most of the north, given name precedes family or clan name.

Use family name on second reference. *Hans Raj Bhardwaj* is *Bhardwaj* on second reference.

Indians in the south often abbreviate their long given names, which include their father's names and the village they belong to. *N. T. Ram Rao* is *Rao* on second reference.

Sikh names are an exception. Male Sikhs follow their given name with *Singh*, which means "lion." Singh may be used on second reference only if there is only one Singh in the story. If there are multiple Singhs, use full names of all throughout.

Never use just the given name of a Sikh.

Indonesia

Javanese, who constitute two-thirds of Indonesia's population, generally have only one name. Example: *Suharto*. In such cases, it's often helpful to note that the person uses only one name.

Change *oe* to *u* and *dj* to *j* unless the person has specified a preferred spelling that includes the antiquated Dutch transliterations.

Most non-Javanese Muslims have adopted surnames, which usually come last and are used on second reference. *Bacharuddin Jusuf Habibie* is *Habibie* on second reference.

Indonesian Christians follow the Western style of naming. *Benny Murdani* is *Murdani* on second reference.

Chinese names follow the Hong Kong convention. They are rendered as three separate words and spelled according to the British style of romanizing the Cantonese dialect. Family name comes before two given names. Use family name on second reference.

Beware: Many families prominent in colonial times adopted surnames. There is no rule to follow on second reference other than the person's preference.

Japan

Surname follows given name in romanized usage. *Taro Aso* is *Aso* on second reference.

Beware: In Japanese, surname precedes given name. Verify unfamiliar names to make sure the switch to Western style has been made.

Korea

Surname precedes two given names, which are rendered as two separate words. Use surname on second reference. *Kim Jong Il* and former president *Kim Young Sam* are both *Kim* on second reference.

There is a standard system of romanization for Korean names, and Koreans seldom use it. The name of the former president, *Roh Tae Woo*, should be spelled *No Tae U*. He prefers *Roh*. Use the individual's preferred spelling.

Kim, Park and *Han* are common family names. If there are more than one of these in a story, use the entire name.

Laos

Given name precedes family name.

Use given name on second reference. *Bouasone Bouphavanh* is *Bouasone* on second reference.

Malaysia

The majority of people are Malay, for whom given name precedes father's name.

Use given name on second reference. *Mahathir Mohamad* is *Mahathir* on second reference.

Omit unnecessary honorific titles that often precede Malay names: *Tan Sri, Datuk, Dato* and *Haji*. Retain the following honorifics: *Tun*, which is the highest, and *Tunku, Tengku* and *Tuanku*, which are reserved for Malaysia's royalty.

When honorifics are used, go with the first name on second reference. *Tengku Razaleigh Hamzah* is *Razaleigh* on second reference.

Some Malays use *Abdul* and *Mohamed* as double-element names, such as *Abdul Karim Ishak*. In such a case, *Karim* should be used on second reference, though some people prefer their first two names. Never use just *Abdul*, which means "slave to the Prophet Muhammad."

In general, *Mohamed* is the preferred general spelling of that name, although prominent people such as former Prime Minister Mahathir prefer to spell it *Mohamad*, which should be observed. The prophet is always *Muhammad*.

Follow the Singapore and India guidelines for Singaporeans of Chinese or Indian origin.

Myanmar

Most people don't have surnames. Most have two given names, such as *Than Shwe*, and some have three, such as *Khin Maung Win*. Use the complete name on second reference.

U is an honorific, as in *U Thant*.

Pakistan

Most people have adopted a surname. Usually, given name first, family name last.

Use family name on second reference. Slain leader *Benazir Bhutto* becomes *Bhutto* on second reference.

Shias often have three names. Use last name on second reference. *Ali Hassan Shirazi* becomes *Shirazi* on second reference.

Philippines

Family name comes last.

Use family name on second reference.

Surnames using the Spanish particulars *de la, del* or *de* carry the particulars with them on second reference. *Renato del Castillo* is *del Castillo* on second reference.

Nicknames are common and a source of amusement to Filipinos and foreigners alike. Generally use the full name and not a nickname on first reference: *Corazon "Cory" Aquino.*

Singapore

Chinese names follow the Hong Kong convention. They are rendered as three separate words and spelled according to the British style of romanizing the Cantonese dialect. Family name comes before two given names.

Use family name on second reference. *Lee Kuan Yew* is *Lee* on second reference.

25

Taiwan

Names in Taiwan are still rendered with the Wade-Giles system of transliteration, with the given name hyphenated and the second element in lowercase. Surname precedes given name.

Use surname on second reference. *Ma Ying-jeou* is *Ma* on second reference.

Beware: Don't refer to a person as Taiwanese unless he or she is ethnically Taiwanese. Though most residents were born in Taiwan, their forebears may have come from Mainland China after the country's formation in 1949—a sore point among the locals, who prefer the distinction be made.

Thailand

Given name precedes family name.

Use given name on second reference. *Prime Minister Abhisit Vejjajiva* is *Abhisit* on second reference.

There isn't any standard English spelling for Thai names. Check past stories to maintain consistency or check with a correspondent in Thailand. Thais did not have family names until *King Rama VI* instituted the policy in his reign from 1910 to 1925.

People with family names of four or more syllables are usually of Chinese origin, such as *Chartsiri Sophonpanich*, who would be *Chartsiri* on second reference.

Vietnam

Vietnamese usually have three names. The first is a family name, and the second and third are given names.

Use third name on second reference. *Nguyen Tan Dung* is *Dung* on second reference.

Many Vietnamese have adopted pseudonyms, including *Ho Chi Minh, Truong Chinh, Le Duc Tho* and *Pham Van Dong. Ho Chi Minh* is *Ho* on second reference. Pseudonyms such as Truong Chinh, which means "Long March," can't be split. Use *Truong Chinh* on second reference. Le Duc Tho, likewise, is correctly named as *Le Duc Tho* on second reference. Before submitting a story with Vietnamese names, check the origin of each name.

Muslim Names

In the Muslim world, stretching from Mauritania on the west coast of Africa to the Philippines, names vary from country to country—and even within the same country—because there isn't a standard way to transcribe them into English.

For this reason, it is always best to ask people how they prefer to have their names spelled. When that isn't possible, use the following guidelines in conjunction with the *Associated Press Stylebook*'s entry on Arabic names to determine the appropriate spelling. Muslim names generally fall into three categories with the exception of those in China and some states of the former Soviet Union:

Arab: Common names are *Mohammed* and *Ahmed*.

Persian-influenced: Common names are *Mohammad* and *Ahmad*.

Turkish-influenced: Common names are *Mehmet* and *Ahmet*.

Arab Names

Residents of Arab countries—Algeria, Bahrain, Comoros, Djibouti, Egypt, Eritrea, Iraq, Jordan, Kuwait, Lebanon, Libya, Mauritania, Morocco, Oman, Qatar, Saudi Arabia, Somalia, Sudan, Syria, Tunisia, United Arab Emirates and Yemen—and Arab residents of Israel usually have three names: given name, father's name and grandfather's name: *Mohammed Ahmed Fahd*.

Most Arab family names in the Persian Gulf region have the prefix *al-*, which is joined to their surname by a hyphen: *Mohammed Ahmed al-Torabi*, or *al-Torabi* on second reference.

In Egypt and Sudan, most people prefer *el-* to *al-*, so the same name would be *el-Torabi* in these two countries. Either article may be dropped depending on a person's preference or common practice. For instance, *Dodi Fayed* was the son of *Mohamed al-Fayed*, the owner of London's Harrods department store.

Some Muslims prefer *bin*, which means son of. *Mohammed bin Ali*, or *bin Ali* on second reference.

Prince Al-Waleed Bin Talal, the Saudi Arabian investor who is a member of the royal family, is an exception. On second reference, he prefers to be called *Alwaleed*, capitalized and unhyphenated because it is his first name.

For kings and sultans, only use one name: *King Fahd* on first reference, and *Fahd* or *the king* on second reference. Similarly, it is *Sultan Qaboos*. There isn't any *al, el* or *bin* here because these are unique names.

Persian-Influenced Names

Most Iranians and residents of countries that once belonged to the Persian Empire—Afghans, Tajiks, Pakistanis, Bengalis and Indians—use only two names. Example: *Mohammad Khatami*. On second reference, use only the family name, in this case *Khatami*.

Some family names in these parts of the world refer to place of birth, country of origin or profession: *Ahmad Pakistani, Ali Irani, Mohammad Hendi, Hossain Bengali* and *Hamid Afghani*.

Turkish-Influenced Names

Turkish names are easier to handle because Turkey adopted Roman letters in the early 1900s, and most Turks have names with standard spelling. The same is true for Albanians and eastern Europeans because their names date back to the Turkish Ottoman Empire, which converted them to Islam.